Conservation Skills

In his work *Conservation Skills* Chris Caple provides an overview of the issues facing conservators of historic and artistic works. This extensive work not only describes the nature of conservation but also provides an ethical framework to which the conservation of objects as diverse as 'old masters' to the ephemera of the twentieth century can be related. Drawing on case studies of well-known objects such as the body of the Lindow Man, Michaelangelo's Sistine Chapel frescoes and the Statue of Liberty, the author addresses the following issues:

- perception, judgement and learning
- reasons for preserving the past
- the nature and history of conservation
- conservation ethics
- recording, investigating, cleaning objects
- stabilization and restoration
- preventive conservation
- decision making and responsibilities.

The conservator has to fulfil a number of roles and make important decisions which are clearly defined in this comprehensive work, drawing on Chris Caple's many years as a conservator and an archaeologist.

Chris Caple is Senior Lecturer in Archaeological Conservation and Archaeological Science and the Director of the Postgraduate Conservation Course at the University of Durham.

Conservation Skills

Judgement, method and decision making

Chris Caple

London and New York

28846

First published 2000 by Routledge
11 New Fetter Lane, London EC4P 4EE

Simultaneously published in the USA and Canada
by Routledge
29 West 35th Street, New York, NY 10001

Routledge is an imprint of the Taylor & Francis Group

Typeset in Goudy and Helvetica by Steven Gardiner Ltd
Printed and bound in Great Britain by TJ International Ltd, Padstow, Cornwall

British Library Cataloguing in Publication Data
A catalogue record for this book is available from the British Library

Library of Congress Cataloging in Publication Data
Caple, Chris, 1958–
    Conservation skills : judgement, method, and decision / Chris Caple.
        p.   cm.
    Includes bibliographical references (p.   ) and index.
    1. Antiquities – Collection and preservation.   2. Historic sites – Conservation and
restoration.   3. Cultural property, Protection of.   4. Historic preservation.   I. Title.
CC135.C29 2000
363.6'9 – dc21   00-032183

ISBN 0–415–18880–6 (hbk)
ISBN 0–415–18881–4 (pbk)

To Roz

Contents

Acknowledgements

I would like to thank Mike Corfield, Mary Brooks and Janey Cronyn for reading much of the initial draft of this book and providing so much useful comment and encouragement and also Ann Bacon, Bob Kentridge, Jennifer Jones, Phil Clogg, Simon Cane, John Bintliff, Sharon Cather, Emily Williams and Andrew Oddy, all of whom read chapters or case studies and suggested improvements.

I also owe an enormous debt of gratitude to all my colleagues in conservation who have been so supportive throughout my career in conservation; they have helped in so many ways. Particular thanks go to David Leigh, Mike Corfield, Mary Brooks, David Watkinson, Janey Cronyn, Kate Foley, Jim Spriggs, Ann Bacon, Jane McKinley, Bob Child, Phil Clogg, Jennifer Jones, Simon Cane, Rosemary Cramp and Graham Morgan.

1 Perception, judgement and learning

1.1 Introduction

The implementation of conservation comprises 'the technical investigation, preservation and conservation/restoration of cultural property' (ICOM-CC 1984). To be successful it depends on the conservator knowing: what the object is, where it comes from and what it relates to (context), the materials of which the object is composed, the decay mechanisms of those materials and a variety of measures which could be implemented to clean, stabilize and preserve the object. It also crucially depends on the ability of the conservator to judge which investigation and remedial measures are most appropriate to implement. Inexperienced conservators do not find the acquisition of knowledge, such as learning different conservation techniques, as difficult as judging which one to apply. Judgement can be defined as 'the weighting of knowledge leading to a decision' and includes: ethical considerations, the best way of achieving the aims of conservation, the extent of cleaning, the extent of restoration, the extent to which limited time or funding should influence the conservation, the wishes of the object owner, risks of damage to an object, the health and safety of the conservator, aesthetic considerations and many other factors. Whilst senior conservators have the benefit of many years of experience in order to help them make this judgement, inexperienced conservators need some assistance. They need to be aware of all the issues but cannot possess this experience until they have gained it through practice. Neither this book, nor any other, can teach you how to make good judgements; however, this textbook does seek to acquaint the inexperienced conservator with many of the considerations which should be raised when approaching the conservation of an object and which lead to good judgement. It uses a number of detailed case studies drawn primarily from the conservation of archaeological and historic objects, to exemplify the judgement exercised by experienced conservators. The underlying principles of conservation are applicable to a wide range of 'cultural property' (Berducou 1996) from fine art to buildings.

The conservator is like anyone operating at a professional level, whether a doctor, lawyer, engineer or curator; they face complex problems, a situation with numerous possibilities. There is invariably no simple answer. The professional is responsible for identifying all the problems, determining the options for dealing with the problems, deciding on the solutions and then enacting them. This is often made more difficult because there is no one to prompt with questions and no standard procedures to implement. In such situations, all actions require careful judgement.

In this initial chapter the way in which the human brain perceives, reasons, makes judgements and learns is reviewed. This highlights some of the inherent limitations which we all possess as human beings when it comes to making judgements and explains how learning and experience lead to better judgement.

1.2 The nature of perception, understanding and learning

Conservators are principally aware of their objects in the visual domain and, therefore, the nature of visual perception affects how a conservator sees and understands their object. The process of perception starts from the continuously changing pattern of light we receive in our eyes. From this we create an initial image, a rough 3-D image of the world around us. This allows us to react with our immediate surroundings, without having to know what they are. This 'fast' or 'actional' form of initial perception is favoured by Darwinian evolution, since having a good idea of what is in front of you very quickly is helpful for survival. Even if the higher functions of the brain fail or are damaged this action system can nevertheless allow us to act and function within our environment.

As we observe we continuously acquire more information, colour, detail and texture in the world around us. This more informative image starts to trigger a second more complex form of perception which seeks to identify an object by comparing the observed image with existing stored images and information. These existing 'patterns' (Margolis 1987) are often referred to as schemata (Abercromby 1960). Where the existing schemata appear to correspond to the received image, we do not continue to observe but use the existing schemata instead. This leads us to visual errors.

When we see this phrase it is read as the phrase we know and not the phrase which is actually written. (Read carefully)

Thus the mind perceives by reference to existing patterns, and seeks the nearest match to the whole image; only when prompted does one look at each element and find a more accurate match. A blurred, distant fragmentary or indistinct image is recognized by matching the image to the nearest familiar sharp image.

Human beings do not normally see single images; the visual image comes as part of a continuous stream of information and with other associated images (i.e. a context). Thus when seeking to identify an object, we are selecting from a group of restricted images those associated with the previous image/situation and which correspond to the surrounding context. The patterns or schemata carry with them cues or links to further patterns and thus humans perceive in a sequence of patterns (images, actions, movements) described as P cognition sequences (Margolis 1987). This develops into a series or cascade of existing patterns, one triggering another, with an inhibiting or checking mechanism which registers the degree of correspondence or lack of correspondence, automatically generating the next pattern which may better correspond with the received image (Margolis 1987). Thus a small white cylinder in a room could be a cigarette or wooden stick, but the cue of a blackboard in association with the room and we identify the white cylinder as a piece of chalk (see Figure 1.1). This type of continuous perceptual hypothesis testing may not simply involve testing a sequence of possibilities one after another; we may continuously evaluate many hypotheses in parallel using information collected over a period of time (Kentridge personal communication). It is, however, through such mechanisms that the conservator identifies the object and in doing so accesses images, actions, information associated with this type of object.

The behaviour of the simplest animals can be explained by simple feedback loops from stimuli which constitute instincts; thus plants and moths head towards light without any

Figure 1.1 The Hippopotamus at the Zoological Gardens, Regent's Park Zoo, London (photographed by Count de Montizon in 1855, courtesy of the Royal Photographic Society). Caged people and a blissful hippo or a caged wild animal and intrepid onlookers. Though we perceive the animal, bars and people, the meaning of the image is entirely derived from our associated information.

consciousness of previous events or consequences. However, this reaction sequence can be modified, by associating consequences such as a pleasant or unpleasant stimuli and the resultant behaviour of the animal can be altered or habituated. These 'learnt' patterns can become more complex and through repetition become unconscious such as young human beings and other higher primates smiling in greeting. The simplest learnt patterns and associated responses are made on a trial-and-error basis. The acquisition of learnt patterns and responses leads to choices and since you have options there are different outcomes, different consequences. The more extensive the memory capacity and the greater the level of experience (older) then, theoretically, the wider the range of options and choices and the greater level of consideration which attends any response.

At higher levels of thought we come to a process which can be termed judgement. Margolis (1987) defines this in terms of an ability to solve a problem not previously encountered and concludes that it requires some form of imagination for its solution. For example, when a chimpanzee is faced with the need to get food suspended high above its head, some can, without having been shown, figure out that putting one box onto another will enable them to gain sufficient height to pick the fruit. This can be explained as the ape running possible actions in its head and working out the consequence, building from an existing pattern of reaching food at a lower level from standing on one box to realize (imagine) the consequence of standing one box on another. This process of judgement is seen as requiring both a concept of 3-D and a perception of self. Thus fiction in the form of imagined images has an essential role in enabling an animal to be capable of judgement and so to succeed in the real world.

The capacity for communication exists in many simple organisms which operate in a social or cooperative manner. The communication of future potential outcomes (judgements) is achieved through the complex communication of language. It permits the equating (or not equating) of concepts against each other (or with reality) to determine the most effective. This is the process we refer to as reason and it enables human beings to use collective judgements to modify or support our own judgement. This comparison mechanism may lead to accurate and planned actions of the group which conform to a reality, thus benefiting the group and favoured by evolutionary processes. The more developed forms of reason are logic and calculation. Margolis (1987) suggests that logic and calculation do not have a direct biological evolutionary basis, but are a construct of cultural development.

There are two routes which can be suggested as leading to pattern recognition and to judgement. Human experience would suggest that both are carried out. In the 'seeing that' approach, an intuitive line is drawn through existing facts and extrapolated to form the complete picture, theory or idea. This provides the intuitive unconscious 'jumps' in understanding which we all experience. The 'reasoning why' approach invariably follows the 'seeing that' process and proceeds by logical reasoned steps through the facts leading to the understanding indicated from the 'seeing that' process. The 'reasoning why' approach will modify the final image or understanding. Within human society it is important to prove why something works, in order to allow communication and explanation to others; thus the 'reasoning why' step has become increasingly important. The speed of the 'seeing that' process is, however, the approach favoured by evolution, but the exactness, executability and reproducibility favoured by our culture demands the reasoned path. There is no guarantee that the 'reasoned why' approach has to define a truth and, though less prone to error than the 'seeing that' approach, it is possible to justify an inaccurate or erroneous thought or action. Evidence of these phenomena may be seen from the fact that the body often sends signals to prepare for action, probably based on the unconscious 'seeing that' process up to half a second before the logical reasoned decision to act. The process of 'reasoning why' can be seen as rationalization whilst the 'seeing that' process can be equated with belief and may, in unconscious form, generate emotions and movement. Where reason and belief correspond we have certainty, where there is belief but no proof or there is proof but no belief there is a paradox and doubt exists. Such states of doubt are frequently encountered in the learning process.

When humans acquire additional information it is incorporated into existing P cognition schemes, skeletons or patterns of understanding. Additional knowledge is more easily added or assimilated into an area where there is already a significant level of thought patterns and understanding. This is far harder in an area where there is little existing thought pattern or understanding. Thus it is easier for an expert to take in additional information and ask probing and relevant questions than a student who is still learning the subject and has yet to establish a pattern of understanding on which to hang additional information. In an area where an individual has expertise, and a large number of thought patterns, almost everything will cue more thought patterns, whereas for students with fewer thought patterns, there are few cues to trigger additional thought patterns. This is why every aspect of an object 'means something' to an experienced conservator, whilst it means so much less to the inexperienced conservator.

The complexity of pattern matching is such that it is desirable not to overburden the short-term memory of our brains, which has limited capacity. Therefore, information is bundled or 'chunked' together where possible (e.g. memories of a given time and place), leading to the creation of 'stereotypes'. Another reduction process is to run together complex sequences of actions (recognized patterns) such as driving. These sequences of patterns are learnt slowly in the first place but familiarity leads to a speeding up of the thinking process, as alternatives to the norm are inhibited. Thus the world becomes an ordered (non-surrealist) place of sequences, such that when watching a game of chess you expect one move to follow another rather than the chess pieces to become fish. Through repetition thought patterns become reinforced sequences which are rarely even raised to consciousness during operation. They become attention-free, automatic processes which consequently require very little reasoning or other time-consuming brain activities and even complex actions can be performed whilst other thinking activities are run in parallel.

The process of learning is seen as being based on using existing patterns which are similar to the new activity. Thus learning to clean a dirty or corroded object with a scalpel may be learnt by basing your hand movements on familiar actions such as using a knife (and fork) for eating or sharpening a pencil. The new patterns are altered by trial and error and improved, new cues adding other patterns to the repertoire until a full activity or level of understanding has been built up. This approach to learning does not differentiate between copying something which is being demonstrated and discovering something from scratch, save in the speed at which the new activity is assimilated. In general, learning is a slow process with many tediously reasoned thought processes and trial-and-error processes. However, once established the thought process speeds up through repetition, as outlined above. In some areas, such as visual recognition, humans are quick to learn, which probably relates to the evolutionary past, whilst relatively recently developed powers of logical thought are very poorly developed.

When learning new ways of doing things, or re-ordering knowledge in a new way, it is difficult to learn to do things the new 'slow' way rather than using the old 'fast track' pathways and there is a constant problem of sliding back into the old ways of thinking (Margolis 1987). Untroubled by an existing pathway fresh young minds find it easier to assimilate new skills and ideas. These problems of re-ordering and relearning support Kuhn's ideas of scientific development, where the occasional genius engenders a paradigm shift in scientific understanding, through proposal of a radical new theory which re-orders all the existing information. This was certainly the case for Copernicus or Einstein whose theories many contemporary thinkers found difficult to accept, but which following generations have enthusiastically accepted.

These models of perception explain, if crudely: the ability humans have to see and understand objects and actions, the ability and need to communicate, the speed of insight and slowness of reason, the problems of slow learning, our ability to learn complex tasks, the problems of relearning and the familiarity which experts have with their subject.

1.3 Limitations and biases in perception and judgement

The desire to make theories and ideas from facts, whether by the 'seeing that' or 'reasoned why' process, means that facts which fit the theories are remembered and fitted into the patterns of understanding or facts are unconsciously falsified to fit the theory. Facts are also discarded or altered in order to reduce detail and become easier to remember. When shown a picture and told a related story, people mis-remember the picture in order that the facts fit the story. Stories are linked and they reinforce images, and theories, and so are remembered more easily in comparison to the seemingly random detail of a picture (Abercromby 1960). To derive a clear understanding of a complex artefact or image, there is a long iterative process of developing ideas, using them to explain the observed facts and modifying or refining the ideas, until all the facts fit. This process forces an appreciation of both the details/facts of the case and the reason behind the presence of such details.

Another method of reducing detail is that of classification. This may be seen as a series of cued images of similar or associated types of object (Abercromby 1960). Thus a series of images which correspond to the image or word 'knife' and cues such as the context or features of the knife allow it to be placed in a particular chronological period or associated with an activity such as eating or as a potential weapon or tool, etc. While classification can lead to a large number of mental references these can come as bundles or stereotypes, and unless conscious efforts are made to focus on the exact nature of the knife and check the assumptions, it is assumed to be familiar and unremarkable and inaccurately or incompletely identified. It is important that the conservator can distinguish between the actual facts, the basic image itself, and the assumptions or conclusions drawn from this information. Recording systems such as FOCUS (Caple 1996) try to ensure accurate observation and analysis

Not all images are equally powerful. Images experienced as individuals are more powerful than those taught or learnt. Images which are more recent are more powerful than those which are older. Scientific presentation of information is believed over informal artistic presentation. Dramatic facts and incidents are more readily remembered than the boring or mundane; thus catastrophic failures loom large and receive undue emphasis as the continuation of the status quo is unremarkable and is poorly remembered. So it is not simply the information or images gained which is important, but also the way in which that information was received which will influence the power and reliability of the image in the mind.

In general, human beings are poor at combining multiple sources of information. Their previous experience in particular tends to dominate their thinking and lead to the repetition of well-used methods. Though this gives significant bias, the experienced individual is using tried and tested methods which they are adept at using.

A model for reaching or changing a judgement was developed by Trevsky and Kahneman (Meyer and Booker 1991). This suggests that judgement is a heuristic process of anchoring and adjustment. The individual starts with an initial decision which is based on previous experience (a 'seeing that' insight based on previous patterns) and this judgement is simply modified with each piece of additional information. This would suggest that a judgement is never recreated from the facts. Having made a judgement, it becomes the dominant fact within the assemblage and cannot be ignored. People are predisposed to regard their own thoughts highly which consequently act as an anchor constraining all future consideration of this problem. The final judgement will invariably show a skew or bias towards the original reaction. This unwillingness to embrace a new judgement manifests itself as stubbornness or fear of new ideas. One of the greatest limitations to better judgement is an individual's own thoughts, which are themselves also the essential building blocks of understanding.

A group of experienced doctors when confronted with a number of X-radiographs, a number of which show signs of TB, will not all pick out the same radiographs. Indeed if confronted with the same set of radiographs a few days later a doctor may not even pick out the same radiographs as on the previous occasion. The error can be either one of observation, failing to see all the important aspects of the image but is more usually one of judgement when all the aspects of the image were seen but not considered significant. In such a case shadows seen in the radiograph were considered within the natural background variation of human tissue. While the errors of observation can be minimized (e.g. through the use of several observers with experience looking at the subject and through consciously stripping away the assumptions), it is possible to assemble an accurate image, it is in the nature of judgement that there will always be errors. Good judgement derives from keeping these 'errors of judgement' to a minimum. Persistent errors of judgement are termed bias and by the nature of their consistency can be detected and counteracted. As mentioned above, one of the most consistent forms of bias is the natural reticence to changing one's mind.

Given the limitations of short-term memory, and the complex process which is thinking, experimental evidence suggests that it is difficult to consider more than seven variables at any one time (Meyer and Booker 1991; Miller 1956). Consequently, when judging the various options or interpretations, it is sensible to reduce the number of options or interpretations to seven or fewer. This is usually achieved by discarding possible options until a manageable number remain. If this is not consciously done the brain will tend to do it automatically, bundling or 'chunking' the information, so variables under consideration are reduced to a manageable number. Greater levels of discrimination can be achieved by directly comparing one thing with another. To improve both perception and judgement the use of calibration or feedback loops, testing judgement against a known, improves accuracy. For many professions such as doctors, weathermen and conservators reality provides a natural feedback loop.

From these present-day ideas about the nature of the recognition and thinking process it is clear that humans perceive in detail by reference to existing patterns or schemata which carry associated cues to other patterns to form cognition sequences, skeletons or patterns of understanding to which additional information can be related. Judgement can be regarded as the mental activity in which an individual 'figures out' a process, which could be in the form of an action or idea, not previously encountered. This is achieved by running potential scenarios in the mind and selecting the one which will work (Margolis 1987). Through communication the skills of reason and logic have been developed to compare and improve judgement by giving access to the best judgement of a group. Through the learning process new judgements are made more efficiently than through experience. Previous thought patterns, dramatic events, personal experiences and the limitations of short-term memory, however, all have a biasing effect on judgement made. Errors in judgement can be made through both the limitations of the perception, pattern-matching process and the ideas of established cognition sequences, derived from 'seeing that' or 'reasoned why' routes.

1.4 Judgement in conservation

When undertaking the conservation of an object, since every object is unique, the conservator should not be performing an oft-repeated process which has developed into an automatic cognition sequence, but should be following a reasoned judgemental process with a large number of options with many possible outcomes. Judgement is 'a decision or conclusion made on the basis of indicators and probabilities when the facts are not clearly (fully) ascertained' (Abercromby 1960). When applying the term judgement to the complexity of the conservation process the facts can be defined as:

Knowledge: a series of facts and the associated understanding which forms them into a coherent meaningful theory. In conservation this may be the knowledge about the object or a conservation treatment sych as mechanical cleaning. This can be described as the substantive expertise (Meyer and Booker 1991).

and the indicators and probabilities defined as:

Weighting factor: this defines the likelihood of a successful outcome through using this technique or the importance of this factor in view of the particular circumstance of the object under consideration. This can be described as the normative expertise (Meyer and Booker 1991).

The weighting of the facts (options or interpretations) is normally done unconsciously and only raised to consciousness when there are a number of options which have similar likelihoods of success or failure. Though it might appear logical to suggest that judgement is made on the basis of selecting the best likely result from a range of weighted options in reality less logical methods are often utilized:

● One or two crucial or higher rank categories dominate the process.

● A selection is made on the basis of the options which minimize conflict, though this is not selected through logic, but through processes similar to the statistical processes in neural networks where any one of any number of good solutions is selected.

As a result of experience experts are often highly proficient at making judgements but it often proves difficult for the expert to say why one option was chosen rather than another. Much relevant information is perceived unconsciously and even the judgement is made unconsciously. It is often difficult to bring the information and weighting factors accurately to consciousness and explain them.

A more conscious and deliberate selection process can be used. For example,

● A ranking is achieved through considering pairs of options and selecting one as preferable to the other. This process continues until one option is seen as preferable to all other options.

It is important to recognize that judgement is a balanced estimate, an extrapolation based on the existing information. It is what is considered most appropriate and there is no certainty in a judgement. It is not a fact until it has been implemented. There will always be alternative views and they are an essential part of judgement, after all if it were certain, a machine could decide rather than an educated, qualified and experienced human being. It is the process of considering the alternatives, becoming comfortable with exercising the balance of probability, and not certainty, in the field of conservation, with which this book is concerned.

1.5 Teaching and learning

The processes of: pattern matching to achieve perception, extrapolation of facts to a future through the 'seeing that' or 'reasoning why' approaches to achieve understanding, the development of new schemata or patterns of understanding to achieve learning, all proceed internally and unconsciously within the mind. However, to be an effective tool such processes must have some correspondence with reality if they are to be useful to us in the real world. An important element within any learning process is not simply the establishment of a sequence or pattern of thought, but also the generation of a correct answer. Thus there is need for reality testing (Abercromby 1960). This takes two forms:

- Communicating your understanding to others and comparing your judgement with theirs. Through the written or spoken word complex ideas can be communicated and this forms a fairly quick and easy method of reality testing. It only approximates to reality, since there could be a misunderstanding by all the individuals involved; the larger and more experienced the group the less likely this is to occur.

- Correspondence of your perception with real objects and real situations. Is what I believe, or have reason to believe, true? For example, if I have worked out, or simply believe, that this object is light enough for me to lift, I can try it to see if it is true. Confidence is gained if the 'learnt' thinking process is proved to be correct. If it is not correct further facts and information are sought and the thinking process repeated with the additional information.

Where subjects are taught through reading and attending lectures there is little opportunity for 'reality testing'. Written essays, which are marked and returned, are the only form of testing normally seen in arts and social-science subjects and such testing seeks only correspondence of understanding with that of the lecturer and the wider academic community rather than truly equating to reality. For the professional training required for conservators this is insufficient. Conservators must have a very close correspondence between their understanding and the reality of the objects they handle and conserve if they are to be effective conservators. They will be judged on the reality of the 'hands on' work they produce. This requirement for constant reality testing means that all conservator training and education courses must contain a substantial component of real work, handling and conserving objects in order to fully test the developing understanding of the student. Working with real objects means that the learning proceeds in an iterative manner, with constant cycles of learning and testing being undertaken. This has the effect of making the students very aware of the additional information they need to know, thus such courses remain very practical and focused on the information and understanding required by the student to work with objects. In order to maximize the efficiency of the reality testing, it is important that conservators discuss their objects, their understanding and their treatments. Reality testing will avoid misunderstandings and misconceptions to which the thinking processes of all human beings are prone, consequently conservation students need to become comfortable expressing their ideas in written and verbal form.

Where there is no reality testing, the patterns of thought are referred to as autistic or fantasy thinking.

The images which we encounter ourselves, through our own experience, are more vivid, have far more associated information and associated cues to other images and are far stronger than those we are taught. This means that we preferentially image and interpret using our own experience. Although it provides rich and deep images, personal experience is a slow learning medium particularly for reasoned ideas. It is far easier to learn reasoned ideas such as Pythogoras's Theorem, than to derive it for yourself, though when people speak of a garden, the personal experience of the garden is remembered and not a written description or definition. To learn efficiently you invariably require an appropriate balance of personal (experienced) and taught (learnt) information. An awareness of the power of personal experience with actual objects encourages conservation teachers to train conservators with actual objects (Caple 1996).

> What you hear you will forget, what you see you will remember, what you do you know.
>
> Swedish Proverb (Kavanagh 1990)

1.6 Improving judgement

There are a number of techniques which are often used in engineering and other subjects for improving the nature of judgement. These include:

- Breaking the subject down into many smaller questions.

- Communicating (e.g. writing down) the evidence and deductions made at each stage.

- Developing a model of the problem.

There has been little exploration or development of these techniques within conservation. The modelling approach suffers from the unique nature of each object. Thus few models are appropriate.

Most conservation tasks can be broken down into smaller units. Frequently this occurs within the teaching courses. Students start on the simplest object (e.g. a corroded nail or simple iron object), then work on more intricate objects with more evidence (e.g. brooches and locks), eventually moving to complex composite objects. Each element in a composite object can be thought of as separate, then the interactions as a result of the proximity of the other materials are considered. When approaching a conservation problem the simplest approach is often to break it down into a series of smaller steps, and solve each separate stage, then explore the problems of increasing the scale or the sequence of processes or the interaction of one material or technique on another.

While an experienced conservator when viewing an object will, because of the numerous patterns and cues already present, frame previous experience and be able to immediately observe many aspects of the object under consideration, the inexperienced conservator must work in a very slow and deliberate manner (see Figure 3.5). Following observation and recording it is usually appropriate to create a proposal for conserving the object. Such conservation proposals can and should be written down by inexperienced conservators. This will help clarify all the various steps which are required. Conservation proposals are often not used by experienced conservators when conserving relatively simple objects, as the procedures involved are often very familiar. When the conservation of a large and complex object is envisaged (e.g. the Albert Memorial in London or the Sphinx in Egypt), the work is so complex and involves such a large number of different conservators and extensive careful judgement, written conservation-treatment proposals are essential. Increased use of treatment proposals has arisen where conservation work is done by contract or through a tendering process, so that the client can also be made aware of the work envisaged and its likely outcome and effect. These written conservation proposals will always have a beneficial effect in supporting and developing the judgement process.

2   Reasons for preserving the past

2.1 The importance of the past

Before discussing how we preserve the past, or even what of the past we should preserve, it is essential to answer the question 'why is the past important'. From our understanding of human perception (see Chapter 1), it is clear that we only perceive or know something by correlating it with an existing image; we only know things by reference to the past. Therefore, a personal past is essential to us. A more distant past also appears to be an essential human requirement, since it provides us with a wider sense of belonging. This manifests in many ways: foster children invariably want information about their biological parents, the need to trace one's ancestors or for emigrants to maintain the traditions of their 'homeland'. Throughout much of the world the system for naming individuals is in the form of an individual name and a family name. Thus I am an individual Christopher of the family Caple, a person recognizable through being part of a family with a known past or history to which I can be related. It is believed that this requirement stems from the need for humans to have some point of contact, a shared experience or shared belief so that there is some basis for communication. The unknown is feared, but things which fit into existing schemes of understanding are explicable and thus not frightening or threatening.

Denial of an individual's past, like the denial of an individual's beliefs, has always been seen as a restriction on individual liberty and UNESCO identifies a cultural heritage as an essential human right, as it does food and water (Lowenthal 1996).

In a similar manner to individuals, groups appear to cherish a past; indeed they invariably define themselves and their traits or qualities by reference to their past. Thus regiments record their battle honours, sports teams record their victories and people erect monuments to celebrate individuals or aspects of their past. This extends to nations and forms the basis of nationalism; thus no sooner is a country created than efforts are made to preserve the places and objects associated with its inception and its past. The house of Chairman Mao was a national monument before his death and Americans sought to preserve Colonial Williamsburg barely 175 years after it had been the capital city of Virginia. A past legitimizes the present, whilst the new is not trusted since it shows things are easily changed. Thus 'heritage' (Lowenthal 1996) goes beyond an individual's need to have a past, to be an essential component of almost every social and political organization (Kavanagh 1990; Fowler 1992).

The past has many forms: oral history, written history, buildings, landscape, objects, pictures, memories, sounds, smells, people, etc. The most common forms for the period prior to AD 1900 are objects and written history. From reading newspapers or advertizing posters people are well aware that written history is not a complete or whole truth; the social and political bias of the writer and their editor ensure that facts are selected and the way they are portrayed supports the social or political beliefs of the writer. This is most clearly seen in the propaganda written during the wars of the twentieth century, but it extends into all written historical documents. Even factual documents such as birth certificates may be economical with the truth, occasionally omitting the father's name. Thus written history has become widely recognized as biased and, as such, always needs to be interpreted. Objects, however, particularly functional objects, are seen as truthful, the real thing, 'the nearest thing to an objective past' (Lipe 1987). They come down to us directly from their creators and are not translated or interpreted by any scribe.

Though an object may be an unbiased, mute witness to every event in its creation, its working life and deposition, there are numerous pieces of information or 'truths' about an object and invariably only some of them are uncovered or explained. An axe can truthfully be described as a weapon, even if it is of a form most usually used for chopping wood and thus more accurately described as a tool. It contains two, or more, truths and the truth which is presented will depend on the interpreter and the context in which they place the axe.

Establishing and maintaining a past consists of three separate processes.

- Researching to discover as much information or evidence regardless of its nature or condition. It is a never-ending process, the truth is constantly sought and there is always additional information to recover (see Chapter 6).

- Preserving a process which holds the object intact so that the evidence, proof of the past, is retained unaltered. Since objects 'do not lie' they represent a reassuringly physical certainty of the past. Preserved objects can form the basis with which a past can be both learnt and taught (see Figure 2.1).

Figure 2.1 Farm carts rusting in the vegetation of the Fulford Store of York Castle Museum 1987 (photographed by the author). The act of collecting an object into a museum's collection is only the first step towards its preservation.

- Display where the objects and information about the past are presented to inform others about the past. The display process selects some of the truths about the object and through written, visual or verbal information, or the nature of the display emphasizes them.

Though I have used the term 'the past' to describe the objects and events of earlier times, Lowenthal, Merriman, Michalski and others (Lowenthal 1996; Michalski 1994) distinguish between two forms of the past:

History: The whole of the past including raw unrefined events. History is ever expanding and all inclusive. It explores and explains the past, its purpose is simply to be and be known. This is the past which is taught in classrooms and lives in books.

Heritage: A personal inheritance of the past, a past which can be used in the present. It is that subsection of the past which an individual inherits: their family, their ancestry, the traditions of their nation. It is exclusive, it is biased, its purpose is to benefit the individual or the state. It is personal memory, an attachment to people, places and things, a past that can be used.

History is factual, detailed and dull; heritage is simplified and personalized. Lowenthal (1996) illustrates this through the example of the Tiv tribe in Nigeria who first recounted their tribal genealogy and history to white anthropologists over 50 years ago. The anthropologists' written record of this genealogy no longer corresponds to the present-day genealogy and 'history' which is told within the tribe. As the oral genealogy and 'history' is their heritage, the past serving the purposes of the present, it will be continually amended and updated to keep its relevance and usefulness to the tribe of today.

In countries such as Greece and Turkey villagers walk through classical ruins, unheeding their antiquity, the stones form a quarry for their houses and they corral their livestock in the palaces of kings. This past is all around them, but like the ground they walk on, it is ever present and, consequently, it has little value or worth. As many countries modernize they are shorn of their roots; people live away from their families, in modern cities built in the last 50 years. Consequently connections with the past are lost, and in losing them they become valued. In times past, when there was no mass production, objects continued to be used and were handed down from generation to generation and the past was fused with the present. All the furniture in the house came from one relative or another, the buildings in which one lived were old and much altered (Brand 1994); thus people were surrounded by their past. In present-day existence most possessions are younger than the owner! Consequently, people now collect and preserve 'freeze' the past which is now too precious to use. People, institutions, buildings, systems, objects all demonstrate the dramatic pace of change and many people seek the certainty of an earlier age. In these circumstances heritage becomes important as society preserves its historic buildings, preserves its objects in museums and revives 'traditional' music and food. Heritage is a poultice for the trauma of loss and the shock of the new. This is not a new phenomena; such reverence and valuing of the past was, for example, described by the writers of Imperial Rome seeking the certainty of the earlier

Republican Age. Industrialization and urbanization have caused considerable change in many countries throughout the nineteenth and twentieth centuries, leading to a consequent rise in the 'value' of the past in almost all modern societies (Lowenthal 1996). It is 'a past' – any past – which is important; many of the tourists found wandering uncomprehendingly around ancient monuments are unable to identify what they are seeing and where it fits into history. For them it is simply the act of veneration, seeing the past – a heritage – which appears to be important.

A demonstration of the importance of the past being determined by the circumstances of the present is provided by the archaeological projects of Mussolini. As a Fascist dictator he sought a popular mandate for his continued hold on power by reminding the Italians of their Imperial Roman past. He excavated major classical monuments in Rome, exposing the Tomb of Augustus and the Faro Argentina by lowering the ground level by 15–20 feet. He recovered the Altar of Augustan Peace (Ara Pacis Augustae) by freezing the boggy ground beside the Tiber in which it was seated, cutting it into sections and dragging each section out, then cleaning it as it thawed and finally reassembling it. His most substantial scheme was to lower Lake Nemi by 112 feet, using huge water pumps in order to reveal three 'pleasure' galleys, which had been used by the emperor Caligula for orgies, feasting and entertaining friends on the lake. These galleys became a popular tourist attraction in the 1930s and were covered by wooden buildings to protect them from the wind and weather. However, changing circumstances sealed the fate of the past as, after Italy's surrender in World War II, retreating German soldiers set the buildings and galleys alight (Chamberlin 1979).

Modern perceptions of the past probably emerge with the Renaissance. The feudal system of the preceding medieval period emphasized conservative values, the church and state actively suppressing new ideas. The past was ever present, laws were based on ancient precedent and objects stayed in use for decades, even centuries. The Renaissance saw the new become fashionable and desirable (Lowenthal 1994). Inventions such as gunpowder and artillery rendered ancient castle walls obsolete and the sciences and arts flourished. The desire for the new led to greater awareness of the past. The medieval past became seen as simple and uneducated, the term 'old fashioned' becoming an insult. The classical past, by contrast, became admired as civilized, educated and cultured. The desire for the 'new' which developed in the Renaissance continued to the eighteenth century, when ideas of the picturesque, rustic and rural Arcadia and a state of graceful decay became fashionable. Subsequently, regular oscillations in fashion have brought the aged look of the past (e.g. Victorian Gothic) back to prominence (Lowenthal 1994).

2.2 The importance of preserving the past

The physical manifestation of collecting has formed the basis of most of the world's museum collections and has consequently been defined and studied by many authors (Pearce 1994a; Belk 1994; Pomian 1994). The simplistic urge to collect, which can be seen as a childlike, even fetishistic urge, may account for personal collecting, but the development of historic and archaeological museums by learned societies, local and national governments is founded upon more generally accepted ideas about the importance of the past and the need to preserve it. I would suggest that there are eight basic motives which underlie collecting and preserving objects of the past.

- *Curiosity*: Inquisitive beings – such as children – and birds – such as magpies and other members of the crow family – seek to acquire unusual and interesting objects which 'catch the eye'. Gaudy, symmetrical, outsized or other unusual items seem to attract attention. Our palaeolithic ancestors collected fossils and bright stones for this reason. They probably collected a wide variety of other unusual objects but only the undegradable stones have survived and come down to us. Collections of the unusual continued into the seventeenth and eighteenth centuries as the contents of 'cabinets of curiosities'. In such collections ideas and myths are as strong as reality and tokens of mythical creatures such as mermaids frequently occur.

- *Understanding* (scholarship): As thinking beings, we have endeavoured to 'make sense' of the world around us. Objects were collected in order to study what they were, how they related to one another and to the world at large. This led to the collecting of objects so that they could be ordered and classified. In the eighteenth and nineteenth centuries there was a particular interest in creating collections of natural-history specimens which resulted in the foundation of many modern sciences such as geology, zoology and botany. Concepts such as evolution, genetics, natural selection, adaptation, stratigraphy emerged in order to explain the observed differences.

- *Control*: Once the past can be collected and understood it can be used to provide explanation. Since the past gives rise to the present, being able to explain the past made it possible to explain, influence and justify the present. Collections of prehistoric artefacts by General Pitt Rivers and others were used to show how far civilization had advanced from 'the savages' (Thompson 1977). These ideas reinforced widespread Victorian beliefs about how civilized Western European societies were and, by implication, how uncivilized were many of the other peoples of the world. In the nineteenth century many national governments sought to emphasize and justify their national status through the establishment and development of powerful national museums (Duncan 1994). Such national pride was re-evoked in national and international conflicts such as the First and Second World Wars; for example, the German *Heimatmuseen* which were blatantly nationalistic and extolled 'national virtues'. When many African and Asian countries gained independence in the post-colonial period they set up national museums in order to emphasize their countries' national identity in terms which were understood by the rest of the world (Duncan 1994). As recently as 1975 the Marcos regime in the Philippines set up a museum of Modern Art in the space of a few months just ahead of the World Bank Conference in Manila. 'Who controls the past, controls the future; who controls the present controls the past' (Orwell 1949).

- *Belief*: Many of those who flew in Spitfires in the Second World War, or were horrified by the concentration camps, or who travelled on a steam train, believe that it is important for people of the present to remember these places, events and machines of the past. Thus they seek to preserve these aspects of the past. Those who have worked in industries which are being closed down seek to preserve the workplace and activities of that industry, no longer as a viable trade but as a museum. They maintain a holistic past, preserving the sights and sounds and smells of the past by keeping the machines running. Through such actions they hope to illicit an empathetic and emotional response from the museum visitor as well as understanding. They want the museum visitor to believe, as they do, that these aspects of the past were important.

- *Aesthetic*: Much of what is collected and saved is not the mundane or the ugly; but the beautiful. Works of art on canvas or paper, sculpture, glass, ceramics, textiles, photographs and buildings are all more likely to be saved because they appeal to the aesthetic sensibilities of the collector. These sensibilities are various: form, colour, composition, ideas, grandeur, simplicity, reality and abstraction and all have led to works of art being preserved. In some instances, such as the Victoria and Albert Museum, collections of 'good art' were amassed in order to demonstrate to the masses what 'good taste' was. Such collections were a mixture of control, belief and aesthetic motives.

- *Value*: Attributes such as age, rarity, beauty, cost and associations with famous people and places can make an object valuable. Objects which are 'famous' or truly unique, such as works of art from a dead artist, will have their value expressed in financial terms. Within present-day society many objects are collected, wholly or in part, because of their financial value. Some are seen as investments and retained in bank vaults; others, through controversy and the publicity of display, have their fame and value increased. The works of an artist invariably rise in value and are more assiduously collected after their death. It is the emergence of a 'valuable' past which has given rise to fakes and forgeries (Jones 1990).

- *Memories*: This is the retention of an object which reminds one individual of another, or of a particular aspect of their personal past. It usually accounts for the short-term survival of an object, often something small and of little monetary value (e.g. a grandfather's medals, a toy from childhood or a souvenir from a holiday).

- *Veneration of age*: Often places, individuals or objects are accorded respect because of their age. The reasons for such veneration are not clear; that something has survived a long time suggests that it is valuable, powerful or different from the norm, important to others if not to ourselves. There may be a respect for the beliefs of others making such longevity effectively sacred. Frequently we find human settlement has reoccurred in the same location for thousands of years or churches are built over henges or other prehistoric ritual monuments.

Many examples of preservation are undertaken for a mixture of motives.

By analysing why an object has been preserved (e.g. through collection), it is possible to discern the key features of this object as far as the owners and curators of the collection are concerned. These are invariably the features which need to be retained or emphasized in the conservation process. Natural-history specimens within important nineteenth-century collections may be 'type' specimens, and as such form the key examples for the classification of species. As such their preservation for future reference is paramount. With such a specimen even the original label associated with the object is likely to be important.

One of the earliest and most enduring ways of signifying the importance of the past was through the erection of monuments. In 1907 the tercentenary of the founding of Jamestown, the first permanent European settlement in the USA, was celebrated through the erection of a large white granite monument at the site of the Jamestown settlement. A change in approach was evident by 1957 when the same event was commemorated by the erection of a brick tower with an interpretation centre attached. By 1992, and the quinquennial anniversary of Columbus 'discovering' America, one of the prime celebrations was the conservation of the Statue of Liberty (see Case study 3A) and the Ellis Island Immigration Halls. The move from celebration of the past by erection of monuments to the active preservation and study of the past marks an important change. No longer does a myth of the past (a creation myth) suffice; the physical reality, the truth of the past, is increasingly important to modern-day societies.

2.3 Reasons for presenting the past

With the exception of private collections not intended for public display, which are usually made for reasons of aesthetics, scholarship or memories, almost all other collections of objects have been collected and preserved for the purpose of presentation. In presenting objects of the past to be viewed, the authors of the presentation are seeking to convince others of their own beliefs regarding the past (or present). Such displays are seen as particularly effective since objects are regarded as 'the real thing', an essentially truthful medium. These displays can be regarded as educational and impartial or biased propaganda depending on the extent to which the viewer subscribes to the viewpoint of the display.

The vast majority of museum displays, though seen as honest and educational, have to make choices in the display of objects and this brings with it bias. For example, displaying a large number of similar objects may be seen to imply that minor variations between similar objects are important. A single object displayed alone invites the visitor to see the object as a work of art with meaning in its form, colour and decoration. When an object is displayed as part of a diorama the object is seen as important in terms of its function and its association with the objects around it. All these displays are derived from the imagination of the curator or designer and may have no relation to the actual or known history of the object. Similarly the limited space on museum labels or explanation panels necessitates the selection of some information about the object and the neglect of other aspects. No museum display is free from bias and every object contains a number of truths of which only a few are revealed in any one museum display. What is revealed depends on the purpose of the display, museum policy, personal bias of the curator, the state of knowledge, what is fashionable in museum/academic circles at that time and what is socially acceptable to display in a public place. These biases change over time but remain a constant topic of debate amongst curators (Pearce 1990; Kavanagh 1990).

An example of the several truths contained within an object and their potential for creating displays can be seen in a display case of native American Indian objects located in one of Glasgow's museums. Objects, including a pair of women's or children's moccasins were recorded as having been collected by an individual after the conflict at Wounded Knee. They were donated at a later date to Glasgow Museums. The Wounded Knee conflict has been described by the American army as a battle and by the native American Indians as a massacre. It appears likely that these moccasins, like many other objects, were removed as trophies from the feet of a dead woman or child. In the original display the moccasins were presented simply as an example of the material culture of native American Indians, emphasizing one element of the truth of these objects, but ignoring other aspects of the history. Future displays may emphasize other aspects or truths about these objects or, given the sensitivity of such issues as the Wounded Knee conflict and the stripping of the dead, they may be removed from display altogether.

The purpose or message behind the presentation of objects of the past can be powerful. Some ideas are felt so inviolate that, like religious beliefs, they are supported by law. It is, for instance, a criminal offence in Israel to deny that the Holocaust took place. Other ideas touch upon modern sensitivities, so language, particularly blasphemy, attitudes to women and race are omitted from period displays. Lowenthal (1996) quotes the example that where slave quarters have been recreated attached to some of the historic houses in USA, they do not have watermelon patches. Even though archaeological evidence suggests they existed, they are felt to be racially stereotypical and provide a demeaning image, so they are not portrayed. The more historically distant the events the less sensitive the issue. Thus Roman slave camps can be interpreted without conscious bias. Some modern sensitivities to sexuality, torture and bodily functions continue to result in omission from display or the failure to label certain objects.

Every generation reinterprets the collections of previous generations and interprets the previous generations through their collecting (Ames 1994; Kavanagh 1990). Thus objects are constantly re-examined and new information and meaning ascribed to them. A process which seems unlikely to ever end. Heritage, as distinct from history, is whatever you determine it to be. This pessimistic view suggests that archaeologists and historians are merely engaged in 'self projection onto an essentially unknowable past' (Bintliff 1988). This emphasizes the need for conservators to carefully distinguish between the facts about an object, a history to which they can constructively add, and the selective subjectivity of interpretation which, though necessary to aid understanding, is, like all heritage, always subject to revision.

The objects in a museum are selectively viewed by the public, who fit them into their existing frameworks of knowledge (myths) about the past (see Chapter 1). Consequently they ignore objects and information which do not fit into their existing pattern of under-standing. They cannot, literally, make sense of it, having no hooks on to which to attach this information. In order to expand people's understanding of the past it is necessary to show how objects relate one to another; for example, through a diorama (Jorvik Viking Centre or Kirkgate, York Castle Museum) or through an explanation panel or picture, which integrates the new object or information with their existing knowledge. This builds into a more accurate holistic view of the past. The more complete and detailed people's views of the past the easier they find it to add on existing information and thus to 'decode' museums (Kavanagh 1990; Pearce 1990) and ancient monuments.

Museums competing for the attention of the public against the intensity of television, radio, computers and newspapers, have sometimes sought to strengthen the dramatic effect of history; for example, in the Washington Holocaust Museum every visitor's identity tag is that of one of the victims of the concentration camp. This level of detail appears to bring one close enough to smell 'the true stench of history', though such 'realism' is not necessarily any more truthful than more mundane displays. It can be suggested that it is important that the 'messages' of the past are preserved and passed on to future generations, no matter how unpalatable. Such ideas have led to the preservation of the concentration camp of Auschwitz. Efforts to preserve the 'original' centre upon the need to remind future visitors of what took place in the camp during the latter half of the World War II. The exact means of preserving any physical form may be seen as secondary to the message; the barbed wire must be on the fences, whether original or replaced matters far less than the overall message which the whole preserved camp portrays.

However, in presenting the past, the process of conservation and restoration can make the past conform with present-day ideas. Lowenthal (1996) quotes the example of a statue of Lincoln inscribed with the words 'Letter to the Working Men of Manchester' which was given in 1920 to the citizens of Manchester by the citizens of the USA, in recognition of the fact that, following a letter from Lincoln during the American Civil war, the working men of Manchester had refused to spin cotton from the Confederacy. In 1986 the statue was refurbished and the inscription was altered to read 'Letter to the Working People of Manchester'. Someone felt they had the right literally to rewrite history, rewrite the words of Lincoln and his commemorators. This inscription now commemorates the political correctness of the 1980s and when the record of the change is lost, the altered words will be mistaken for the truth. If an accurate history of the past is to be preserved it is clear that where an object is conserved or restored, it must be done as exactly as possible, no matter how worthy the reasons for alteration may appear at the time.

There are more obvious examples of the tastes and ideas of an age resulting in the amendment of major works of art. Following the Council of Trent (1545–63), the clerics of a prudish age had fig leaves painted on to cover the genitalia of the figures in Michelangelo's *Last Supper*. The Victorians continued this prudish approach to nudity amending numerous paintings and statues with a selection of fig leaves and other coverings. Present-day Western civilization holds 'truth' and 'artist's intent' in high esteem, and these obscurations are being removed. A future society may have them restored.

The presence of many truths about an object, some of which are more socially acceptable than others can give rise to problems when dealing with objects of the recent past. For example, do Nazi war memorabilia celebrate their views or remind of the dangers of a totalitarian regime? There are actually two separate questions:

- Should they be collected and preserved as a record of the period and what happened at that time?

- Should they be displayed and brought to the attention of people?

It is more usually the display and the nature of the display which raises questions of taste and morality. Accurate, truthful understanding of the past requires that there is a case for collecting all forms of material, even that which is seen as highly offensive in order to have a complete record of the past. This argument is seen to justify the collection of pornographic, racist and other forms of offensive material (i.e. it represents a truth in our present or previous cultures). The difficulty of explaining the use of public funds for this purpose invariably remains.

2.4 The truth in the objects of the past

If the display of the past has bias, are the objects themselves inherently biased or an absolutely truthful record of the past?

- Some materials such as stone and bronze are robust and survive well. They are consequently over-represented in museum collections whilst organic materials, which decay quickly, are very under-represented. The pewter dishes of the sixteenth and seventeenth centuries have frequently survived to enter museum collections but as a result of breakage and decay only a few ceramic dishes and very few wooden dishes, which were originally the most common, now remain.

- Unusual objects such as wedding dresses have often been retained, but few examples of mundane or typical clothing such as everyday overalls or work wear are treasured and preserved.

- The valuable – gold jewellery – is retained whilst the cheap costume jewellery typical of a period fashion is discarded. The good suit is often retained whilst cheap fashion garments are not.

- The unusual and valuable are often studied giving a bias to scholarship. We are consequently more aware of the variation in such objects and this highlights the interest and consequently the collectability of such artefacts. The common and mundane are often under-studied and consequently rarely collected.

The present-day collections are thus inaccurate records of the material culture of the past.

Our perception of the distant past is primarily through fragmentary archaeological remains which must be interpreted through written or pictorial record, with all interpreters biased to some degree. Therefore, the truth about the past is relative; some interpretations are deemed more accurate than others. It is obvious that the less functional an object, the older it is and the more numerous the phases of use and reuse, the greater will be the difficulty in accurately interpreting it. Thus ritual prehistoric monuments which were used over a long period of time, such as Stonehenge, which will have experienced constantly changing ceremonies as well as changing stone configurations, will be some of the hardest objects to accurately interpret (Chippindale 1983).

The desire to own objects of the past, especially those which are scarce because of the effects of age and decay or of high aesthetic value, has led to the creation of fakes and forgeries to satisfy the demand (Jones 1990). The fact that not all objects are what they seem emphasizes the burden which the conservator bares to be accurate in their investigation of objects and the need to be truthful in reporting those findings (see Case study 2A: The De Walden Collection).

2.5 Destroying the past

By making the past important, we not only give reasons for preserving something, but also for destroying it. If an object is important in the expression of a country's national identity, when an aggressor seeks to reduce or eliminate that identity, then such objects will be removed or destroyed. Thus the Nazis deliberately destroyed Warsaw following the Warsaw Uprising (Chamberlin 1979), whilst in 1991 invading Iraqi troops removed the contents of the National Museum of Kuwait. This process has been prevalent throughout history especially when there are changes in belief such as the Reformation which swept through North-West Europe in the sixteenth and seventeenth centuries and which engendered the destruction of many religious statues and relics. This can be seen on a personal scale with the destruction of images or representations of an individual. For example, the obliteration of the name and image of Hatshepsut, the powerful eighteenth-dynasty queen of Egypt who proclaimed herself as Horus (i.e. a king), by her nephew and successor Thutmose III, who appears to have considered the concept of a female king a blasphemy (Quirke and Spencer 1992).

The sense that something is not your heritage robs it of any value for you and thus you either acquiesce or participate in its destruction or fail to use valuable resources to preserve it. Egyptian peasants of the nineteenth century did not consider that the remains of Pharaonic Egypt was their past so they looted tombs and aided their destruction. Indeed, their heritage was robbing Pharaonic tombs, a tradition which had gone on since antiquity. The problem is exacerbated by what is viewed as heritage; many lands split with tribal, racial and religious differences find difficulty in agreeing a common heritage, and countries which have gained their independence in more recent decades find it difficult to see their colonial heritage as important as their native heritage. This appears manifest by the present crumbling buildings of the British Raj in India.

Interest by collectors in specific aspects of the objects of the past has distorted the nature of the preserved past. Thus Mussolini cleared away much of the medieval archaeology of Rome in order to expose the Roman ruins beneath. Similarly Heinrich Schliemann cleared away the later levels at Troy in order to find the city of the Greek heroes Achilles and Ajax (Lowenthal 1996).

Though there has been almost as much destruction as construction in human history, traces of such activity are rarely preserved. Occasionally human conflicts throw up icons such as the bombed shell of Coventry Cathedral, which are preserved to remind the generations which follow of the destructive power of wars. Such monuments are rare; almost all of the debris of war is swept away, there is no guiding hand, no national curator, to preserve the traces of destruction. Such destruction is undoubtedly an important element of the development of civilization, thus preserving the traces of damage or graffiti becomes an important element in preserving the 'truth' of an object. It remains difficult, almost counter-intuitive, to seek to preserve traces of the damage or decay inflicted on objects (see Section 11.6).

The extent of the destruction of two world wars and the speed of nineteenth-century industrialization and urban redevelopment of the twentieth century has had the effect of making people aware of the loss of their past. Lowenthal (1996) has argued that it is the loss of the past, or the threat of loss, which is the primary mechanism for making people value their past. This is exemplified by the threatened loss of Tatershall Castle in 1911 (see Section 11.4) which led to the protection of ancient monuments through scheduling in the UK.

2.6 Visitors and tourists

Those who care for historic buildings and artefacts have a love–hate relationship with visitors. They require visitors in order to generate money, directly by admission charges or indirectly through souvenir purchase, to fund the continued care of the collections. However, 'people are bad for objects'; they bump, drop, rub, scratch, breathe on, cause light to be shed on objects, all of which harms or potentially harms the objects. The visitors have considerable economic power and the economic pressure applied by tourism is an unstoppable force. Even if they damage the building or ancient contents it is difficult, indeed frequently impossible, to stop them. The Temple of Zeus at Olympia had 100 visitors in 1932, in 1976 it had nearly 1 million and sites such as the Sistine Chapel were receiving 1.8 million visitors annually by the late 1980s (*Apollo* 1987). Visitor numbers can have substantial impacts on monuments, Canterbury Cathedral noted that its stone floors had been worn down 1.5 inches by the constant stream of visitors (*Apollo* 1987).

Modern-day authorities perceive heritage as an industry, generating economic growth and providing the livelihoods of many of today's voters. In such circumstances you do not 'kill the goose that lays the golden egg'; thus damage to a monument will rarely be prevented by reducing the number of visitors. Other methods are chosen, replacing worn steps and pathways, installing air conditioning, creating surrounding attractions to divert attention and smooth out visiting loads, removing damageable or removable objects, covering or protecting vulnerable surfaces, replicating or replacing vulnerable objects. Examples of many of these strategies can be seen in the conservation and restoration of the Statue of Liberty (see Case study 3A). This can be seen as reducing the accuracy of the visitor experience, though others might describe it as modifying or managing the experience.

Every monument has a different carrying capacity for visitors (i.e. the number of visitors it can withstand over a given period without perceptible levels of damage to the monument). For example, some ancient aboriginal desert encampment sites are very ephemeral and even a few visitors a year would damage them; consequently to minimize visitation the locations of these monuments are kept secret. Other monuments, such as the Tower of London, can handle millions of visitors per year. Organizations responsible for many monuments such as the National Trust are starting to monitor the effects of visitors on their properties (e.g. visitor-impact assessments, Ashley-Smith 1999) whilst English Heritage have already started to concentrate visitor facilities and publicity on monuments which are easily accessed, easily marketed and which can withstand the visitor pressure (Corfield, personal communication).

2A Case study: The De Walden Collection (Wollny 1996)

Thomas Evelyn Scott Ellis 8th Baron Howard de Walden and 4th Baron Seaford was born in London on 9 May 1880. Educated at Eton and The Royal Military College, Sandhurst he inherited his full titles and estates when he came of age in 1901. He was a wealthy man and throughout the first half of the twentieth century he indulged his interests in art, genealogy, heraldry and in collecting arms and armour. He built up a considerable collection of weapons and armour with a wide range of periods and cultures represented, though he was particularly interested in the classical period. There is little information about how he acquired the objects in his collection. The collection was initially displayed at his home in Kilmarnock, then later at Seaford House in London and after 1911 in Chirk Castle in Wales, where Lord Howard De Walden was based for most of his life.

In April 1945 Lord Howard de Walden offered his collection of antiquities to the National Museum of Wales for an initial loan of 10 years, with the stated intention that the collection should pass to the National Museum of Wales upon his death. He wrote to the director of the National Museum of Wales, Sir Cyril Fox, 'there are certain pieces you may not wish to have, such as a few oriental specimens and several specimens of doubtful authenticity'. We do not know how many objects were held back on these grounds, but the vast bulk of the collection was deposited with the National Museum of Wales in November 1945. Following the death of Lord Howard de Walden on 6 November 1946, his son confirmed his father's wishes and the whole collection passed to the National Museum of Wales in October 1947. In 1990 Kate Hunter, the antiquities conservator, surveyed and repackaged the 136 objects of the collection. Amongst the most notable pieces in the collection were a number of ancient antique helmets, all of corroded or patinated copper alloy, many appeared fragile and there was evidence that many had been crudely 'restored' in the recent past. In 1990 the first two helmets of this collection were examined by Daniel Bone, a student from the Durham University Masters Conservation course, and in 1996 Katharina Wollny, another student from the course, recorded, investigated and analysed a further six helmets (see Figure 2.2) which are discussed below.

De Walden Collection No. 7.19   This helmet had the form of an inverted shallow bowl with a pair of ears or wings riveted on to the side. No comparable example of this type of helmet can be located in any other museum collection. The metal of the helmet is

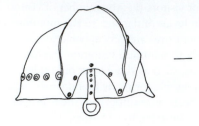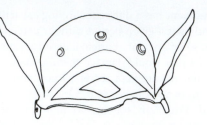

7.19

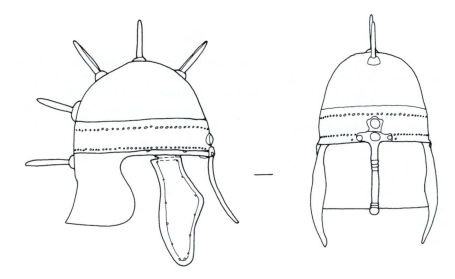

7.23

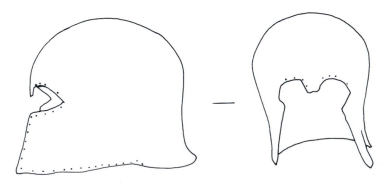

7.33

Figure 2.2 Helmets from the De Walden Collection, National Museum of Wales. Redrawn by
Y. Beadnell (from Wollny 1996).

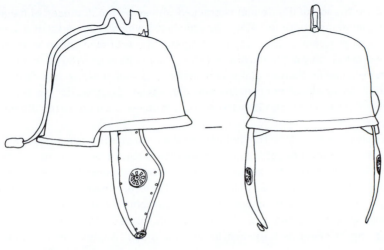

7.20

7.25

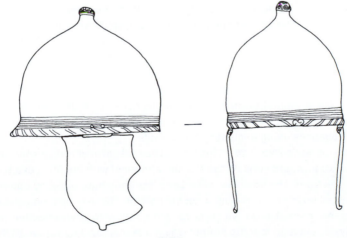

7.34

0.55 mm thick and the top of the helmet is cracked with some small pieces of metal missing. The golden metal of the helmet was analysed which revealed that it was composed of a 35 per cent zinc brass. The Romans, the first civilization to make extensive use of brass, only achieved brass with zinc contents of up to 30 per cent, as a result of the technical limitations of the cementation process of brass manufacture (Craddock 1978). Brass with 35 per cent zinc was only seen in Europe after the seventeenth century (Pollard and Heron 1996); therefore, this object is a modern (nineteenth century) forgery.

De Walden Collection No. 7.20   This helmet had the form of an inverted basin with deep sides. On top of the helmet was a damaged sinuous figure forming a crest probably initially in the form of a hippocamp or centaur and curved cheek pieces, attached through hinges, to the sides of the helmet. This form of helmet is not readily paralleled by any ancient known examples. X-radiographic examination revealed that the helmet was of unusually poor construction formed by a shallow bowl soldered to a ring of sheet metal which formed the sides. Analysis of the metal revealed that it was composed of a 5–10 per cent tin bronze, consistent with ancient metal. Analysis of the corrosion products using Fourier Transform Infra-Red Spectroscopy (FTIR) identified copper acetate (verdigris) as one of the principal minerals present. This is an extremely rare corrosion product which hardly ever appears in normal burial conditions. Since it can form very quickly, in a matter of weeks or months and looks similar to many more natural slowly formed corrosion products such as malachite, it is frequently deliberately created by forgers and fakers to make new objects appear corroded and ancient. Therefore, it appears likely that this object is either a modern (nineteenth century) forgery or a pastiche, composed of a number of pieces of ancient metal which have been formed into a helmet and re-corroded.

De Walden Collection No. 7.23   This helmet has the form of an inverted basin which curves down the back of the head with a line of five, originally six, square-section spikes with domed bases protruding 50–60 mm from the central line of the helmet. There is a thin nose-guard and hinged cheek pieces attached to the sides. Again no comparable example of this helmet form can be found from antiquity. Radiographic examination revealed that the helmet was formed from a shallow cap with a series of four bands of metal soldered one to another to form the deep sinuously contoured sides of the helmet. The whole helmet had also been split along the crest, presumably to assist in inserting the spikes and then soldered back together. This helmet, formed of ten separate plates soldered together, was an extremely weak form of construction which would have provided little practical protection for the wearer. Analysis of the metal composition revealed that the sheet metal of the helmet was low tin bronze and the spikes were of leaded bronze, compositions constant with an antique origin. On the basis of the unusual form and weak construction the helmet is probably a modern forgery or a pastiche using ancient pieces of metal.

De Walden Collection No. 7.25   This helmet has the form of a very shallow inverted bowl with a two pronged hook on the top and a roundel with the form of a female face attached to the front. The bowl is cracked and has been supported by adhering some crudely painted textile on to the inside of the helmet. There is no comparable ancient example of this helmet form which is far too shallow to give effective protection. Metal analysis revealed that the helmet was made of a low tin bronze. FTIR analysis of the corrosion products again yielded copper acetate (verdigris) together with possible copper cyanates and copper silicate (chrysocolla). Chrysocolla is rarely seen in copper corrosion crusts, but was a commonly used artist's green pigment which, like verdigris, is used by forgers to fake copper corrosion patinas. Therefore, it appears that on the basis of form and faked corrosion products this is a modern (nineteenth century) forgery.

De Walden Collection No. 7.33 This helmet has the rounded open-fronted skull form of the Corinthian helmet frequently depicted as worn by Greek hippolytes. The nose-guard is broken off as is the front of the left-side protective neck guard. The cracking on the top of the helmet has been crudely repaired with a cement-like gap filler and internal supports of adhered textile and metal are observable. X-radiographic exam-ination indicated that the helmet had been formed from a single piece of metal. Many small indentations, hammer marks from the extensive shaping, were visible. Around the eyeholes and the lower edge of the helmet were numerous regular small holes for the attachment of internal and edge padding. Metal analysis revealed that the helmet was made of a typical ancient bronze with 8.6 per cent tin. FTIR confirmed the presence of normal copper-alloy corrosion products principally malachite plus traces of chrysocolla. This is almost certainly an original Greek helmet which has endured some nineteenth-century restoration.

De Walden Collection No. 7.34 This helmet, which has a roll-formed rim and cheek pieces, has a top which curves upward to form a knob in a form identical to that used by the early Republican Roman legions circa 400 BC (Robinson's Montefortino Type A). X-radiographic examination showed the slight irregularities of hammer marks on the main part of the helmet, which was formed from a single piece of metal. The cheek pieces have many small bubbles apparent in the metal suggesting they were manufactured through a poor-quality casting process. Metal analysis revealed that the helmet was made of a typical bronze with 7.7 per cent tin, the cheek pieces of a leaded tin bronze; 5 per cent tin, 5 per cent lead – a typical casting metal composition with a raised lead content. The form, methods of manufacture and composition of this object clearly suggest that it is an original unrestored object.

Lord Howard de Walden, a collector fascinated with the study of arms and armour, had amassed a very variable collection of ancient helmets as part of his collection. He recognized that some of his collection may not have been original. Modern analyti-cal techniques, a clear set of comparable analyses of ancient artefacts and an under-standing of ancient technology and the practices of nineteenth century fakers have enabled the modern conservator to reach a judgement about which objects in this col-lection are fakes (7.19), which are probable fakes or pastiches (7.20, 7.23, 7.24, 7.25) and which are likely to be genuine (7.33, 7.34). It is clear that the actions of this collector have preserved some original objects from antiquity, but his concern and interest in the past created a value for the objects of the past and thus also promoted a market in fake artefacts. The extent and nature of the faking was judged to deceive those who were potential purchasers who had limited information available to them. The developments in technology and knowledge now allow us to deduce the 'real thing'. There is also now a fascination in the art of the fakers of antiquities, who have been operating since the Renaissance when modern interest in the past began. The fakes created for this collector reflect rather romantic Victorian notions of the past with winged helmets (7.19) and helmets with cruel and viscous spikes (7.23). This suggests that we can easily influence the past through our own perceptions. If such 'ideas' are given solid form they risk become regarded as real objects, part of the incontrovertible proof of the past. It is clear that when collecting, cataloguing, researching, preserving or explaining the past there is a need always to investigate objects closely to ensure that an accurate picture of the past (history) is derived rather than a modern-day fiction.

3 The nature of conservation

3.1 Objects as historic documents and aesthetic entities

Objects of the past are important and are preserved because of the information they contain and for what they represent (see Chapter 2). This can be translated into regarding objects as historical documents and aesthetic entities.

Every object is in part a *historic document*. It contains information about the materials from which it was made, the way in which it was assembled, and every incident which occurred in its life. It could have traces of DNA and fingerprints from everyone who handled the object or damage from the light which fell on it when on display. In reality we do not yet have the technology to 'read' all of this information, and much information is lost, obscured by later activities. Many activities and uses of an object do, however, leave detectable traces, from the smooth surfaces or scratches created by wear to the nailholes of previous attachments.

Every object is in part an *aesthetic entity*, an entity (a physical reality) which provides an aesthetic experience for everyone who senses (sees, feels, touches, smells or hears) it. Every object which is consciously made or selected by a human being contains shape, colour and texture which that individual has created or chosen from a range of possibilities. A steel tool may be left unpainted, for that is how its manufacturer wishes it to look, rough and functional, whilst another is given a coat of paint so that it appears finished, clear and neat. Many functional objects have minimal aesthetic input; thus a coat of paint is functional in preventing rust, and may be brightly coloured so that it is easily seen, but there is still an aesthetic in selecting the colour. Some objects' very function is aesthetic; an oil painting has little other function than to create a visual image and stimulate an idea, emotion or reaction in the viewer. The aesthetic entity is that aspect of the object deliberately created by the artist or manufacturer in order to communicate with the user or viewer and as such can be considered the physical manifestation of the 'artist's intent'. This aesthetic quality of objects has been expressed in many ways; for example, William Morris regarded craftsmen as putting their 'genius' into the objects they created, so endowing the object with a 'soul-like quality'.

As all objects contain aspects which are definable as being 'documents of the past'

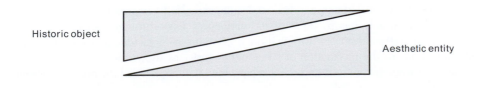

Historic object   Aesthetic entity

(Jedrzejewska 1976) and aspects which are 'aesthetic' (Riegel 1996; Kirby Talley 1996), no object is totally devoid of either aspect, and thus all objects lie between the two extremes It is essential that the conservator fully appreciates all aspects of the object as a historic document and aesthetic entity, prior to conservation

- In order that these aspects can influence the nature of the proposed conservation.

- To ensure that none of these aspects is lost during the conservation process.

- To ensure that a complete record is made of all aspects of the object and that the complete record is available to all who wish to study the object (see Chapter 6).

As a historic document the conservator would seek to determine the materials of which the object is composed, the decay processes at work, the form and original nature of the object, its function, who had owned and used the object and what had happened to it through its life. This information would be created as a record and wherever possible remain preserved within the object itself. The nature of the aesthetic entity will also need to be fully appreciated by the conservator (Kirby Talley 1990), so that the 'true nature' of the object can be seen and understood. It may be necessary to clean the object in order to reveal the aesthetic entity which can then be experienced by present day and future viewers. If the aesthetic entity is fragmentary it may be necessary to restore some parts of the object or image in order to ensure that the aesthetic impact of the object is fully experienced by the viewer.

Since all objects are both historic documents and aesthetic entities it will be necessary to balance out the actions of investigating the object to reveal the evidence it contains as an historic document, preserving the object and associated information for future study and revealing, through cleaning and restoring, the aesthetic character of the object, so that the best compromise is achieved. Pursuing only one aspect will limit the extent to which another can be achieved. In reality those objects with high levels of aesthetic entity such as works of art on canvas and paper, musical instruments and machines such as cars, are often restored and used. Those objects with high value as historic documents, such as historic monuments and archaeological objects, are preserved in their ruined or decayed state (see Figure 3.1).

The fact that all objects are aesthetic entities and historic documents is recognized in their conservation treatment. A painting or other object being restored is fully investigated and recorded prior to restoration, so that the record of the object provides the full testimony of the object in its pre-restored form as a historic document. Similarly, when an archaeological object is simply preserved in its present damaged or degraded state, a reconstruction drawing is done in order to show the original form of the object, which would form part of the object's conservation record. When considered in this manner the importance of the record of the object becomes clear.

Early collecting by Renaissance princes focused primarily on objects such as classical statues which were sought for their aesthetic values. The financial value of objects continues to be primarily influenced by their aesthetic entity and how present-day society values that aesthetic. Such financial value and appreciation of the aesthetic gives impetus to the process of restoration. Increase in financial value can also be related to the history of an object, which invariably has to do with its uniqueness (e.g. through association with a famous person), rather than the information it contains as a historical document. Such an emphasis leads to the production of fakes and forgeries as shown in Chapter 2.

It is modern academic interest and scholarship which has emphasized the nature of objects

Figure 3.1 Gravestone in the churchyard at Llangarren, Herefordshire (photographed by the author). The face-bedded carved stone slab is losing its inscription and decorative relief carving because of the weathering and decay of the stone. It is losing both its appeal as an aesthetic entity and its importance as a historic object.

as historic documents (see Chapter 6). This has led, as Kirby Talley has pointed out, to conservation students seeing a painted image in terms of the pigments and techniques used by the artist rather than the image which is depicted.

> The students had not started their examination of the picture as a work of art, but as an object, a thing with ailments. They were oblivious of its demand to be experienced aesthetically. There was no sympathetic attention and they may as well have been looking over a used car.
>
> (Kirby Talley 1990: 61)

In addition to having access to scientific facilities to successfully analyse an object's composition and a knowledge of material culture history (art and archaeology) in order to appreciate the importance of the object and place it in its historic and artistic context, the conservator also needs to have developed the critical faculties necessary to receive and appreciate the aesthetic attributes of objects. There is a world of difference between the aesthetic appreciation derived from a clear message obtained by a well-tuned receiver and the noise and interference received on a poorly tuned one. Every conservator should have eyes trained to fully appreciate the beauty of every object on which they work, even the graceful lines and period detail of a used car (cf. Kirby Talley 1990).

3.2 Conservation: A definition

A number of authoritative conservation organizations and individuals have at various times in the past defined conservation:

Conservation is the means by which the true nature of an object is preserved. The true nature of an object includes evidence of its origins, its original construction, the materials of which it is composed and information as to the technology used in its manufacture. Subsequent modifications may be of such a significant nature that they should be preserved.

(UKIC 1983: 2)

The primary goal of conservation professionals, individuals with training and special expertise, is the preservation of cultural property. Cultural property ... is material which has significance that may be artistic, historic, scientific, religious or social ... an invaluable and irreplaceable legacy that must be preserved for future generations.

(AIC 1994: 1)

The activity of the conservator–restorer (conservation) consists of technical examination, preservation and conservation/restoration of cultural property.

(ICOM-CC 1984)

[The term conservator–restorer is often used in Europe since in many countries of southern and eastern Europe the term restorer is used to describe those who undertake conservation work.]

The act of preservation is undertaken by almost all human beings for anything they treasure, 'putting it in a safe place'. The importance of this first impulse is reflected in the prominence which preservation receives in the AIC (American Institute of Conservation) (1994) and UKIC (United Kingdom Institute of Conservation) (1996) codes. However, preservation usually occurs in order to show others (or remind ourselves) of the importance we attach to the object and to show them what it means to us (see Chapter 2). Thus inherent in the conscious act of preservation is the desire to show or reveal this aspect of the past to others. The nature of the importance of the object, the things it reveals, are frequently not self-evident. It is essential through investigation to uncover why the preserved object is important, what is important about it and how it can be preserved. Thus although preservation may be at the core of what conservators do, it does not define it fully.

Preservation in perpetuity, if taken to its logical conclusion and done with 100 per cent efficiency, would theoretically result in objects being stored at absolute zero, halting all chemical and physical processes of degradation. Preservation in a cryogenic vat would preclude easy observation or examination of the object (see Sections 8.4 and 11.3). Simply preserving objects makes us no wiser about the past. To have any purpose it is essential to use the objects to further our understanding about the past and reveal their truths either through research or as an exhibit demonstrating what the past was like.

It can be seen that preservation does not override all other considerations and is tempered with the need to investigate objects and the need for them to be used to reveal their truth to a wider audience (e.g. as part of a museum display). Definitions – e.g. 'conservation is the technology of preservation' (Ward 1986), 'conservation is the means by which collections are preserved and cared for' (Keene 1996) – do not convey the full range of the conservation process. Hence the emphasis on the aspects of showing/revealing and investigation/examination which are given equal prominence in the opening sentence of the ICOM code.

Whilst conservators are definable as the professionals involved in this process of preservation/investigation/revelation, there are many other professionals such as historians, archaeologists, museum curators, private collectors, etc. who through their actions and expertise such as collection, research, excavation and display also fulfil the process of, or aspects of, preserving, investigating and revealing objects (see Sections 13.1 and 13.2).

3.3 Revelation, investigation, preservation (RIP)

Whilst much has been written about the ethics of conservation (see Chapter 5), less has been written about the aims of conservation. Before worrying about whether the conservation treatment being undertaken is 'reversible' or 'minimally interventive' it is essential to have established what one is seeking to achieve through treatment. The aims or principles of conservation derive from the definition of conservation (see Section 3.2) and can be expressed in the form of three almost opposing aims: revelation, investigation and preservation.

Revelation: Cleaning and exposing the object, to reveal its original form at some point in its past. The visual form can be restored to give the observer, typically a museum visitor, a clear visual impression of the original form or function of the object (see Chapters 7 and 9).

Investigation: All the forms of analysis which uncover information about the object, from visual observation and X-radiography to complete destructive analysis (see Chapter 6).

Preservation: The act of seeking to maintain the object in its present form, without any further deterioration. This will typically involve a full range of preventive conservation practices and the stabilization processes of interventive conservation (see Chapters 8 and 11).

Any conservation process can be seen as a balance of these three activities. At the extremes these activities are mutually exclusive; thus to best preserve an archaeological object it may not be excavated or even cleaned and an object subject to the fullest form of examination may be dissected or dismembered to achieve as complete a file of information on the object as possible. In almost all cases conservation involves all three of these activities to a certain degree, virtually never carried to an extreme. Thus, conservation activities can be characterized as lying in the space between these extremes (Figure 3.2). All the individual conservation activities – such as cleaning, gap filling, X-radiography, etc. – can be plotted in this RIP triangular space. It is useful in reminding the conservator of the balance and compromise they strike in undertaking conservation; for example, in cleaning (revealing) an object they will have less of the original object and its evidence to preserve. Some activities such as recording, though dependent upon investigation and used for education and revelation, are intended primarily as a means of preservation (see Chapter 6).

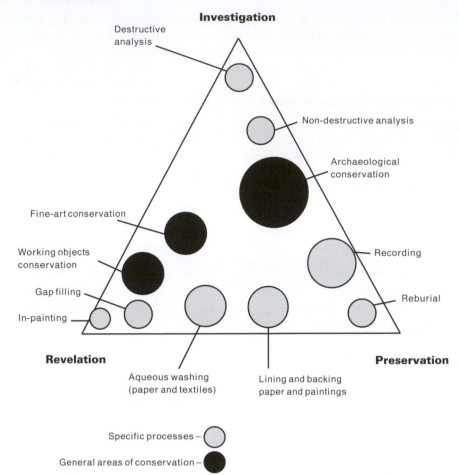

Figure 3.2 The aims of conservation: RIP balance triangle.

It is possible to describe both the entire conservation process as well as individual aspects of the conservation process within the RIP balance triangle. In cases of an entire conservation process the specific location derives from all the separate processes carried out as part of the conservation process; that is, the sum of all the different processes: cleaning, recording, analysis, the use of a reversible adhesive and storage with inert buffered materials. It should be emphasized that this is a relative measure with no numerical scales or absolute values. The relative ratios of the different processes may allow the suggestion that the balance differs for different types of object. Archaeological objects will usually have higher ratios of investigation and preservation than revelation, whereas an object with considerable intrinsic aesthetic properties such as a work of art may have a higher ratio of revelation to preservation or investigation work (see Figure 3.2).

Whilst the acts of preservation and investigation are easy to identify as two of the goals of conservation, the other goal is more difficult to define. Activities such as cleaning and restoration are seeking to show the 'true nature' of the object, with a conscious selection of what is the most important truth to be viewed. The process of cleaning is a choice, removing some of the evidence of the past in an attempt to reveal more important information beneath (see Chapter 7). The process of revelation recognizes that the present visual form of an object is not necessarily the most informative for the viewer: the most important form of the object's 'true nature' may only be revealed as a result of the processes of cleaning and restoration. Restoration is enacted through the infilling of missing areas of the object and some level of duplication of the colour and texture of the original, for which there is clear evidence. This restores a clear approximation to the original visual form and coloration of the object and the viewer discovers how the present fragments of original material relate to the original object as a whole. The aesthetic entity of the original object (see Chapter 9), can consequently be appreciated. Regardless of whether adding (restoring) or subtracting (cleaning) material, the object moves from a form created by the indiscriminate hand of fate to a form which it had during its life, one which the conservator can justify as important and informative to the viewer.

Processes such as cleaning do not serve a single purpose, the removal of dirt and corrosion products will often help to preserve the object; for example, removing corrosion promoters such as chlorides from metal-corrosion crusts and removing acidic, hygroscopic dirt from the surfaces of textile, paper, glass, plastic, ceramic and metals. The removal of such material will expose more of the original surface of the object (see Section 7.4), allowing closer, more accurate and more detailed examination revealing information about the use and manufacture of the object. Thus cleaning processes can occupy a number of points within the RIP balance triangle depending on the relative contribution the cleaning makes to the preservation and investigation of the object as well as the revelation.

Ethical concepts such as 'minimum intervention' and 'reversibility' can be described as forces moving towards the extreme of preservation, whilst concepts such as 'true nature' can be seen as moving towards investigation and revelation. The RIP balance is drawn at a single moment in time; as further additional information is uncovered during the conservation process the balance may be amended.

Decision: The establishment of the RIP balance and thus the aims of conservation is not made by the conservator alone but also normally involves the curator or owner of the object (Ramsay-Jolicoeur and Wainwright 1990). The wide range of reasons which have led the owner/curator to consider an object worthy of collection, study, preservation and display (see Chapter 2), have also usually led to the desire to have it conserved. Numerous factors enter into the consideration, the most common of which are listed in Figure 3.3. The intended use of the object (e.g. for display) is often the primary consideration. Factors such as the context and object condition also weigh heavily in the balance. The range of factors and their weighting are different for every object, which is why every object and its conservation is unique. The conservator in discussing the work with the owner/curator needs to have a well-developed and clear understanding of the aims of and ethics of conservation as well as the technical possibilities and health and safety considerations for any proposed conservation work. The conservator should always derive a clear point of view on what is appropriate in terms of conservation for the object, and ensure that they are not merely acting as a technician, implementing the wishes of the owner/curator. The establishment of the balance (or weighting) of revelation, investigation and preservation factors is the crucial part of the judgement process which the conservator makes

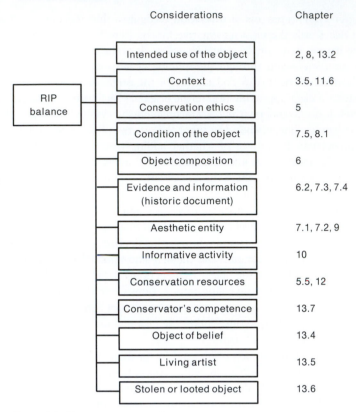

Figure 3.3 Conservation considerations.

and which leads to the decisions regarding the actual conservation work which will actually be carried out. The work envisaged will only be conservation if it includes consideration of the factors of revelation, investigation and preservation (i.e. it lies within the RIP balance triangle).

3.4 Context

Context is the relationship that an object has with other objects which surround it and other forms of historical information. Context sees the object as part of a larger entity (e.g. the room of an historic house or part of a historic landscape). The object provides both historic information about the larger entity and crucially is part of the aesthetic entity of the whole. Thus the Victorian upholstery of an antique Georgian chair may be preserved if present as an individual object since this would preserve all parts of the history of the object. However, if it was part of a room of Georgian furniture, a strong case may exist for restoring the chair to its original Georgian upholstered form. For common objects – e.g. blankets (Kavanagh 1990) or a safety pin (Tilley 1994) – context is uniquely crucial to the correct interpretation of the object. The gravestone in Figure 3.1, remains it its original context in a Herefordshire churchyard informing people, through its presence and surroundings, of the continuity of burial in the churchyard since the eighteenth century. The conservation balance recognizes the importance of context and thus will focus on preservation of the object *in situ*. Continued exposure to wind and rain would mean that any conservation measures would slow rather than halt the decay of the object. If the gravestone were present in a museum, an example of the art of eighteenth-century rural England, it would be protected from the elements, consolidated to prevent further decay, mounted on a sloping plinth to reduce the stress on the stone and elements might be restored to aid the clarity of understanding of the object. Context is crucial when considering any conservation work (Eastop 1998), particularly crucial when considering objects being preserved *in situ* (see Section 11.6 and Case study 11A: The Laetoli Footprints).

Brooks *et al.* (1996) and Jaeschke (1996) have suggested that sometimes identical objects which come from different contexts can receive different conservation approaches. In such cases the balance of revelation, investigation and preservation is clearly different for each object. The archaeological example will be conserved with an emphasis on the information on the context to which it relates: latrine, rubbish dump or grave, period of use and discard. The historic object, usually devoid of original context, will be conserved with an emphasis on its role as a display item, demonstrating the aesthetic sensibilities and the impressive needlework of the period.

3.5 The conservation process

When engaging in the conservation process there are two approaches which can be adopted:

Preventive conservation: aims to retain the object in ideal conditions, so no further damage and decay will occur. This can take numerous forms: protecting historic sites or objects through legislation, purchase by caring organizations or management agreements, through public education and advocacy or through direct preservation of the object. This would include preventing access and handling of the object (e.g. through security, recording, packaging), physically supporting the object (e.g. appropriate packaging and mounts), ensuring that the atmosphere which surrounds the object does not promote decay (e.g. environmental monitoring and control, testing packaging and display materials for stability). The establishment of private collections from the seventeenth century onwards, national and major public museums in the nineteenth century together with the legislation to protect ancient monuments can be seen as significant early preventive conservation activities. The development of environmental care of artefacts championed by Gary Thomson (Thomson 1978) and the articulation of the concept of preventive conservation (Roy and Smith 1994) has led in recent years to a higher profile for this branch of the subject. Many aspects of preventive conservation such as basic storage and simple cleaning, often defined as good housekeeping, can and are undertaken by volunteers or staff not specifically trained in conservation. Other aspects such as legal protection, object collection for public bodies, research and environmental monitoring are of a more specialized nature and are undertaken by heritage professionals.

Interventive conservation also known as remedial conservation (Keene 1994): aims, through physical and chemical mediation with the object, to prevent further decay and reveal information about, and the earlier appearance of, the object. Interventive conservation activities are tailored to each object, depending upon its composition and the extent and nature of the decay to ensure its preservation and revealing the information (investigative conservation) which it contains. Interventive conservation is done by those with specialized expertise, usually conservators, practising the ethical standards of conservation in approaching such work. Almost all early textbooks (Rathgen 1898; Plenderleith and Werner 1971) are based on interventive conservation.

Interventive conservation is predominantly focused on individual objects, whilst preventive conservation is predominantly focused on collections of objects. The range of practical activities in which a conservator might engage when working with an object or objects are outlined in Figure 3.4. These activities, whether preventive conservation described in

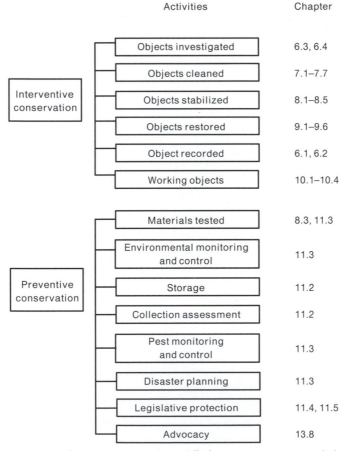

Activities	Chapter
Interventive conservation	
Objects investigated	6.3, 6.4
Objects cleaned	7.1–7.7
Objects stabilized	8.1–8.5
Objects restored	9.1–9.6
Object recorded	6.1, 6.2
Working objects	10.1–10.4
Preventive conservation	
Materials tested	8.3, 11.3
Environmental monitoring and control	11.3
Storage	11.2
Collection assessment	11.2
Pest monitoring and control	11.3
Disaster planning	11.3
Legislative protection	11.4, 11.5
Advocacy	13.8

Figure 3.4 Conservation activities. All these activities may include creating, maintaining and consulting records as an integral part of the process.

Chapter 11 or interventive conservation which is described in Chapters 6–10, should all be conscious actions determined by what is judged the most appropriate balance between the aims of conservation: revelation, investigation and preservation.

3.6 The sequence of interventive conservation

For an object undergoing interventive conservation a generalized sequence of actions and decisions can be envisaged (see Figure 3.5). Not all the steps in the sequence are enacted. At every step in this process the conservator is required to exercise judgement, no step is automatic.

Any form of *Object* can be conserved, from a matchbox to a mansion. In the *Initial investigation* the conservator makes an initial assessment of the object considering what the object appears to be made of and the levels of damage and decay. Working with the *Curator/Owner* of the object a series of *Initial aims* are established. These broadly centre on whether the object is to be *Stored*, *Investigated* or is capable of being *Displayed*. If the object is not *Stable* it will need to go through a conservation process, as it will if it is to be displayed, but is not currently in a displayable condition. Initially a complete *Record* of the object is made using written and visual formats. This requires detailed investigation of the object. As a result of this investigation a detailed *Conservation proposal* is created (see Section 1.6). This may be referred back to the *Curator/Owner* or other senior conservators for comment or approval. An interactive dialogue can be held between the conservator and *Owner/Curator* at any stage during the conservation process, but it is essential when determining the aims of the conservation work. The object, if constructed from several parts, may be *Disassembled* making all parts of the object available for *Analysis*. When the composition of the materials, the decay products and any other appropriate features of the object have been analysed and researched, the conservation proposal may be modified in light of this information. The various parts of the object are, if appropriate, then *Cleaned* and treated to *Stabilize* them and so prevent further decay. If the object is to be displayed, is it now, or will it be when it is reassembled, in *Displayable* condition? If not then the object may be *Restored*. The object may then be given a *Protective* coating to help maintain its stable condition. Any disassembled object is *Reassembled* and the *Conservation record* is *Completed*. An object intended for display may have a *Display mount* created and a stable display *Environment* is assured. Any object being stored will be given suitable stable *Packaging* and placed in an appropriately stable *Environment*. At the end of these processes the conservator has created either an *Object on display*, or an *Object in storage*, and a complete *Conservation record* plus any *Reports* based on aspects of the analysis, conservation or research work which was undertaken as well as retaining any *Samples* taken for, but not destroyed by, the analytical process. The *Conservation record* like a medical record continues to be added too over the succeeding years as additional information about the object is recovered and additional conservation measures are applied.

3A Case study: The Statue of Liberty (Baboian *et al.* 1990)

The Statue of Liberty, formally entitled Liberty Enlightening the World and known colloquially as 'Miss Liberty', was conserved between 1982 and 1986. As the quintessential symbol of the most powerful nation of the world in the late twentieth century, this conservation project was carried out in the full glare of international publicity and exposed many of the ethics and ideals of conservation to a wide public audience. The object was conserved as part of the American quinquennial and the statues own centennial celebrations. This object is important to the people of America for what it represents rather than its artistic merit, though as the only statue of this size made in this period it represents a major artistic and technical achievement.

The Statue was envisaged and initially sculpted at reduced scale by Auguste Bartholdi. The French nation paid for the fabrication of the full-scale statue, which was created between 1874 and 1884 at the workshops of Monduit & Co. The statue is composed of 2.5-mm-thick copper sheet which was hammered into moulds to form the shape. Three hundred copper panels were shaped in this manner and then riveted together and on to a wrought-iron armature. This thin bar iron was attached to an angle-iron frame which was in turn attached to a central 'A' frame wrought-iron pylon composed of four substantial vertical girders. The iron frame was probably designed by Gustav Eiffel. This 'curtain wall' form of construction and the use of wrought iron for the armature allowed the statue to flex slightly in high winds and through thermal expansion and contraction without any weakening of the structure.

To support the statue the American public paid for the erection of a substantial hollow concrete plinth sheathed in polished granite blocks in the centre of Fort Wood on Bedloe's Island, subsequently renamed Liberty Island, in New York Harbour. The American engineering work was directed by General Charles Stone. The statue was sent in pieces from France which were assembled on top of the plinth. The 151-ft-high statue atop its five-storey plinth was officially inaugurated on 28 October 1886. From its opening there was public access into the statue and up to the crown and the statue was lit as a symbol of the freedoms of the New World (see Figure 3.6).

To prevent galvanic corrosion, the iron armature was attached to the copper skin by a series of copper strips or saddles which ran over the iron-bar armature and were riveted to the copper skin. A layer of asbestos soaked in shellac was inserted between the iron bar and the copper saddle and skin, separating the two metals so reducing the possible opportunities for galvanic corrosion. Immediately prior to the opening, circular holes were cut through the skin of the torch and an electric light installed inside the torch, so that the statue radiated light and acted as a harbour light. Consequently the statue was under the control of the US Light House Board up to 1902. It was subsequently under the care of the War Department between 1902 and 1933, after which time it became one of the earliest national monuments in the care of the National Park Service. Originally the copper metal inside the statue was left bare. In 1911 it was covered in a coal-tar emulsion sealing compound which was in later years covered with a total of eleven layers of paint: aluminium flake paint (1932), lead paint, enamel paint (1947), alkalyd paint and in the 1970s, vinyl paints. In 1916 the flame had numerous holes cut in it and stained glass was inserted in order to give a more brightly lit and highly coloured appearance.

By 1982 there were a number of problems with the statue:

- In many places the asbestos was degraded and had adsorbed salt-water spray so creating very active galvanic cell-corrosion conditions and the iron armature was extensively corroded. The iron-corrosion products were pushing out the copper skin and the retaining copper saddles.

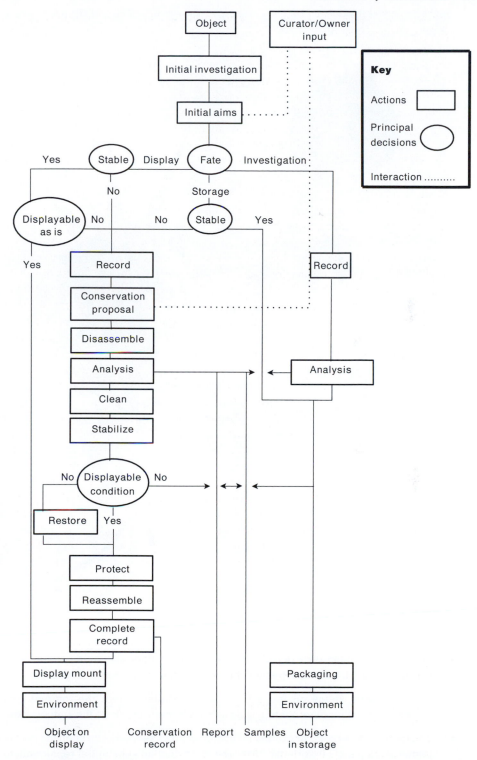

Figure 3.5 Generalized sequence of interventive conservation actions and decisions.

Figure 3.6 The Statue of Liberty (photograph courtesy of Robert Baboian).

- In a few areas there was severe corrosion of the copper skin of the statue. This was usually where water collected or on edges from which water dripped.

- Rust and paint stains on the exterior of the statue, where the internal iron corrosion or earlier paint coatings had seeped through cracks in the statue's skin.

- The torch was severely degraded. A lot of water had seeped in through the poorly joined glass panels inserted in 1916. The torch needed substantial repair and, to stop the problem reoccurring, the torch flame needed to be redesigned to be fully waterproof.

- The paint in the statue's interior was peeling.

- The crown and spikes showed evidence of deterioration and required repair.

- The junction between the torch arm and the shoulder of the statue had been re-inforced in 1932 with the addition of steel plates. This junction again required strengthening.

In 1982 a Centennial Commission was set up to oversee the conservation of the Statue of Liberty and Ellis Island (the principal immigration point to the USA throughout much of the nineteenth and twentieth centuries). The Commission utilized the existing Statue of Liberty – Ellis Island Foundation to acquire funds and commission work. This work was principally done by private contractors and overseen by The National Park Service, many of whose workers were directly involved with the project and who continue to manage the monument to the present day. Over the 4 years of the project the Foundation raised $66 million for the conservation work with further funds coming from the National Park Service.

This statue is a national icon, a symbol of belief, even veneration, so conservation had the potential to arouse strong feelings. The conservators on this project judged that the visual image of the statue was the most important aspect of the object and that major visual changes would be viewed as desecration. The initial decision, therefore, was to leave the present external green patina of the statue intact. It would have been possible to strip it off and leave the statue 'penny bright'; however, this appearance was not viable in the long term since it could not be easily maintained in the corrosive coastal environment. Crucially the presence of the patina retarded the rate of corrosion, thus the statue would last far longer by retaining its present corrosion. The patina of the statue, which is principally composed of the copper sulphate minerals brochantite and antlerite and the basic copper chloride atacamite, was simply washed with freshwater to remove dirt and accumulated salts. Paint and rust stains, which had run through cracks from the interior of the statue, were mechanically removed. Within the statue the internal iron armature was suffering from corrosion; the continued pressure from this corrosion was continuing to damage the external copper sheeting. After testing a number of metals, the whole of the iron armature was replaced with stainless steel type 316L (UNS S31603). This material is corrosion resistant, has similar physical properties to wrought iron (e.g. thermal expansion and strength) and could be cut to exactly the same size as the wrought iron which it replaced. The removal of the pieces of iron armature had to be accomplished in full protective suits because of the health problems from asbestos dust. All the 1,800 pieces of iron were replaced. Each piece of stainless steel was indi-vidually shaped to match the wrought-iron piece it replaced and after shaping was annealed, cleaned and passivated before being riveted into place with a layer of Teflon between the stainless steel and the copper skin and saddle limiting the electro-chemical contact which could occur. A sample of the original wrought-iron armature in good condition was left in the right foot of the statue as a record of the original materials and structure used in the construction of the statue.

In order to replace the iron bars all the paint, much of which was now failing as a protective coating, had to be removed from the inside of the statue. This removal could not involve any vigorous mechanical cleaning because of the potential damage to the copper metal skin and its outer patina. It was hazardous to use chemicals in the sealed confines of the statue because of the fast build-up of toxic fumes. After experimentation the outer layers of paint were removed by blasting the paint with liquid nitrogen ($-196°C$) which made them brittle so the force of the blast and attendant ice particles flaked them off. Traces of the initial coal-tar initial paint layer remained but these could be removed by abrading it in a stream of compressed air (60 psi) containing sodium-bicarbonate particles. This worked well; though if the sodium bicarbonate spilled out through existing cracks on to the exterior it tended to turn the patina blue. This was countered by washing the exterior so removing the sodium bicarbonate. It was decided, since there had originally been no paint applied to the inside of the copper skin of the statue, to leave it in the original unpainted condition. To stop the water getting into the statue through the cracks between the copper plates these were sealed with a silicon sealant. The central iron pylon and rods connecting it to the armature had originally been covered with red lead primer and six further coats of paint, much of which was now flaking off. This was blasted clean with an air abrasive system using aluminium-oxide powder and an inorganic zinc dust and potassium-silicate coating applied within 8 hours to the freshly exposed ironwork. This NASA-developed coating gave excellent corrosion protection and was subsequently sealed with three coats of 'Diamondite', a water-borne two-part epoxy-polyamide coating. This gave a very tough, irreversible, glossy, vandalism-and-graffiti-resistant coating.

The torch and flame was so degraded that most of it was replicated and replaced employing the traditional methods and materials used to create the original. The flame of the torch was recreated in the original completely solid form, based on photographs and drawings. The exterior surface of the flame was then gilded as the original had been prior to 1905. When lit from spotlights on the ground and in the rim of the torch it gave the effect of a glowing flame, the original intention. This created luminescence without the need for any holes in the skin which could admit water and thus promote corrosion within the monument. This restoration was judged by the project conservators to be the best option to the long-term solution for the preservation of the monument. It restored the artist's original intentions and the original form of the monument, though it did remove part of the monument's history. The original flame and upper part of the torch was cleaned and placed inside the museum in the plinth of the statue so this evidence was preserved.

In the area of the statue's shoulder additional strengthening bars in stainless steel were added to provide better support for the torch arm. The possibility of remounting the arm into a slightly more secure position, possibly originally intended by Bartholdi, was not enacted because it was clear that the statue as originally erected had the arm in the present position. Any visual change in the statue would not have been appreciated by the public since it would not have preserved the true nature of this statue, which was as much to do with the history of the statue greeting the immigrants to America, as in the artistic conception of the piece. The armature and the skin of the rays from the crown were brass rather than the pure 'tough pitch' copper used throughout the rest of the statue. They were extensively restored and other holes in the copper skin – such as the tip of the nose which had been holed as a result of the thin beaten nature of the metal and the extensive corrosion – were repaired. Any new metal piece and all the new rivets used in the replacement of the armature were patinated to blend in with the present exterior visual form of the statue.

In addition to the direct conservation and restoration of the statue measures were taken to improve public access to the structure, improve the visitor experience at the monument and modify the interaction between the visitors (ca. 2.5 million annually) and the statue. A museum about the statue, its creation and conservation was placed in the plinth, so diverting some visitors from ascending the statue and explaining more about the monument. The spiral staircase which gives visitors access up to the crown level was strengthened in stainless steel and cleaned. Air conditioning to cool the statue's interior, reducing the relative humidity fluctuation in the statue and making it more pleasant for visitors, new lighting, security and fire-protection systems were installed. Where it was possible for visitors to touch the copper skin at the crown level it was protected with three coats of epoxy-polyamide paint on an acrylic-polymer base coat.

The conservation of this statue involved the conservators in careful judgement of a wide variety of factors. A balance needed to be struck between the revelation of the statue (torch replacement, patina retention, exact form of the iron-armature replacement, cleaned unpainted internal surface of the copper skin), investigation (of the preservative effect of the patina, the form and construction of the replacement torch, specification of the stainless steel for armature replacement) and preservation (original torch, the replacement of the torch and sealing the cracks stopping water ingress, patina retention, painting the iron support pylon, air conditioning). This has meant that the statue in its present form is a restored compromise, with the patina of 100 years, the new flame in its original form and an open internal structure with modern air conditioning, stainless steel on the stairs and glossy epoxy-painted ironwork. It has thus not been restored to an original condition, nor a thoroughly modern form, but a compromise, which gives much of the visual impression of the original, but contains the modern safety requirements essential for any public space, and retains the patina of age as a cherished symbol.

4 History of conservation

4.1 History of museums and collections

The earliest collecting of objects of the past is represented by the occurrence of fossils in palaeolithic graves. Such tokens supported the idea of a supernatural and something beyond the present. Like many of the rulers of ancient kingdoms, the Egyptian pharaohs massed collections of old, unusual and interesting objects such as Tulimosis III's collection of Asian flora and fauna. Such collections celebrated their power to own the rare and consequently valuable, and to have an understanding of things beyond the experience of other men. However, in the sixth century BC, En-nigaldi-Nanna, the daughter of Mesopotamian king Nabonidus, had a collection of ancient objects in a building which has been interpreted as a school (Lewis 1992a) and thus this is perhaps the earliest museum, a collection used to educate others.

This creation of collections of old and unusual objects became one of the expected functions of Greek temples, such as that established in 490 BC in the temple of Delphi to celebrate the victory of the Athenians at Marathon. These collections in the 'treasuries' of temples were both 'inventoried' and 'conserved' and represent some of the first attempts at good museum practice, and certainly preventive conservation. Greek philosophers had private collections of objects as did early educational institutions such as the Alexandria 'museion' founded in 290 BC by Ptolemy Sotor I. The Romans copied the Greek idea of temple treasuries as well as having personal collections of old and unusual objects. A fashion for the ancient Greek led to copying and faking ancient Greek statuary and indicates a widespread appreciation for the appearance of the past by the Roman elite.

The centres of worship continued to house old and unusual objects in their treasuries, regardless of the religion. For example, the Toji treasure house in the Kyoto Buddhist temple and the collection of the widow of the Japanese emperor Shomu (724–756 AD), housed in a treasury 'Shoso-in' dedicated to the Buddha Vairochana. Similarly Islamic shrines housed collections of objects such as that of Aliar-Rida, a Muslim martyr (765–818 AD), housed at Meshed. The churches and cathedrals of western Europe received numerous gifts which they assembled into treasuries such as that at Conque in southern France, on the pilgrim route to St James de Compostela. The collections housed in these religious centres were gifts from believers who wished to venerate the deity through their gift. Both the individuals and the religious authorities felt that power and value rested in these collections of old and treasured objects. The collections mentioned above are known because, as places of sanctity, they have survived. Where there was religious upheaval, such as the Reformation in North-West Europe, these collections at religious sites have often been dispersed as in the case of the treasury of Aachen Cathedral (Corfield, personal communication).

The tradition of powerful rulers amassing collections of unusual, old and interesting artefacts also continued. Julius Caesar, most of the Chinese Emperors, Henry III of England (1207–1272) all developed large private collections of artefacts. Such individuals appear to have placed a higher value on knowledge than their contemporaries, and they invariably also had substantial libraries. The concept of a knowledgeable ruler (e.g. Solomon), rather than merely a powerful one, became a more prevalent attitude in the Renaissance when private collections of the old and curious, but particularly the antique, increased substantially. Collections, such as that by the Medici family, were both a means of displaying their wealth, a fashionable pastime of the Renaissance wealthy and of genuine enquiry and appreciation of the arts. The creation of the upper floor of the Uffizi by Francesco I (1541–1587) to house and display his collection of pictures reflects an appreciation of the need to care for the objects and for ensuring people could visit the collection. Similarly Albrecht V, Duke of Bavaria, created a purpose-built building (1563–7) to house his art collection and in 1569–73 a purpose-built museum to house his antiquities collections.

In Europe the development of a professional or middle class through the late Middle Ages and Renaissance period created men who had money and power because of their wits, rather than their ancestry. Members of this class as well as the aristocracy acquired 'cabinets of curiosities' to delight friends as a fashionable diversion. A number of individuals from this professional/middle class also started to pursue the intellectual quest of classifying resulting in the earliest encyclopaedias: Samuel Quiccheberg's *Inscriptiones vel tituli theatri amplissimi* ... (Schulz 1994) and the attempts to produce a coherent historical narrative (Pearce 1990). They documented and studied their collections seeking to use them as a means of explaining part of the world around them. Specialised collectors included Luca Ghini (1490–1556) of Padua and Olaf Worm (1588–1654) of Copenhagen. After their death many of these men bequeathed their collections to the towns, learned societies or universities which were springing up around Europe. Amerbach's collection was purchased by the city of Basel in 1661 to form the earliest public museum, swiftly followed by Elias Ashmole's gift of his collection to Oxford University in 1683. As this 'age of enlightenment' progressed, learned and scientific societies were established (e.g. The Royal Society in 1660) and later books, such as *Museographia* by Neickel, *Museum museorum* by Valentini (1704) and *Systema Naturae* by Linnaeus (1735), started to draw some understanding from these collections. This ultimately led to later texts and ideas, such as the Three Age System, a division of prehistory into stone, bronze and iron ages by C. J. Thomson in 1836, which started the classification and discipline we know as archaeology and the work of Darwin, which by 1859, led to theories of evolution. The efforts of numerous gentlemen intellectuals of the nineteenth century such as General Pitt Rivers resulted in the establishment of many thousands of assiduously catalogued and studied specimens in private collections, which eventually formed the basis of public museum collections. These emphasized the belief system of their collectors; the ability to classify and thus explain the ancient and natural worlds (Pearce 1990). A need to preserve or 'fix' specimens, particularly 'type' specimens, was important to support the order of the newly emerging disciplines of geology, biology, zoology, botany, archaeology, etc.

During the period 1600–1900 AD the power of royalty, the aristocracy and the church diminished and consequently many of these earlier royal and ecclesiastical collections were lost or broken up. The new power which emerged was that of national governments, which led to heightened sense of nationalism and to the establishment of national museums such as the British Museum in 1759 and the Louvre in 1793. Though, even these national museums were often founded on the collections of a single individual; for example, the collections of

Sir Hans Sloane which formed the basis for the collections of the British Museum. The three dominant nineteenth-century powers of Europe – Germany, France and Britain – spent much effort filling their national museums with the treasures of the ancient world. The economic strength of these powers, like Rome before them and America in the late twentieth century, enabled these museums to amass substantial important collections.

During the Renaissance wealthy individuals had collected the antique, driven by a sense of the aesthetic and veneration of the ancient culture and its ideals. However, the changing national and political boundaries of eighteenth-century northern Europe generated a need to define national aspirations. The definition of nationalism became the crucial development in using the past, thus defining heritage. In Denmark the symbols of the ancient inhabitants of the land, the prehistoric mounds and stone monuments, were seen as the national past and were protected as 'ancient monuments' as early as 1807. The French similarly defined and protected ancient monuments in 1836. Throughout Europe symbols of the potency and legacy of the past began to be gradually drawn in to establish the concept of nationalism, and ancient monuments and national museums were the crucibles in which part of the national identity was formed.

The first museum in the USA was established in Charleston, South Carolina in 1773. Like many small museums of the late eighteenth and early nineteenth century it was established and supported by the local literary and philosophical societies which sprang up during this period. In Britain many museums and art galleries were established in the mid- and late nineteenth century for the purposes of public enlightenment. There was free admission into these institutions which displayed 'fine art' in order that the public would learn about 'good taste' and together with libraries were part of a Victorian ideal of self-improvement. This increasing number of museums was aided by the passing of the Museums Act of 1845 which permitted local authorities to set up museums using the local rates (taxes). This established a network of local and regional museums, many of which have acquired important collections and acted as a regional focus for efforts to preserve local heritage.

Following World War I, German influence declined and that of America grew, but it was the development of train, plane and ship transportation systems as well as film and radio communications which started a more international approach to museums. Many emergent countries in North Africa, South America and Asia started to develop national museums. The International Museum Office, which later became the International Council of Museums, held its first conference in Rome in 1930. The presence of journals on collecting and caring for objects such as *The Museums Journal* (UK) (established 1901), *Museumhinde* (Germany) (established 1905), *Museum News* (US) (established 1924) and *Museion* (Germany) (1927–47) later *Museum* (UNESCO) (1948–) provided a useful source of information to both emerging and established museums.

The concern for the loss of historic buildings and places as a result of the social and industrial development of the nineteenth and twentieth centuries led to efforts to preserve such buildings and places (see Figure 4.1). In Great Britain this resulted in the establishment of The National Trust in 1894 as a charitable body dedicated to preservation of places and buildings of natural and historic beauty. Through the parliamentary acts in 1907 and 1971 it acquired the status of a statutory body whose property and possessions were inalienable and thus protected for all time. After its first 40 years of existence it only had 8,000 members, demonstrating that even up to the 1930s the protection of the heritage was a minority interest of the educated, middle and upper classes. The rise in leisure time during the 1950s led to large increases in visitor numbers to museums and historic houses throughout the UK. Consequently, by 1968, the Trust had 400,000 members and the preservation of 'the

Figure 4.1 Plaque commemorating the restoration of a dun (fortified place) known as The Borg
at Kirkandrews Bay, Kirkcudbrightshire in 1905 (photographed by the author). A
stone-walled prehistoric fort, part of a local heritage, restored by a local landowner
to ensure its survival and enhance local tradition.

heritage' was a mass movement. The rise in leisure time and the interest in heritage has
continued to the present day with 1 million visits to National Trust properties in 1959
increasing to 4 million visits by 1976 (Chamberlin 1979).

Following World War II, the pace of social and industrial change quickened. The folk-
museum tradition, which had started in 1891 with the establishment by Artur Hazelius of
the first open-air museum at Skansen (1891) in Stockholm, was a reaction to the loss of local
culture and tradition (particularly agriculturally based) overcome by the first waves of the
industrial revolution (Kavanagh 1990). By the 1970s large numbers of local museums, folk
and industrial museums were springing up around the world, but particularly in Britain. Most
substantial and successful of these were the folk museums based on nineteenth-century
industries such as Ironbridge Gorge and Beamish. In a time of considerable social change
many local communities sought to emphasize the importance and permanence which those
nineteenth-century industries had represented through the establishment of museums (Lewis
1992b; Kavanagh 1990). The continuing development of local museums and the emergence
of museums for native peoples in the last quarter of the twentieth century were reactions to
the growing globalization of 'Americana' culture, which appeared to be swamping the older
locally based cultures and belief systems.

Keene (1996) usefully identifies the present continuum of museums as fulfilling roles
defined by the nature of their collections and resulting in different display policies.

- Art galleries have small collections, most of which are out on display. They preserve the
  idea of temples to beauty, places where good taste is displayed. Display is the primary
  function of these institutions.

- Natural-history museums and archaeological museums have massive collections, many thousands or millions of specimens, only a small percentage of which are out on display. The vast collections of small fossils and sherds of pottery represent a storehouse of knowledge, the means by which we understand the natural world and the past. Preservation and curation of this collection is the primary function of these institutions.

- Technology/science museums and folk parks or social-history museums have large collections, a substantial proportion of which is out on display. The emphasis is on the educative role of the displays, encouraging the visitors to enter the world of the recent past, or the scientific process. The use of 'working objects' and involving displays is paramount in engaging the interest and thus informing the visitor. Education is the primary function of these institutions.

The role of collecting has already been shown to be the historic root of museum collections. Curators appear to have an emotional need to collect, expressed by Sir David Wilson 'A museum which does not collect is a dead museum' (Keene 1996). However, with finite financial resources, and an associated cost in cataloguing and storage which is concomitant with collecting, many museums cannot afford to keep collecting and many museums now function principally through investigation and display of their existing collections. Thus this statement defines the emotional response of an acquisitor and not a central tenant of a museum's existence. More balanced views of the nature of role of museums are provided by ICOM's definition of a museum as 'an institution which acquires, conserves, researches, communicates and exhibits', whilst Ward (1986) defines a museum simply as having four functions: 'they collect, they preserve, they conduct research and they present or interpret their collections'.

4.2 History of conservation

Whilst the earliest 'conservators' could be regarded as the priests who cared for the objects in the Greek temples or the 'muntadors' who cleaned Michelangelo's frescos on the ceiling of the Sistine Chapel (see Case study 7A), such work was done without any scientific basis, recording, analytical investigation or identification of the causes of decay of the object. Thus it is more accurately described as cleaning.

There are numerous examples of ancient objects which have been repaired, such as Roman Samian bowls which have been repaired with lead rivets and straps (Corfield 1988a), and although these may be seen as restoring the function of the object, it is more likely, given that such vessels were no longer waterproof, that this was the repair of a treasured object, repaired more for its own sake than any function. This work was again done without any scientific basis, recording, analytical investigation or identification of the causes of decay of the object; thus it is more accurately described as repair than conservation.

A reverence for objects of the past is described by Pliny the Elder in his *Natural History* as the reason for the 'restoration' of both objects and monuments which were undertaken by the Romans (Sease 1996). In subsequent periods, wherever there was a reverence for the past, there were attempts to uncover, retain, clean and restore artefacts from the venerated past. The act of recovery, retention and cleaning the object became the means of expressing reverence for the past; such work being well beyond the financial value of the object.

This veneration of the past is perhaps most apparent in the Renaissance, where artists of the day such as Michelangelo and Cellini were employed to restore classical antiquities, particularly statues. Cellini records chiselling off the earth and corrosion products on classical bronze statues (Cellini 1878; Sease 1996). Restoration of classical statues was undertaken to restore the aesthetic vision of the whole. Though Cellini regarded such restoration work as the province of inferior artists, he did undertake such work himself (Sease 1996). Coremans (1969) described this phase of conservation/cleaning as 'some form of aesthetic surgery, which gave a work of art a pleasant appearance, even if such surgery greatly accelerated decay'.

Works of art such as paintings were, even into the late medieval period, regarded as working art (Hartin 1990). Early restorers such as Neri di Bicci would restore such art as the client wished. In 1471 he restored an altarpiece for Tomaso Soderini altering a figure of St Fredianus to St Margaret (Thomas 1998). The value of art began to be more greatly appreciated in the seventeenth century with many of the works of the Flemish artists protected with curtains or even shutters (Campbell 1998). This rising importance of original art was seen in the veneration of 'old art' and the concept of 'old masters' through the eighteenth century. Restoration work could still be extensive, and artists of the ability of van Dyck and Sir Joshua Reynolds undertook restoration work (Kirby Talley 1998).

By the late eighteenth century the taste for classical Greece and Rome was taking hold in England and aristocratic young men were starting to make the Grand Tour visiting Rome and the lands of the Mediterranean. This was stimulated the excavations at Pompeii, which started in 1748, and unearthed many unstable and partially damaged objects which required attention. The charred papyri from Pompeii and, in particular, from the Villa of the Papyri uncovered in Herculanium in 1752 were a source of interest to many scholars. Work in the late eighteenth century by Antonio Piaggio, a Genoese monk and sub-librarian at the Vatican, led to the development of a technique for very gradually unrolling and supporting these papyri scrolls by gluing them onto a thin backing of parchment (Seeley 1987). This technique was not always successful but quite a number of the least badly charred papyri were unrolled and translated. The British Prince Regent was fascinated by these discoveries and acquired copies of the translations. After he had become King George IV in 1818, he instructed the President of the Royal Society, Sir Humphrey Davy, to study the remaining papyri. Davy, who had previously analysed classical wall paintings and vases, undertook a coherent body of research seeking to examine the condition of these papyri, looking for the cause of their decay, prior to devising a solution to the problem (Davy 1821). This is an approach which we would recognize as modern conservation research, a tradition of investigating the material and determining its process of decay. It was copied in 1826 by Sir Humphrey's brother Dr John Davy in his investigation of the corrosion of the copper alloy of an ancient Greek helmet (Davy 1826). Similar scientific thoroughness in exploring the relationship between a material's composition, environment and decay was shown by Sir David Brewster in his work on iridescence on glass (Brewster 1861) and James Fowler in his extensive work on the corrosion of glass (Fowler 1880).

In Denmark the collections of The National Museum in Copenhagen, founded in 1807, were classified and catalogued by C. J. Thomson (Three Age System), who cleaned objects in the collection using vinegar and carborundum and paid others to wash clean the runestones in the collection (Brinch Madsen 1987). Thomson was an archaeologist who, working with colleagues such as Herbst, Stenstrup and Jorgansen, developed or utilized techniques for conserving freshly excavated finds; for example, leaving soft freshly excavated prehistoric pots to stand and dry in order to harden, and saving the fragile finds of the Hvidegard grave at Lyngby through coating them immediately upon discovery with shellac and preserving the waterlogged wood by twice boiling the wood in a solution of alum and coating, about a month later, in purified linseed oil. This marked the start of the conservation work on waterlogged archaeological materials though it has often received little recognition since it was published in Danish (Brinch Madsen 1987). The need to clean and preserve finds coming up from archaeological excavations began to be widely appreciated and in 1888 Flinders Petrie published a paper 'The treatment of small finds' in the *Archaeological Journal*, whilst Albert Voss, the director of the Berlin Museums, published *Merkbuch, Alterthumer Aufzugraben und Aufzubewahren* (Caldararo 1987; Seeley 1987).

In 1843 Michael Faraday undertook research on the decay of leather book bindings in the vicinity of gas-lamp burners (Faraday 1843), the phenomena we now know as 'red rot' which is caused by high levels of SO_2 (Caldararo 1987). The problem with gas burners continued to receive attention in later years (Woodward 1888) and marks an awareness about pollution and the environment which has remained with those engaged in preserving libraries and archives.

In 1836 the British Museum employed Mr John Doubleday as a craftsman to clean and repair objects in the collections and, after he died, Mr Robert Sparrow (locksmith) was employed as locksmith and cleaner and repairer of objects in the museum. Doubleday was mentioned, by Sir Henry Layard, as being particularly skilful in conserving the ivories from his Nineveh excavations, and he is famous for reassembling the Portland Vase smashed by a vandal in 1845 (see Case study 4A). These appointments were typical of the craft base which was originally perceived as the necessary background to ensure that the collections were, as specified in the British Museum Act of 1753:

> preserved and maintained, not only for the Inspection and Entertainment of the learned and the curious, but for the general Use and Benefit of the Public.
>
> (Watkins 1997: 223)

This craft tradition for the care of artefacts was established in many of the national museums and art galleries springing up through Europe in the late nineteenth century, and which continued in some institutions until the 1970s. Throughout the mid-nineteenth century, in addition to the craftsman cleaner, the British Museum also consulted notable British scientists such as Faraday, William Brande, Professor Hoffmann and Dr Frankland to advise on specific aspects of problems related to the corrosion of metals and the problem of salts in stone (Watkins 1997). In fine art conservation work such as the refurbishment of Polish religious polychrome statues, eminent artists, sculptors and scholars were consulted as to how far the craftsmen undertaking the work should proceed with their cleaning and restoration work (Slesinski 1993).

In the mid- to late nineteenth century, the fashion for Gothic architecture swept through the UK. Blessed with too much money many churches, in particular, were altered and amended to remove many original features and recreate imagined gothic interiors and exteriors. In order to prevent such desecration William Morris and others founded the Society for the Protection of Ancient Buildings (SPAB) in 1877 (see Section 9.3). In the first report of this body Morris wrote:

> Restoration of ancient buildings ... a strange and most fatal idea – which by its very name implies that it is possible to strip from a building, this, that and the other part of

history, of its life that is, and then to stay the hand at some arbitrary point and leave it still historical, still living and even as it once was.

(Morris 1996: 319)

In early times this kind of forgery was impossible ... If repairs were needed, if ambition or piety pricked on to change, that change was of necessity wrought in the unmistakable fashion of the time ... But those who make the changes wrought in our day under the name restoration, while professing to bring back a building to the best time of its history, have no guide but each his own individual whim to point out to them what is admirable and what contemptible.

(*ibid.*: 320)

Such clear expressions of the historic importance of all aspects of these ancient buildings have helped to define modern approaches to conservation (Morris 1996). The SPAB received support at the time from academics, architects and the public. Schemes to renovate the tomb of Edward the Confessor in Westminster Abbey or the front of San Marco in Venice were halted through SPAB pressure (Chamberlin 1979).

It was, perhaps, only in 1888 that conservation as a professional discipline can truly be seen to have started with the appointment of Friedrich Rathgen to a post in the Royal Museums of Berlin. Rathgen was a young chemist who was asked to solve the problems of ancient Egyptian artefacts which had been excavated by the German archaeologist Lepsius in the 1830s, brought back to the Royal Museum in Berlin and were now starting to decay. Rathgen created a laboratory, and devised many of the earliest conservation treatments such as the desalination of stone, the baking of the unfired clay tablets so preserving their legends, the use of synthetic polymers for adhesion and coating of artefacts; all of which are still done to this day. Crucially, Rathgen carefully diagnosed the nature of the decay of the artefacts and kept records monitoring progress. Thus he was able to start building up a record of knowledge about successful techniques which could then be repeated. Consequently in 1898 Rathgen produced one of the first textbooks on conservation *Die Konservierung von Altumsfunden* (The Conservation of Antiquities) (Gilberg 1987).

In 1890 Georg Rosenberg was appointed to the National Museum in Copenhagen. Trained as a sculptor, he taught himself the science he needed and established conservation laboratories and procedures in the Danish National Museum. He was one of a group of scientists and conservators who worked for national museums around Europe and who developed conservation techniques built upon the scientific approaches of Rathgen and other colleagues. In 1889 Finkener developed electrolytic reduction to treat corroding bronze objects, whilst in 1892 Krefting developed electrochemical reduction for cleaning corroding antiquities. Rathgen used and developed these methods and utilized information from the work of Berthelot who, in regular papers to the French Academy of Sciences, had identified chloride ions as causative of high rates of decay in copper corrosion. Rathgen himself pioneered the use of Zapon (cellulose nitrate) in 1903–4 as an adhesive and coating polymer and in 1913 the use of Zellon (cellulose acetate) for similar uses. In 1905 Rathgen's first book was published in English as *The Preservation of Antiquities* and it served as the basis for much of the subsequent scholarly work on conservation published in English. In 1915 he revised, enlarged and republished his textbook on conservation which was published in German, entitled in translation *The Conservation of Antiquities with Special Reference to Ethnographic, Folk Art and Museum Objects*. The German loss of power and influence after World War I meant that few read the later work of Rathgen, consequently the work of British and American authors on conservation became better known (Gilberg 1987).

Following the discovery of severe problems of mould, corrosion and soluble-salt damage affecting the collections of the British Museum, which had been stored in the damp conditions of the London Underground system during World War I, Dr Alexander Scott of the British Government's Department of Science and Industrial Research was seconded to the British Museum to provide greater scientific input to the preservation of the collections (Plenderleith 1998). He published a number of reports in the 1920s under the general title *The Cleaning and Restoration of Museum Exhibits* and helped to found the British Museum's Research Laboratory in 1931 (Johnson 1993; Oddy 1997). With a strong scientific background and working on some of the most important archaeological finds of the age, this laboratory generated individuals and publications which shaped conservation for the rest of the century. Alfred Lucas, the senior chemist working for the Egyptian government who together with Arthur Mace undertook the conservation work on the finds from the excavation of Tutankhamen's tomb, was in frequent touch with the Research Laboratory (Plenderleith 1998). Lucas subsequently wrote a book *Antiques: Their Restoration and Preservation* in 1924, based on his work on the Tutankhamen finds. He later went on to study and write *Ancient Egyptian Materials* in 1926 based on many years of interest, study and analysis of Egyptian antiquities (Gilberg 1997). There has subsequently been a strong tradition of conservator–ancient technologists such as Hodges (1964) and Oddy (1980) who have studied and produced key texts on ancient technology as well as conservation.

By the late 1920s the Americans had begun to contribute to the field of conservation with research on the patina of ancient bronzes (Seeley 1987) and preserving natural history and anthropological specimens (Leechman 1931). At this time the international museum community also began to publish articles on aspects of care and conservation of museum artefacts in the new museum journals (e.g. *The Museums Journal, Mouseion* and *Curator*). The International Museum's Office of the League of Nations, which eventually became ICOM, hosted international conferences on aspects of museum studies which commenced in Rome in 1930 and Athens in 1931 (Oddy 1997). The 1930s saw a considerable number of new conservation and analytical laboratories devoted to the care and study of paintings established throughout Europe (Roy 1998). In 1938 this office also called the first meeting devoted to conservation entitled 'First International Meeting for the Study of Scientific Methods Applied to the Examination and Conservation of Works of Art', which was held in Rome and devoted almost entirely to paintings (Coremans 1969). The continuing leading role for the British Museum Research Laboratory and its staff in the English speaking world was confirmed by the widespread use of the textbook on conservation *Preservation of Antiquities* written in 1934 by Harold Plenderleith. This was revised and republished in 1956 as *The Conservation of Antiquities and Works of Art* which, in turn, was revised and republished as a second edition by Plenderleith and Werner in 1971 (Caldararo 1987). These last two books became the textbooks to the emerging subject of archaeological and artefact conservation.

After World War II, the conservation community around the world was of sufficient size to establish its own organization, The International Institute for Conservation of Historic Objects and Works of Art (IIC) in 1950. This organization has grown and spawned regional groups (such as the UK group established in 1953) which have themselves then split off to become strong national associations, such as the United Kingdom Institute for Conservation

(UKIC). In 1952 the IIC began to produce *Studies in Conservation*, the first journal identified as being devoted to conservation. In 1959 UNESCO founded ICCROM (International Centre for the Study of the Preservation and Restoration of Cultural Property) in Rome, which in turn supported ICOM (International Committee of Museums) in an attempt to develop international standards in the care of cultural property and provide a forum for interchange of ideas on best practise in all aspects of curating cultural heritage. From the 1960s onwards both IIC and the Conservation Committee of ICOM (ICOM-CC) have held and published regular international conferences. This started to produce a considerable body of literature on the subject of conservation and as specialist conservation literature developed in the 1970s it appeared far less frequently in the general museum journals.

Since the 1970s there have been an increasing number of books on various aspects of conservation and an increasing number of small specialist conference publications from groups such as AIC, UKIC and the ICOM-CC Working Groups. This has greatly expanded the literature on conservation. Several organizations around the world are dedicated to developing the subject of conservation, such as The Canadian Conservation Institute and the Getty Conservation Institute, who have funded research, publication and major conservation projects. It is now researchers – such as Grattan, Larsen, Wolbers and Michalski, funded by these organizations and the major museums of the world – who are responsible for moving conservation forward into the era of antioxidants, laser cleaning, solvent gels and the numerous aspects of preventive conservation.

Conservation's scientific origins started with the research of Davy in the 1820s, the fieldwork element with Herbst and Thomson in Denmark and Petrie, Schliemann, Voss and others in the Middle East and as a professional laboratory-based discipline with the appointment of Rathgen in 1888. Its craft and artistic origins, particularly in the care, cleaning and restoration of works of art, such as paintings and textiles, is far more obscure, stretching back through practitioners such as John Doubleday to the artists of the Renaissance such as Cellini. It has been the melding together of the two traditions which has created conservation. Much of this evolution has, since World War II been effected through the training courses for conservators which have increasingly been established in higher education institutions.

It has been suggested (Coremans 1969) that conservation could not exist as a discipline until it had grasped the ethical concepts, articulated by Morris and SPAB in 1877, of the importance of original evidence of the past, and the need to preserve it for future generations. Equally it could not exist until there was a widespread acceptance of the need to explain decay in terms of the chemical reactions between the object and the surrounding environment, work which emerged in the late nineteenth century through the efforts of Rathgen and others. It also required the ability to analyse materials, characterize them in terms of elemental composition and microstructural form, and to develop some understanding of the use of physical evidence to interpret the past (i.e. the discipline of archaeology), all of which also occurred throughout the latter half of the nineteenth century. Thus the discipline, which we now know as conservation, could not have existed much before the 1890s. Its roots stretch back to the earliest collectors of the past whose patronage helped develop the art and craft skills of restorers to clean and restore objects, but it is the development of the ability to investigate and the scientific understanding and ethical basis for preservation as well as recognition for the need to record (see Chapter 6), which generated the modern discipline of conservation.

4A Case study: The Portland Vase (Smith 1992; Williams 1989)

This Roman glass vase, composed of a white cameo cut glass depicting a classical scene on a deep blue background, was probably created in the first century AD or BC. Clearly a piece of the finest craftsmanship it had always been a prized object, and was disinterred in 1582 from a marble sarcophagus located beneath the huge burial mound at Monte del Grano, south of Rome. This was, in all probability, the tomb of the Emperor Alexander Severus (222–235 AD). The vase passed through the hands of several owners, including the British Ambassador at the court of Naples, before it was bought by the Dowager Duchess of Portland for 1,800 guineas. In 1810 the 4th Duke of Portland loaned the vase to the British Museum for display and safe keeping. In 1845 a young man calling himself William Lloyd, who was described as 'in a state of nervous excitement after a week of drinking' used a heavy object to smash through the museum case and shatter the Portland vase into hundreds of fragments. He could provide no reason for his vandalism and was sentenced to pay £3.00 or serve 2 months hard labour for the destruction of the museum case. He could not be prosecuted for the destruction of the vase since there was no law to cover such wilful destruction of valuable property, the Wilful Damage Act only applying to objects up to a value of £5.00. Subsequently, and in response to this crime, Parliament passed The Protection of Works of Art and Scientific and Library Collections Act (Smith 1992; Williams 1989).

In 1845 the restorer at the British Museum, John Doubleday, reassembled the vase, though thirty-seven of the fragments could not be fitted into the restoration. The vase was displayed in this form until 1948 when, following its purchase by the British Museum from the Portland family in 1945, it was decided to conduct another restoration. The vase was 'taken down' and reassembled by the museum's chief restorer J. H. W Axtell; thirty-four fragments could still not be incorporated into the restored vase. By 1988 the adhesive used in the 1948 reassembly had begun to turn yellowish brown in colour. Tapping the glass gave a dull knock, rather than a ringing sound, which indicated the presence of unadhered cracks in the restored vase and areas of the 1945 gap filling had also visibly shrunk. Therefore, Nigel Williams and Sandra Smith, senior conservators in the Glass and Ceramics section of the British Museum Conservation Department, undertook the reconservation of this vessel.

There were no records from the 1845 and 1948 restorations of this vase, only the watercolour by T. Hasmer Sheperd immortalizing the smashed fragments and the occasional image of the conserved vessel. The adhesive used in the 1948 restoration was consequently unknown and analysis was required to show that it was an early epoxy resin. The gap fills were made of pigmented wax. Following the creation of temporary inner and outer moulds of blotting paper the inner one stiffened with a thin wash of plaster of Paris, the vase was left in an atmosphere of water vapour and methylene chloride (1,1,1-trichloromethane) for 3 days which softened the adhesive and allowed the glass fragments to be removed one by one. The fact that the epoxy resin was so degraded that it softened in the atmosphere, composed largely of water vapour, vindicated the judgement that reconservation was needed because of the weakened state of the object. After mechanically removing all the remaining adhesive from the edges of the sherds and cleaning the dirt and dust from the surface, through gentle washing in a solution of non-ionic detergent, a total of 189

Figure 4.2 The Portland Vase after restoration (photograph courtesy of the British Museum).

separate sherds were ready to be reassembled. In reassembling the sherds it was essential to have a stable adhesive which would not discolour and which hold the vessel together effectively for many decades. Such adhesives are by their nature irreversible. It was also necessary to hold the glass fragments together in exact registration so that there were no cracks or ledges between the fragments. Following testing it was found that the most effective way to achieve these criteria was to use two adhesives: one, a slow (7 day) curing epoxy resin (Hxtal NYL) as the principal adhesive, the second a quick-setting UV cured acrylic resin applied in small patches just to hold the glass sherds together in the correct position whilst the epoxy resin gradually set. This necessitated the use of a strong UV source to ensure the acrylic set quickly. It proved difficult to line up the pieces of glass accurately whilst wearing protective gloves and goggles, essential when using the UV source (Smith 1992). The reassembly continued well up to the level of the shoulder; however, above this level around the neck of the vessel the sherds did not always fit together well, and closer examination revealed that, in a previous restoration, in order to 'make the pieces fit' they had been abraded with a file (Smith 1992). Thus when this more exact modern restoration was being undertaken, there were gaps between some of the sherds. In order that the correct original shape of the vase could be achieved, these missing areas were subsequently gap filled. All but seventeen (Williams 1989) minuscule fragments were fitted into this reconstruction of the vase. These fragments all came from heavily damaged areas, where actual glass was missing as a result of the damage caused from the original breaking of the vase in 1845. The missing areas of glass were filled with the epoxy resin which was tinted to resemble the glass. In creating the gap-filled areas, whilst the original shape of the blue background was clear, the details of the white cameo-cut figures was more uncertain. However, plaster casts made in the sixteenth century and drawings of the vase from the same period provided all the required information to enable an exact copy of the original lines and decoration of the figures to be created. The whole vessel was subsequently given a coat of microcrystalline wax in order to restore the sheen to the surface of the glass (Smith 1992; Williams 1989) (see Figure 4.2).

The decision to dismantle and reassemble the vessel was judged necessary on the grounds of the fragility of the 1948 restoration and the clear risk to its continued survival. It was also apparent that considerable improvement in the visual appearance of the object could be effected through the use of modern more stable materials and as a result of increased experience in the restoration of glass and ceramic vessels. The conservators judged that the need for good adhesion between the glass fragments and a stable restored vessel outweighed other considerations such as reversibility, and thus an irreversible epoxy resin adhesive was used. The vase was gap filled and given a surface coating of wax to restore the visual integrity (aesthetic entity) of this beautiful object. The modern conservation work revealed the deficiencies of the earlier restorers, both in terms of the lack of records and in terms of damaging the object. These practices were not unusual for the time, but do show how conservation standards have improved.

5 Conservation ethics

5.1 Ethical codes

Ethics are definable as 'the principle of good or right conduct' which is predicated on 'a series of moral principles or values' (Edson 1997). Such ideas of right and wrong and the values to which they refer are determined by the society in which one lives, and are designed to modify the behaviour of the individuals in that society for the benefit of that society. Ethical codes are operated by every individual and all groups within a society. All professions have specialized codes of ethics. Ethical codes for a group are drawn up by consensus from the ethical codes practised by individuals. The laws of a country invariably represent a minimum series of ethical ideas agreed for that society and are enforced through punishment for transgression. Ethics or moral principles are a function of a society and as such vary from one society to another and alter through time within a society. Thus as Butler suggested 'cannibalism is moral (and hence ethical) in a cannibal country' (Child 1997).

Codes of ethics are necessary in order to provide a basis for making choices. As such they form the conceptual basis of the conservation profession and all forms of professional practice (Jedrzejewska 1976; Brooks 1998; Ashley-Smith 1982). The twentieth-century improvements in conservation techniques and materials have been accompanied by increasing restrictions on time and finance. This means that, although more choices are available, an increasingly limited number of them can be enacted. Thus there has been, in recent decades, an increased need for an awareness of the ethical basis on which conservation decisions can be seen to be made. Keene (1994) suggests that ethical codes are of particular relevance for inexperienced conservators in order to provide a framework and rules by which such practitioners can operate. Every profession realizes that it cannot police the actions of all its inexperienced practitioners. Educating or indoctrinating them in the ethical codes ensures they operate the rules without the need for policing or supervision. There is always uncertainty within any group as to how strictly the ethical codes of the group should be followed. Some treat them as absolute rules whilst others treat them as guidelines. Such variations in approach can be particularly confusing to new members of the group.

By 1950 conservation had become sufficiently specialized that a group of expert practitioners who described themselves as 'conservators' and 'restorers' founded the first conservators' organization – the IIC. This and subsequent groupings of conservators, UKIC and AIC, grew to became accepted as a specialized profession with its own high level training courses, conferences and journals. In forming an exclusive grouping conservators accepted a common series of aims or objectives and defined acceptable and unacceptable behaviour for members of that group (i.e. the ethics of the group). The first code of ethics for a group of conservators appeared in 1963 with the AIC 'Standards of practice and professional relationships for conservators', published in *Studies in Conservation* in 1964. In 1978 ICOM-CC published *Definition of a Conservator–Restorer* which was further developed for approval by ICOM in 1984 (ICOM-CC 1984). Whilst this was not a code of ethics, it helped to define what a conservator/restorer does and thus helped to define the role of the conservator/restorer. In 1981 the UKIC developed an ethical code which was revised and published in 1983, *Guidance for Conservation Practice* (UKIC 1983). These have been further revised and developed to create the 1996 UKIC *Code of Ethics and Rules of Practice*. In 1979 the AIC developed a code of ethics which it revised and published in 1985, *Code of Ethics and Standards of Practice*. This was further revised in 1994 to form the *Code of Ethics and Guidelines for Practice* (1994). Many other national conservation organizations have created codes of ethics such as the Australian Institute for the Conservation of Cultural Material who adopted and published a *Code of Ethics and Guidance for Conservation Practice* in 1986 (AICCM 1986) and the New Zealand Professional Conservators Group who adopted a 'Code of ethics' in 1988 (NZPCG 1988). The members of these associations are expected to abide by these ethical codes and in most cases can be penalized for their contravention by expulsion. All students of conservation should be familiar with these various codes since they form a series of coherent statements of the ethical basis for approaching conservation work. The fact that these codes have been frequently redrafted and revised make it clear that ethics in conservation are both complex and evolving.

Redefinition of a group's ethical code, whilst it may aid clarity, particularly in a time of change, can jeopardize the uniqueness and permanency of the group's identity. An overlong or elaborate ethical code can become too cumbersome and difficult to use and thus loses the support of the group. Overlong ethical codes may develop as a result of the inclusion of 'good practice' (Oddy 1996) or political ideals (Scheiner 1997) which dilute the strength and reduce the permanence of the ethical code. Some conservators (Oddy 1996) feel that the problems of defining right and wrong, which can vary from one group of conservators to another, creates an 'ethical relativism' (Edson 1997), effectively making the concept of an ethical code for conservation redundant. There is, however, widespread support for the creation of such codes and the modern AIC, UKIC and AICCM documents on ethics (AIC 1994; UKIC 1996; AICCM 1986) are composed of separate 'ethical codes' and 'codes of good practice'. It is recognized that whilst they are not yet universally applied, seeking to implement ethical codes and codes of good practice over a wide range of situations encourages their use and respect by an increasingly large group of practitioners. Expression as an ethical code indicates the fundamental nature of these beliefs which are accepted by large bodies of conservators in organizations such as the AIC, UKIC and ICOM-CC.

All conservators should become familiar with the current ethical codes issued by the principal conservation organizations. The key elements in conservation's ethical codes, distilled principally from ICOM-CC (1984), AIC (1994) and UKIC (1996) are:

- In the 1984 ICOM-CC definition of a conservator–restorer 'the activity of the conservator–restorer (conservation) consists of examination, preservation and conservation–restoration of cultural property'. By 1996 both AIC and UKIC had opted for preservation as the primary goal. These codes, whilst emphasising the primary aim of preserving material culture preferably through preventive conservation, recognize the need to balance this with the need to use, understand and appreciate cultural property.

- These codes emphasize the need for a conservator to work with archaeologists, historians, curators, ethnographers and others on the object and to recognize its importance to these disciplines.

- The 1988 NZPCG and 1983 UKIC code expressed the conviction that the conservator was to reveal and preserve the 'true nature' of the object. By the 1990s the UKIC and AIC codes have dropped the concept of 'true nature' and are emphasizing the conservator's responsibilities both to the 'owners and custodians' of cultural property and 'to the people or person who created it'. This emphasis on others' rights over objects, which conservators should respect, is carried further by the AICCM 1986 Code of Ethics and Guidance for Conservation Practice. This asserts that the conservator has a responsibility to 'maintain a balance between the cultural needs of society and the preservation of cultural material'. This sensitivity to the rights of others over objects has been heightened by the activities of native peoples and others seeking greater rights to objects of their past cultural heritage.

- In the codes there are clear statements about: operating to the highest standards, the importance of recording the object, recognition of the limits of personal skill, the promotion of the profession, the need to support education, professional conduct towards one's colleagues and the importance of the integrity of the object.

- In both the UKIC 1983 code and the AIC 1979 code there is mention of reversibility of treatments and materials. The UKIC 1983 code states 'techniques and materials which affect the object least and which can most easily and completely be reversed should always be selected'. The term 'reversibility' is not used in the 1990's codes which generally have less to say about methods and more emphasis on aims. The UKIC 1996 code states 'Each (UKIC) member must strive to preserve cultural property for the benefit of future generation(s)'. The emphasis is clearly on preservation for the future. The AIC 1994 code emphasizes stability: 'The conservation professional must strive to select methods and materials that . . . do not adversely affect cultural property or its future examination'.

- There are specific statements in AIC, UKIC and the 1986 AICCM codes of the need to use, or consider using, preventive conservation measures wherever possible.

- The codes of ethics are all accompanied by codes of practice, which invariably describe in greater detail the nature of the relationship between the conservators, owners, curators and fellow heritage professionals.

- There is no mention of minimum intervention in any of these codes of ethics, though the UKIC 1994 Rules of Practice instructs 'Each member should not undertake any treatment which is more extensive than necessary'.

- The codes clearly distinguish between conservation and restoration. Statements regarding restoration work or 'compensation for loss' are usually in the codes of practice and not mentioned in the ethical codes.

The judgements which a conservator has to make often revolve about the conflicting needs which these ethical aims create in practice.

Over the years a number of terms or phrases have sought to express a single quintessential guiding ethic for conservation such as: minimum intervention, reversibility, true nature. The problem which emerges with many of the guiding ethical ideas of conservation is the extent to which any of them can realistically be applied in any given situation. The extent to which any single ethical idea should be followed is difficult to judge when used in isolation. For example, the desire to preserve all the evidence following Oddy's stricture *'nothing should be done to an object which compromises any original part of it'* (Oddy 1996) can leave the inexperienced conservator too worried about evidence preserved in corrosion products to attempt any cleaning of a corroded iron object. A more constructive method of approaching the ethical considerations of conserving an object is for the conservator to identify the balance desired to be achieved between revelation, investigation and preservation (see Chapter 3), and then explore the most ethical way of achieving it.

5.2 True nature

The earliest cleaning of classical objects in the Renaissance by artists and sculptors such as Cellini can be seen as a desire to see the true beauty of the classical world (Cellini 1878). The cleaning and often substantial restoration work can be regarded as aiming to reveal the 'true nature' of the object as the fifteenth/sixteenth-century sculptor and his wealthy patron understood it. Thus the concept of revealing the true nature of an object was perhaps the first identifiable aim or ethical concept of conservation.

This desire to see the true form of the object was used in the mid- and late nineteenth century by restoration architects to justify the work of stripping away the poorer quality layer and post-medieval additions from higher quality high-medieval buildings and then restoring to what they believed to be the true, original and complete form. At the same time William Morris and John Ruskin decried any restoration believing that the true form of a building included all elements of its history, none more sacred than the other. Thus what constituted 'true nature' was the first ethical controversy of conservation (see Section 9.3). The UKIC Guidance for Practice (UKIC 1983) defines conservation as 'the means by which the true nature of an object is preserved. The true nature of an object includes evidence of its origins, its original construction, the materials of which it is composed and information as to the technology used in its manufacture'. Though perhaps originally intended to define a moment in the object's past before it decayed, this definition does not include evidence of use or of addition or alteration. It presumes the object is still as its creator intended it. However, no object exists just for a single moment. Every object has evolved through its creation and use; any, and every, point within an object's working life could be described as 'its true nature'. Every sword eventually becomes a piece of scrap iron and both states represent the true nature of the object. Thus every object contains numerous truths, making it impossible to define any one point as the true nature of the object as opposed to any other. The purpose of this concept was undoubtedly to try to express the desire to remove later alterations and additions which obscure the initial purpose of the object and to remove decay and dirt from periods of burial or neglect. Problems in definition of any one exact state of an object as being the true nature led to the demise in the use of this term and it vanished from the ethical codes of the 1990s. It continues to be a useful concept expressing a desire to move towards revealing the truth(s) about an object and away from the obscuration of dirt, decay or inaccurate and inappropriate restoration (see Figure 5.1 and Case study 7A: The Sistine Chapel).

Figure 5.1 The graveyard at Strata Florida, mid-Wales (photographed by the author). The gilding of the incised inscriptions on many of these Welsh gravestones was recently renewed. This returned these objects to the condition in which they were originally intended to be seen, restoring their true nature.

5.3 Reversibility

By the mid-twentieth century conservators had learnt to deal with many of the threats which man and nature posed to objects. However, it was clear that a number of the objects arriving in the laboratories were being adversely affected by earlier conservation treatments. These included problems in removing some of the conservation work of the late nineteenth and early twentieth century where materials such as cement, plaster of Paris and shellac were permanently bonded to fragile antiquities. Further problems of a similar nature were also being posed by a wide range of new polymers, such as soluble nylon and polyvinyl alcohol, which became available in the 1950s and 1960s. To counter such problems the concept of the reversibility of all conservation materials and methods began to be espoused. Reversibility was enshrined in the earliest 1961 AIC Code of Ethics and was still present in the 1983 UKIC 'Guidance'. It demonstrated the continued faith which people still had, in the post-World War II period, in the capabilities of science and technology to create desirable polymers (i.e. ones which were stable and readily removable). It also indicated that people had begun to lose their faith in the permanence of things. It was beginning to be appreciated that in the twentieth century nothing stayed the same for very long, but this would not matter provided that you could undo what had previously been done.

The principal architects of the 1960's AIC Code of Ethics, in which the term reversibility was used, were paintings conservators (Appelbaum 1987). They were no doubt thinking of processes such as infill painting, varnishing and lining of paintings. The concept of reversibility was easily understood by the public and the rest of the heritage profession. It indicated that a more careful approach was being adopted by conservation and this created a distinction between conservators and the repairers and restorers of the past. The work of conservators was now intended as much for the future as for the present.

The terms 'soluble' or 'removable' were subsumed into the term reversible and applied to materials and processes alike (Appelbaum 1987). As the use of the term grew during the 1970s it became increasingly obvious that in reality virtually nothing the conservator did was in the strict sense reversible (Jedrzejewska 1976). In reality all cleaning actions, such as washing paper or textiles, were irreversible. Excavation of archaeological objects caused irreversible chemical changes and analytical techniques increasingly showed that any contact with a material left a few molecules present on the object (Horie 1983). The extent of the irreversibility of impregnating, even with stable polymers, was demonstrated by Horie's consolidation of a modern earthenware ceramic with polymethyl methacrylate. Fifty per cent of the impregnating polymer was retained in the ceramic even after it had been refluxed with solvents in a Soxhlet extractor for 8 hours (Horie 1983). In another example the use of enzymes to treat stains on paper has been shown to leave up to 2 per cent of the enzyme in the paper even after extensive careful washing (Andrews *et al.* 1992).

Therefore, in the 1980s the term reversibility began to gradually pass out of use and terms such as minimum intervention started to appear. In 1987 Appelbaum considered the fate of the term 'reversible'. It was clear that the term could be potentially harmful since, when conservators should have been considering the aesthetic appropriateness or stability of the conservation material (Feller 1978) which they were using on an object, they were still relying on the impractical notion of reversibility to allow them to remove any material which proved unsuitable (Appelbaum 1987).

Whilst reversibility was clearly not a realistically achievable aim, especially for consolidation using polymers, the desirability of being able to undo conservation work and then re-treat it at some point in the future clearly remains a desirable goal. The concept of reversibility if it is regarded as meaning retreatable and the desirable aim of 'being able to undo what you have previously done' continues to be a valid expression of a conservation ideal.

> Nothing ought to be done that cannot be undone. It is an impossible goal, but it is one for which we all strive and are surely closer to attaining it than our forerunners.
>
> (Hedley 1986: 2)

What of the future of the term reversibility? It will be seen, perhaps, as the 'mother' of the ethical ideas of the present. A simple, certain ethical comfort for a young profession in the 1960s, the use of the term reversibility showed how much conservators valued the past, not wanting to change it permanently. The discipline of conservation has grown older and wiser and realized that ideas such as true reversibility were not practical. From it have sprung a new generation of ethical ideas such as: retreatability, minimum intervention (see Section 5.3) and stable materials (see Section 8.3). Reversibility represented a laudable if unachievable perfection. It, like much of the past, has value and can be used. Though conservators should be aware of the limitations of the term reversibility, it has widespread acceptance and it remains a useful concept when trying to explain the aims of conservation (advocacy) to a wider audience.

5.4 Minimum intervention

Whilst the aspiration of doing the minimum necessary to preserve a building (or object) can clearly be ascribed to William Morris (Morris 1996) and colleagues who founded the Society for the Protection of Ancient Buildings in 1877, the phrase using the 'minimum of needed intervention' was articulated by Cesare Brandi in 1963 (Brandi 1996; Vaccaro 1996b). Minimum intervention received prominence as an ethical approach to conservation in the 1980s when the concept of reversibility was declining in use.

Minimum intervention has been defined or rephrased a number of times. Pye and Cronyn (1987) found it difficult to define minimum intervention and compared it with homeopathy, where reversibility was standard medicine. Corfield (1988b) considered that to practise minimum intervention 'the conservator is required to weigh carefully every process that is proposed to apply to an object and decide whether or not it is really necessary', 'the less that is done the better – minimum intervention'. Brooks (1998) defined it as 'doing the least possible consistent with the future safety of the object'. It was described as the 'minimalist principle' by Hanssen-Bauer (1996), who considered that together with the 'principle of reversibility' and the 'principle of stability' it formed the three principles to guide any intervention.

The problem with minimum intervention is that it is not a complete statement. The minimum intervention to achieve what? Though Morris may clearly believe that it is the minimum necessary to preserve the object, the question is, however, context dependent; that is, for how long and in what conditions remain unstated. It is possible to define minimum intervention as that which enables an object to safely endure being put on open display or to go on travelling exhibition. The conservation measures required for such rigours would hardly be what Morris envisaged as 'the minimum to preserve'. Minimum intervention to preserve an object for 10 years standing outside in the rain is very different to minimum intervention to preserve an object for a few days in a controlled internal environment. Minimum intervention must therefore be defined for a given object over a given time in a given set of conditions. The alternative is not to use the phrase but for it to exist as a question which, as suggested by Corfield (1988b), could be used in assessing every proposed conservation action.

It appears likely that much of the enthusiasm for the concept of minimum intervention, arose, like that of reversibility, from a realization of the unsatisfactory nature of earlier approaches to conservation. Loss of evidence from overcleaning, increasing potential for gaining information from objects and problems experienced in achieving truly reversible treatments led to a drive for a more sympathetic approach to object conservation. Incidents, such as the oil pollution from the Torrey Canyon disaster (1969) and the radio-active pollution from Chernobyl (1986), appear to have resulted in a loss of confidence in science and technology, by some sections of the public, by the 1980s. This led to a rise in ideas about ecology, green politics and a far more minimal approach to the use of chemicals. In such a social climate a conservation approach based on minimum intervention found widespread acceptance.

5.5 Pragmatism and prioritization: the money ethic

There is a rarely stated but ever present truth that what can be achieved in terms of the conservation of any object is dictated by the resources available (Staniforth 1990; Ashley-Smith 1999). Thus with limited time and budget, the conservator often selects the most suitable adhesive at hand in the laboratory, rather than engaging in a full regime of testing to find the best adhesive available. This constraint of the available resources is present in all aspects of life, not merely conservation, and the emphasis should always be on achieving the best possible result within the time, expertise, funding and facilities available. When the limitations imposed by the lack of time, money and facilities are so great as to damage or pose unacceptable risks to the object the conservator should then consider whether it is appropriate to continue. Lack of resources should not be used to justify slipshod work or inadequate research. It is, however, important to consider the null hypothesis: What will realistically happen to the object if no conservation work is carried out? Sometimes the object can be left safely stored and untouched. In other instances, this may be the only chance to record an object before it is lost. It is also important to recognize what other activities the conservator could be doing. Rather than spending a long time conserving and restoring a single object, they could be undertaking preventive conservation work safe-guarding the long-term future of many objects. The example in Chapter 12, on the cleaning of archaeological iron objects, demonstrates the variety of options which the conservator faces in judging how to make use of limited resources.

The limitations posed by lack of funding frequently justify using the conservator's time to obtain additional funds. Regardless of whether they are grant applications for national funding or a cost-benefit analysis (see Chapter 12) for one's employer it is essential that the conservator raises sufficient funds to ensure that they can do their job effectively and efficiently.

5.6 Stewardship

Early collectors of antiquities, in keeping with the social values of the time, believed they had absolute rights over the objects they owned. This could result in brutal restorations and a cavalier attitude to their objects. This arrogance can afflict owners, museum curators and conservators even in the present day. One ethical concept which takes a fundamentally different view to the ownership of objects and which has gained ground in recent years is stewardship. It is borrowed from those looking after historic houses and cathedrals, buildings and contents which have such a long past and potentially long future that no present owner has the arrogance to dismiss the aspirations of the past or deny potential to the future.

The term derives from the medieval period; when the lord or master of the house was away his steward was responsible for the safe keeping of the house and its contents. When the master returned, the steward was expected to be able to hand back the household intact, in good order, exactly as the master had left it.

The concept of stewardship reminds any custodian of an object that they hold the object in trust for the next generation and that they have responsibility for its care and well being. It diminishes the concept of absolute ownership recognizing a higher unstated authority which could be termed posterity. It is designed to discourage permanent alteration of the object, encourage the present owner to leave it as they received it but, having taken good care of it in their period of stewardship, ensure that no damage or harm has come to it.

5.7 Implementing ethics

There is little written information as to the way in which ethical ideas should be considered or implemented. Child (1994) has suggested that they represent an ideal towards which conservators should aim. Alternatively Ashley-Smith (1994) has suggested that they are intimately involved with every single action carried out in the laboratory, and he and his staff at the V&A Conservation Department developed a checklist of ethical questions which every conservator should be asking themselves before engaging in any decision making regarding an object. This encourages the use of ethical actions in practice at every stage of the conservation process (see Section 14.2).

A wide range of ethical concepts deserve consideration by the conservator. Balancing these ethical considerations is a key aspect of judgement. When exploring the case studies in this book it is possible to see how other conservators have balanced ethical considerations. Thus whilst minimum intervention may have been practised on the exterior of the Statue of Liberty (see Case study 3A), inside the statue a far more pragmatic series of options associated with working objects were chosen (see Chapter 10). In the case of the Portland Vase (see Case study 4A), the concept of the true nature of the vase can be seen to have outweighed the desirability for a reversible adhesive.

5A Case study: Colonial Williamsburg Garden (Olmert 1985)

The New World's colonial township of Williamsburg was established in 1663 and became the capital of Virginia in 1699, a position it retained until 1780 when the city of Richmond took that honour. During the succeeding centuries Williamsburg became a sleepy backwater. In 1926 Revd W. A. R. Goodwin of Williamsburg convinced the millionaire J. D. Rockefeller Jr of the need to preserve the colonial town, suggesting that eight-eight of the buildings still present in the centre of Williamsburg were of eighteenth-century date. In 1927, using funding from Rockefeller, Goodwin started to purchase these buildings. Over the following years there was an extensive purchasing and rebuilding programme. The Governor's Palace, the Capitol Building and houses and shops (e.g. Raleigh Tavern) were reconstructed in exactly the form they possessed in the eighteenth century and in their original location. Equally important was the demolition and removal of the nineteenth and twentieth-century buildings so that an accurate eighteenth-century townscape was recreated. Between 1926 and 1976 over $100 million, of which Rockefeller contributed over $68 million, were poured into this restoration and reconstruction of an eighteenth-century town. At approximately 1 mile by 0.25 mile it is the largest heritage reconstruction, recreation project ever undertaken.

To fund the running and development of this heritage park, hundreds of thousands of visitors are required each year. The visitors learn about life in the eighteenth century, not from labels, since there are none, but from guides in period costume, who take on the persona of eighteenth-century characters and talk to the visitors. These 'interpreters' are backed up by numerous professional and technical staff all of whom are employed by the Colonial Williamsburg Foundation who run this endeavour. Every aspect of the town's life has been recreated to match that of Virginia in the late eighteenth century, from the goods sold in the shops and the food served in the taverns to the trades practised in the workshops and the flowers grown in the gardens. This is in marked contrast to other American views of the past such as Henry Ford's Greenfield Village and William Randolph Hearst's San Simeon both of which have an unspecific 'scrapbook' approach to history, collecting together items from a variety of different periods, countries and cultures (Chamberlin 1979).

In contrast to much of Europe and especially Britain with its numerous ancient castles, churches and country houses, the USA is a country which has a short history and consequently it has a limited number of surviving relics of the past. Colonial Williamsburg addresses this need, with a very complete, intense involvement with the past which is well researched and as accurate as the economic realities of the late twentieth century permit. Its size allows it to provide well-marketed mass consumption of the past; it can compete in tourist terms with the theme parks of Disney, whilst the originality of some of its buildings and objects, and the accuracy of its replicas gives it the academic role of a museum. Colonial Williamsburg has a single central theme of preserving or recreating the eighteenth century. As with many folk museums, in order to develop the illusion, the difference between the real eighteenth-century buildings or objects and the replicas is not emphasized to the visitor. As time has passed the ideas about what was present in the late eighteenth century have been modified and improved, and Williamsburg has adapted wherever possible to the new information to remain faithful to the concept of accuracy. However, because of its age and status as a heritage park and museum it now contains examples of heritage interpretation which have themselves become historically important.

One such example is the garden of the Elkanah Deane House. This was one of the earliest gardens laid out on the site in the mid-1920s. It reflected the knowledge of that period about the eighteenth-century colonial period. Interest in the colonial period in the 1920s, particularly celebrating the 150 years since independence, had generated a fashion for recreating early colonial-house interiors and exteriors and has subsequently become known as Colonial Revival style. Modern knowledge, however, indicates that even the more well off and influential members of eighteenth-century colonial society would have had gardens which were largely functional containing a cookhouse, hen house, kitchen garden with just a small ornamental area, as seen in the garden of the Wythe House, just around the corner from the Elkanah Deane House. The garden of the Elkanah Deane House is completely ornate, and thus is now perceived as an inaccurate representation of the garden associated with the occupant of the house, who was a skilled craftsman, a coachbuilder. The style of the garden, as well as some of the plantings, reflect the Colonial Revival rather than actual eighteenth-century plantings (see Figure 5.2). By 1997 it was demonstrably not an accurate recreation of the period garden and was ready for substantial alteration to create a more exact reproduction of an eighteenth-century garden. However, the importance of the existing garden, in terms of developing ideas about the past, has led to suggestions that it should remain as it is: a significant example of the Colonial Revival style. Is this the thin end of the wedge? Many of the houses and gardens in Colonial Williamsburg contain the first examples in America of historic recreation and reproduction. Will Colonial Williamsburg continue to alter and update inaccurate examples of recreation and maintain its identity as the most accurate example of an eighteenth-century American colonial capital town or will it start to become a monument to itself and the history of 'heritage'? In this discussion, context is crucial. Were the garden of the Elkanah Deane house not in the middle of an eighteenth-century town, then the initial garden restoration might be paramount and little lost by its retention. However, with the context of Colonial Williamsburg, anything not eighteenth century appears out of place, disruptive to the aesthetic entity of an eighteenth-century township, potentially misleading to the public. For this reason nineteenth-century buildings had previously been removed from the town and if the true nature of the eighteenth-century townscape is to be honoured the garden would need to be re-restored.

Figure 5.2 The Elkanah Deane House Garden, Colonial Williamsburg, USA (photograph
   courtesy of The Colonial Williamsburg Foundation). A Colonial Revival style
   garden in a restored colonial township.

6 Objects
Their recording and investigation

6.1 Purpose and nature of recording

As indicated in Section 3.5, recording is a key element in conservation work. The creation of a conservation record recognizes that conservation and restoration work is not an end in itself but part of a series of ongoing processes which last for the whole of the object's life. It also acknowledges that there are many people who will come after the present conservator who will need information about the object and who will undertake further investigation, revelation or preservation work. Thus in the history of conservation the creation of conservation records marks one of the crucial changes from a craft to a profession.

Making a record of the object and its conservation serves a number of separate purposes:

- Conservators are forced to examine the object in detail. This ensures that they are fully aware of all aspects of the object's composition and decay and that the proposed cleaning and conservation work is appropriate. It minimizes the unexpected discoveries which can lead to accidental damage or delays in the conservation process.

- All the information discovered about the object is recorded. This is an essential element in the investigation process, ensuring that all the information uncovered is available to others. The record provides a location for a wide variety of different types of information about the object: X-rays, photographs, analyses, observations and published references.

- A body of evidence is created which can be examined rather than the object itself. This may provide more information than the object and forms a preventive conservation measure limiting the need to handle and observe the object directly (e.g. the costume collection of Warwick Museum, Kavanagh 1990).

- A visual and written record of the object at a given point in time is created in order that changes, such as corrosion, loss or damage which occur during conservation or during subsequent storing, handling and display, can be detected.

- A record of the conservation work and materials used on the object. Details of all chemicals, treatment times and coatings are recorded so that, in the future, the success of a particular conservation treatment or chemical can be established (Sully and Suenson-Taylor 1996). It will also provide health-and-safety information on the exposure levels of various chemicals such as biocides and solvents which objects and conservators have endured. This may lead to the establishment of greater certainty over safe working practices and exposure limits and identifies any risk still posed by an object to any future conservator as a result of hazardous materials used in its conservation.

- A record of the information necessary to allow an object to be successfully reconserved.

- A valuable example to other conservators proposing to treat similar objects.

- Identifying the object, should its unique identifier (e.g. museum number or site code) be lost or deliberately removed.

The importance of the record is often only recognized when it is shown to be the only source of information. For example, cleaning an object removes evidence/information about the object's past and leaves the conservation record as the only remaining source of that information.

6.2 A conservation record

Whilst the need for a conservation record is unquestionable, the nature and extent of the recording is a matter of judgement. Consequently the information recorded in a conservation record can vary enormously (Oddy and Barker 1971; Corfield 1983; Bradley 1983; Perry 1983; Down 1983; Corfield 1992; Dollery and Henderson 1996). No single recording system is universally used. This is due both to the variation in the type and nature of the object and the fact that the conservation record is often part of a larger sequence of records maintained by an institution such as a museum (Roberts 1985). The individual facts recorded in the conservation record provide information relevant to one or more of the functions mentioned above. The following list indicates the principal facts normally recorded:

Institution name: so that if this record card is misplaced it can be returned.

Object number: every object should have a unique alphanumeric sequence which is permanently placed on the object and which uniquely defines the object. This usually relates to the museum or collection where the object is housed or the place from where it was excavated or recovered. Some objects have several numbers, all of which should be recorded on the conservation record.

Laboratory number: in some institutions this may be the object number, in others every object coming into the laboratory is given a unique number. The object or laboratory number ensure that information, unique to each object, is associated with the correct object.

Owner (curator) of the object: the individual to whom the object belongs or who is responsible for the object and who has agreed to the conservation.

Museum location: (where appropriate) where the object is normally kept.

Numbers or references to further information: this will include the numbers and location of photographic negatives or positives, X-Ray plates, published references, excavation details, records of analysis.

Drawing of the object: every object should be drawn, though the appropriate level of detail will vary. It can be a quick sketch or a full technical drawing (Adkins and Adkins 1989; Griffiths *et al.* 1990). Annotated sketches or drawings are a particularly effective way of providing information about an object.

Photograph: for many objects, in order to depict accurate detail quickly one or more photographs is advisable (Dorrell 1989). Scales, colour card if appropriate and object or laboratory numbers should be included in the photograph. This image supports but does not replace the drawing. All sides of the object are often photographed.

Other images: all corroded archaeological iron objects must be X-rayed, and it is highly advisable for corroded silver and copper-alloy objects. Paintings may often usefully be X-rayed or have an infrared reflectogram taken. Many complex historic and artistic works are also usefully X-rayed, CAT (computerized axial tomography) scanned or γ-radiographed to reveal their method of construction, internal mechanism and condition.

Name: the type of object being recorded. The common or short name, the full or correct name, any trade names, maker's marks or numbers should all be recorded.

Origin details: where is the object from, what culture created it, what date is it?

Dimensions: maximum dimensions of the object expressed as any three of: length, height, width, breadth, depth and thickness. Weight is also sometimes recorded. Measurements should be in SI (metric) units: millimetres and metres, grammes and kilogrammes.

Materials: the principal materials used in the construction and decoration together with the method of identification.

Detailed description: a full description of the object ensuring that details, such as the materials of which each piece of the object is composed, are listed, the presence of paint or other coatings is referred to, the technology of manufacture is noted, information of wear or use is noted, the colour of the various pieces of the object is noted.

Condition: the extent and nature of dirt, damage, corrosion, fading, loss and how fragmentary or fragile the object is should be described. The source of the dirt, damage or decay should be determined and noted.

Conservation treatment: all aspects of the conservation treatment should be recorded, together with who undertook the work and when. Details of the chemicals used, their concentration and any specific temperatures or pressures used should be recorded. Any additional information about the object which comes to light during the cleaning and conservation process should be noted. Basic reasoning behind the conservation work undertaken, especially the initial aims of the proposed conservation work should also be recorded. All this information should be filled in as the conservator goes through the conservation process. Dates for commencement and completion of the treatment should be recorded.

Storage and recommendations: the appropriate conditions in which the object should be stored or displayed should be recorded together with details of any container created specifically to house or support the object and any restrictions on the object's handling or use.

Wherever possible reference should be made to standardized recording systems and thesaurus of terms and definitions where they exist (MDA 1997; Szrajber 1997). All conservation activities should be recorded, even simple cleaning such as washing china or brushing insecticide on to wooden agricultural items. This will aid the interpretation of soiling on the object (see Section 7.3), and the long-term assessment of chemicals, health and safety information, etc.

When treating a large number of similar objects much of this information is repetitive so many conservators have some form of codification or shorthand to describe aspects such as standardized conservation treatments (Corfield 1992). Whilst this can save time there is a risk that the conservation record becomes unintelligible to anyone not familiar with the code. Therefore, the information on the codes must be displayed very prominently beside the conservation records. Computer-based recording systems enable you to economically create records, especially those using standard phrases, in full and can ensure that you use words in a standard thesaurus so ensuring that the record created can readily be located through word-based searching.

The physical form of the record can vary from plastic or paper wallets containing all photographs, written details, X-radiographs, etc. as used in the British Museum up to the 1990s (Bradley 1983) on an A4 or A5 card, with the photographs and X-radiographs in separate indexed storage (University of Durham) to a computer record, backed up by a hard-copy record card (York Archaeological Trust). When computer memories are sufficiently powerful, and a large number of high-quality images can be retained, conservation records will become primarily computer based. Three-dimensional holographic images may eventually form part of the conservation record. The long-term stability of electronic media, hard and floppy discs and magnetic tape, is suspect because of the potential instability of the materials used to construct them (Westheimer 1994); for example, the polyurethane used to adhere the magnetic particles on to the substrate. Even CD-ROMs have a finite life as a result of their polymeric components. Any loss of fidelity would result in potentially undetectable information loss. It is also already clear that rapid software and hardware evolution can leave data stranded on obsolete systems. The computerized data from the 1960 US Federal Census was, by 1975, only capable of being read by two computers, one of which was already a museum exhibit (Westheimer 1994).

The frequent use of paper records, and the importance of maintaining these records, means that they should correspond to the standards developed for libraries and archives (i.e. BS (British Standard) 5454, Walker 1990). Colour is an important component of many objects and it is essential that colour is accurately recorded. This is best achieved through colour photography on good quality film or through using a standardized colour recording system such as L*a*b* (Minolta 1988). One particular area of concern is the stability of colour transparencies (Lavedrine *et al.* 1986; Townsend and Tennent 1993). For all colour photography a standard colour scale should be included, so that the extent of any differential colour fading of the recording medium can be established.

Conservators are the individuals who will study an object most closely, so the responsibility of reporting all the details concerning an object's form, decoration, method of manufacture, composition and state of decay rests primarily with them. They are frequently the only person who examines the object with microscope facilities so should ensure that microscopic details, such as wear, and the identification of materials are recorded. It is important to ensure that the curator, owner or archaeologist responsible for the object should be made aware of any pertinent facts regarding the object which are discovered during the conservation examination. Whilst the conservation record is normally retained by the laboratory which has treated the object, a copy of the record is often made to accompany the object, especially in private conservation work. Separate reports on the composition or condition of the object or proposals for the conservation treatment (see Section 1.6) may also be created.

The key role of records within conservation means that it is essential that time is made in the working day to ensure that the record cards are completed and that any filing and indexing of photographs and X-rays is carried out. The conservator exercises considerable judgement in the extent of the recording for any object. It is possible to waste a large amount of time illustrating and describing the most inconsequential details of an object, information which will never be required. Equally it is possible to ignore information which is crucial to the understanding of the object and neglect to record information which is lost when the object is cleaned. It remains particularly difficult to judge what information will be considered essential by a future generation of conservators.

Referring to Lowenthal's (1996) definitions of history as that which actually happened in the past and heritage as the past used for present-day aims, it is essential that the recording of any object is as near to history as possible. It is research and documentation of the facts. Any interpretation of the facts to enhance understanding about the object should be identified as interpretation and done as objectively as possible. Heritage will be that selected part of the information which is used to accompany the object on display, and is written by the curator conscious of their present-day aims for the exhibition.

6.3 The object

> Before any treatment is carried out the object should be placed in its historical, archaeological or artistic context.
>
> (Coremans 1969: 14)

The complex relationship between an ancient society, the material culture of its objects and the way in which members of a modern Western society interpret the ancient society from its artefacts has been the subject of considerable study (Pearce 1994a). In the nineteenth century Pitt Rivers and others initially interpreted objects as having a simple functional role, the form and construction of the object being directly related to the technological development of the society which made and used the object. The work of twentieth-century anthropologists such as Malinowski and Radcliffe Brown (Leach 1994) showed that complex social structure was invariably reflected within objects, whilst twentieth-century archaeologists have shown that there is a complexity between social belief and the expression of form and decoration of an object – even to the point of detecting the influence of individual craftsmen (Deetz and Dethlefsen 1994). This has led to an awareness that all objects are culturally and contextually sensitive (Tilley 1994), and that even the materials of their construction have complex meaning and symbolism (McGhee 1994). Thus objects must be understood in terms of the culture and date from which they derive. Objects should also be seen as palimpsests, having an evolving series of meanings over time (Ames 1994). Hodder (1994) has proposed that objects can be seen as possessing three forms of identity:

- An object: raw materials shaped by technology to form an object which performs a function within a given society. It contains information about its origin in 'technomic', 'sociotechnic' and 'ideotechnic' forms.

- Part of a context: associated with other objects it is part of a code or communication which signifies and reinforces a social order or context.

- Embodying and signifying past experience: through its appearance it carries ideas of the past into the present.

As such awareness has developed, systems have started to be developed which assist museum curators, archaeologists and anthropologists investigate and analyse objects, helping them extract both evidence and meaning (Elliot *et al.* 1994; Pearce 1994b; Prown 1994; Batchelor 1994).

For the purposes of conservation there is a need to focus on the information which can be obtained from studying the object directly, both as a historic document and as an aesthetic entity. This is particularly important in order that no information is lost or destroyed without record during the conservation process. Of the object recording and investigating systems proposed by conservators Jaeschke's seven ages of an object (Jaeschke 1996) seeks to highlight the continually changing nature of artefacts, whilst Caple's formalized object construction and use sequence (FOCUS) derives a detailed sequence of events from construction through to its present use, for which there is evidence (Caple 1996).

The study of an artist or craftsman, the work they produced, their materials, technique, the subjects they depict, the style or expression of their work as well as a full appreciation of the time and culture in which they worked can be regarded as connoisseurship (Kirby Talley 1989). Conservators usually have limited time and cannot devote a lifetime's study to a single object, or craftsman. Consequently they use: advice from experts and connoisseurs, existing published information and detailed examination of the object in order to assemble as complete an understanding of the nature of the object as possible. Though the exact details of the object may be initially unfamiliar to the conservator, they will, as a result of their education and experience, have a good background knowledge about the types of material of which the object is composed. To prompt more detailed appreciation of the object two generic systems, which can help make the conservator aware of different aspects of the object as they examine it, are here proposed.

Historic Object Production Sequence: The object is considered as the product of a production process. An object produced from raw materials using the expertise of craftsmen. This alerts the conservator to the skill of an object's manufacture, the materials and facilities required to produce the object and some of the non-visible properties which the object may possess, or which it indicates existed. This approach has similarities to that used by Eileen Hooper Greenhill in her representation 'learning with objects: discussion and analysis' (Pearce 1990, figure 12.4).

Visual Evidence Sequence: The object is considered purely as a source of evidence, focusing on the addition and subtraction of forensic information too and from the object surface. This alerts the conservator for the need to search for, and record all traces of, visual evidence which remains on the object's surface as a result of its manufacture, use, burial and previous conservation activities.

In addition there are a wide variety of analytical techniques, detailed in Section 6.4, which can be used to assist various aspects of these investigations.

Historic Object Production Sequence (HOPS)

Objects are physical manifestations of the thoughts and ideas of a culture. Everything which is created, as opposed to being found, is formed by the action of tools which includes machines (which are in reality complex tools) upon raw materials. The other essential element is the craft or expertise to use the tool or operate the machine. The outcome of this process can be described as the product. This simple classification can be applied to the use of tools such as a carpenter's tools on a piece of wood (raw material) to create a piece of furniture (product). It can equally be applied to less tangible products, thus the blowing of air (the raw material) through a musical instrument (a complex tool) can with the ability of a skilled musician (expertise) be formed into music (product). An author (expert) can, through a pen (tool) paper and ink (raw materials) create a written document (product). Even a machine as complex as a computer uses the raw material of electricity, through the expertise which is the software programme, to calculate or create images or words.

Raw materials	Tools	Expertise	Products
Wood	Carpenter's tools	Joinery	Furniture
Ink, paper	Pen	Ability to write	Writing
Wind	Instrument	Musicality	Music
Electricity	Computer	Software	Images/action
Petrol	Car	Ability to drive	Movement
Coal, water	Steam engine	Ability to operate the machine	Movement
Ingredients	Kitchen implements and cooker	Cookery	Food
Light, film	Camera	Photography	Photograph

Evidence for each of these categories is unevenly represented in the record of the past. A carpenter's tools and even his furniture may survive, but his expertise, his knowledge of joinery, does not survive directly. It must be deduced from the surviving tools and furniture. Where we have survival of the product – such as a painting or a piece of fine furniture – we are familiar with archaeologists or art historians deducing the level of expertise of the artist

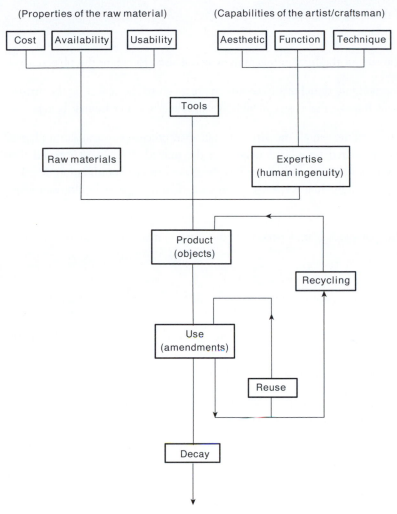

(Properties of the raw material)　　　(Capabilities of the artist/craftsman)

| Cost | Availability | Usability |

| Aesthetic | Function | Technique |

Tools

Raw materials

Expertise
(human ingenuity)

Product
(objects)

Recycling

Use
(amendments)

Reuse

Decay

Recovery and conservation

Figure 6.1 Historic Object Production Sequence.

or craftsmen who made the object. Where the product does not survive (e.g. music, or food) the expertise must be deduced from the instruments or tools which remain, such as the surviving kitchen utensils and our knowledge of ingredients which were used. Direct evidence of the expertise is occasionally partially preserved in the form of written description, musical notation and sound, film and video recordings of artists or craftsmen at work, or describing their work. Direct evidence of expertise is extremely patchy until the evolution of mass recording and communication in the nineteenth century. A product can also form raw material for a subsequent process, thus petrol is both the product of an oil refinery and the raw material for movement.

When this holistic view of objects and their genesis is applied in practice (see Figure 6.1), it can be expanded into a fuller sequence of factors which can be explored. With reference to Figure 6.1 we can define:

Capabilities of the artist/craftsman:

Expertise: the sum of the human ingenuity which is used to create the object.

Aesthetic: the non-functional attributes which are given to the object by the artist or craftsman, which make the object notable or appealing to other human beings.

Technique: the abilities which the artist or craftsman processes to transform physical materials into a desired form. It derives from the individual's experience and their knowledge of materials and tools as well as their hand-to-eye coordination. Much of the knowledge an individual possesses is determined by the age and culture in which they live.

Function: the purpose, as understood by the artist/craftsman, which the object is meant to serve.

Properties of the raw materials:

Raw materials: the materials from which every aspect of the object is created, from the pigments used to colour the object to the metal used in the construction of the fastenings in the object. There may be numerous materials used in any one object.

Usability: the properties or physical characteristics of the raw materials selected for use, their toxicity, strength, ease of working, etc.

Cost: the dominant criteria which governs the materials which are selected for creating an object. The material with the most desirable property may well not be selected because of cost. Factors such as cost of creating the material or transporting it to the place of use all affect the cost at the place of manufacture.

Availability: even if a material with the required properties is affordable, if it is not readily available it cannot be used. Often scrap materials which are lying around a workshop are used in manufacture, since they have ready availability and low cost.

Tools: tools can be the simplest objects – such as lumps of stone – through to the most complex machines, which are used to form the object being created. This factor also includes workshop or factory facilities which are used to support the manufacture of the object. The tools and facilities constrain what can be made.

Product (object): the product that is created from the raw materials, using the tools available with the know-how of the artist or craftsman. The product of this process is a specific completed form with function, whether it be movement, sound or has the physical reality of an object such as a chair.

Use: Every action leaves some imprint upon an object. Every use of the object will induce scratching or wear of its surface, leaving or removing traces of the materials with which it has come into contact. The traces are often so small we cannot detect them, or if detected cannot interpret them. Frequently evidence of later use obscures or obliterates evidence of earlier use.

Reuse: the object retains its basic form but is improved; for example, resharpened or rehafted to allow it to become functional again. This requires input from an artist/ craftsman and their associated expertise.

Recycled: the object is reduced to its basic materials and re-formed into a new product; for example, metal is melted and recast. Reused and recycled materials can be involved in the construction of almost any object. The input of recycled material into new objects is determined by similar constraints to those of the raw materials and involves a similar input of expertise from the artist/craftsman.

Eventually the object is discarded, buried, destroyed or taken out of use. If recovered it may then start a new cycle as a product selected for collection and display.

Visual Evidence Sequence (VES)

It is possible to look at objects in many other ways. If an object is examined for the forms of visual evidence derived from the object's surface for the creation and use of the object, eight forms of evidence (A1–D2) in four distinct phases can be identified and recorded for every object.

Manufacture

A1 Material deposited during manufacture and indicative of the technology of manufac-ture. This includes the material from which the object is made plus traces such as the grit derived from polishing the object or traces of mould material on the surface of a metal casting.

A2 Surface indentations which are caused by the technology of manufacture; for example, tool marks such as punchmarks (Larsen 1987).

Use

B1 Material, sometimes known as ethnic or ethnographic dirt (Oddy 1994), which is deposited on the object's surface from the use of the object or derived from, and characteristic of, the environment through which the object has passed. Examples include: the deposition of a silica sheen on flint implements, food residues found on pots, sweat, urine and faeces on textiles (see Section 7.2). There can be a series of periods of use and alteration. This is most clearly seen in the painted interiors of houses where cross-sections through paint layers can reveal a complex series of repaintings. Layers of dirt particles are often seen to accumulate on any surface which is exposed for a long period. Some regularly applied substances such as leather dressings are adsorbed into the substrate of the material and thus, though present as a record of the use and care of the object, cannot readily be detected.

B2   Damage to the surface of the object caused by wear, or scratches which are related to hard materials impinging on the object during use. These may be hard materials – such as the grinding wheel used to sharpen an axe – or persistent use of soft materials which wear away or polish an object's surface. Such wear marks reveal how clothes were worn or stone axes were hafted. The wear patterns in shoes can reveal the diseases of the feet.

There can be numerous phases of use, repair and reuse.

Decay

C1   Materials accreted during decay: dust, dirt, soil particles, corrosion minerals (e.g. as mineral-replaced organics, see Case study 6A). Such deposits potentially provide information about the burial or storage environment.

C2   Materials lost during decay, especially noticeable in terms of the loss of metal during corrosion or organic material during microbial decay. Such processes lead to considerable loss of evidence of use and manufacture.

Conservation

D1   Materials deposited during the conservation processes such as coatings used to stabilize or protect the object. It is possible to regard the writing on the object of a museum number as a process for the preservation of the object and its associated information.

D2   Traces of processes such as cleaning or repair which result in some form of loss or damage to the object.

Visual evidence of manufacture, use, decay and conservation is present on almost every object's surface. This emphasizes the importance of retaining the original surface of the object (see Section 7.4).

6.4 Scientific analysis

The materials and construction of the object and the decay processes and products of the materials are determined through various analytical, microscopic, imaging and dating techniques in order that:

- The correct conservation treatment will be used to safely arrest the decay of the object and minimize any risk of damage to the object in application of the conservation treatment.

- To confirm the date or cultural affinity of the object. If there is a mismatch between the materials and construction methods used and the envisaged date and cultural affinity of the object, fakes can be discovered (see Case study 2A).

- To add information to the body of knowledge about ancient materials and technology or the materials and technology used by a particular craftsman or artist.

Analysis would be necessary in the case of an unidentified white metal disc since it could be made of silver or its alloys, iron, aluminium, lead, nickel or its alloys, tin or its alloys, zinc, platinum or even some gold alloys. The resistance of that metal object to decay and its importance as a piece of historic information could vary enormously depending on the metal of which it was made. For example, in the early nineteenth century Napoleon had medals struck in aluminium since it had a higher value than silver. It would also potentially affect the conservation methods and chemicals used to stabilize a decaying object.

Prior to commissioning or undertaking analysis the conservator should consider whether:

- There is a sufficiently good reason (i.e. supporting the conservation aims) for doing the analysis which justifies the expense. Analysis is costly and time consuming.

- The analytical method selected can provide the information required.

- The importance of distinguishing between qualitative information; the presence or absence of a particular element, and quantitative information; the amount of an element present. Quantitative information is more difficult and consequently expensive to obtain.

- The conservator has the ability to understand and interpret the information that is obtained. This usually requires detailed background knowledge and comparative samples or data against which the unknown can be compared. Therefore, it is often as important to get comparative data or expert advice and interpretation as it is to get the initial analyses. There may be several explanations for any particular observed analytical phenomena. For example, the detection of titanium in a rosy pink-coloured painted decoration. Titanium is a naturally occurring impurity in iron oxides and could be present as an impurity or it could be present as titanium (dioxide) white, a strong white pigment mixed with a red to form the pink. In such cases the quantity of titanium involved and/or its mineral form need to be determined to resolve the question.

- The object has a date and cultural context, since this fundamentally affects the interpretation of the analytical information. For example, titanium white was only commercially available after 1918 (Laver 1997). If the object is of pre-twentieth-century date it could be a fake or have later added decoration.

- There are reasons for not examining, sampling or analysing an object. This may be due to an excessive level of damage which would be caused to the object or because of ethical constraints (e.g. where it is inappropriate to damage or otherwise desecrate a sacred object).

Instrumental Analytical Methods (elemental and molecular): Conservators should be familiar with a range of scientific analytical techniques (Pollard and Heron 1996; Skoog and Leary 1992) and their application to conservation (Bromelle and Thomson 1982; ICOM-CC 1993; ICOM-CC 1996).

For analysing metal-corrosion products and minerals, such as pigments, the crystalline properties of the material is the most useful attribute of identification; therefore, X-Ray Diffraction (XRD) is appropriate. There is increasing use of Fourier Transform Infra-Red Spectroscopy (FTIR), which characterizes interatomic bonds, for mineral identification. Because of the large volume of existing information, elemental composition is the most useful form of analysis for metals, glass and ceramics. A wide range of analytical techniques can be used for this. Some of the most common include Energy Dispersive X-Ray Fluorescence (EDXRF), Energy Dispersive X-Ray Analysis (EDX) (invariably mounted as part of a scanning electron microscope), Atomic Absorption Spectroscopy (AAS) Proton Induced X-Ray Emission (PIXE), Induction Coupled Plasma Emission Spectroscopy (ICPES) and Induction Coupled Plasma Mass Spectroscopy (ICPMS). Many of these techniques especially ICPMS and ICPES can detect trace amounts of elements (ppm). Such information can occasionally be used for characterizing the origin of raw materials as a result of the unique occurrence or level of trace elements present. Detecting major and minor element concentration is usually most crucial to conservators; for example, detecting the colouring elements and overall composition of glasses and enamels.

For analysing organic molecules such as 'plastics', dyes, binding and coating media, techniques which determine molecular properties can be used. Such techniques include Mass Spectrometry (MS) which determines molecular weight, High Performance Liquid Chromatography (HPLC) or Gas Chromatography (GC) which determines molecular weight and chemical affinity, Ultra-Violet, Visible, Infra-Red (UV/VIS/IR) spectroscopy or Fourier Transform Infra-Red Spectroscopy (FTIR) which determines molecular bonding. The degradation of materials can make the results of any organic analysis difficult to interpret. It is also possible to test for specific elements or molecules using wet chemical tests and there is increasing use of bioassay techniques to detect the presence of specific complex organic molecules such as enzymes or specific micro-organisms. Thermal-analysis techniques such as Differential Scanning Calorimetry (DSC) or Thermo-Gravimetric Analysis (TG) are increasingly used to resolve the structure and nature of complex compounds whilst techniques such as pyrolysis, GC and MS are useful in identifying the composition of complex organic molecule mixtures.

Conservators should be cautious about the analytical data they receive. They have to judge whether the information provided by the analyst is meaningful and if so what it means.

- The apparent accuracy of many analytical techniques which may quote figures to two decimal places may be illusory since, for certain elements or molecules present in low concentrations, the system may only analyse to an accuracy of ±20 per cent.

- The operating conditions and sensitivities of analytical instruments can vary enormously. It is important to be aware of the sensitivities and abilities of the analytical system being used.

- The minimum detectable limit of the element, mineral or molecule being analysed should be known. This will ensure that non-detection is not necessarily interpreted as absence; for example, XRD systems may require over 5 per cent of a mineral in crystalline form before it can be detected.

- Some techniques cannot, because of their analytical method, detect certain elements (e.g. Neutron Activation Analysis (NAA) cannot determine lead content), whilst others such as Atomic Absorption Spectroscopy (AAS) only determine the elements they are set up to analyse.

- An element can be present in many different forms (species). For example, copper may be detected in a liquid as metal particles in suspension, as an oxidized mineral form (e.g. $CuCO_3$ in suspension), as a reduced mineral form (e.g. Cu_2O in suspension), dissolved in solution as a soluble ion Cu^{2+}, held in the form of a sequestered complex or deposited in some form against one of the sides of the vessel.

- There is often a need to combine techniques to ascertain a complete picture. For example, to determine the amount and nature of the minerals present in a waterlogged chair it was found to be necessary to ash the samples to determine the total amount of mineral present, to determine the mineral forms through XRD and to determine the elemental composition, quantitatively, using EDXRF (Caple and Murray 1994).

- It is important to ensure that the samples and the analytical equipment are not contaminated since this can lead to misleading results. This should always be checked by running a blank or a control sample of known composition.

- It is important to be aware of natural background levels. Many elements are present in small quantities in the soil, groundwater or atmospheric dust. The level detected must be significantly above background levels in order to have any meaning.

- Samples from archaeological or historic objects are often aged, dirty, oxidized and degraded. They consequently rarely provide simple clear analytical results. Many analysts will not have analysed samples similar to those provided by the conservator and can have difficulty interpreting the results.

Consequently it is essential that conservators are familiar with the capabilities of various analytical techniques and ask sensible questions to which these techniques can provide an answer.

Visualization and imaging: Many visually observed features, structures and patterns are uniquely created by specific tools or manufacturing techniques. Examples of such informative structures include weave details on textiles, laid lines of paper, jointing in wood and the jointing and fabrication methods of manufacture in metal. This form of examination can be extended through enhancing the range of visualization:

- X-radiography. This will reveal changes in the thickness and density of materials enabling features such as: iron objects buried in a mass of corrosion; wormholes and other structural features in wooden objects; earlier images under paintings; and incised designs or decorative metal inlays in corroded, dirty or overpainted metal to be seen (Gilardoni *et al.* 1994; Graham and Eddie 1985; Lang and Middleton 1997).

- Infra-Red Reflectance Imaging. Many minerals and polymers differentially reflect or adsorb infra-red radiation. This has led to the use of infra-red photography for visualisation of paintings to detect under drawing and earlier images beneath the visible latest image (van Schoute and Verougstraete-Marcq 1986; Walmsley *et al.* 1992).

Features observed in 2-D images, such as X-radiographs, are interpreted by the conservator as 3-D images. It is important to seek additional evidence for such interpretations since there are often several possible explanations for features seen on X-radiographs and other 2-D images.

The visual qualities of a material are only one of a large number of physical attributes which it possesses including density (weight), smell, surface texture, hardness, elasticity, drape, reflectance, magnetism, even taste. Through their experience, or comparison with known 'hand specimens', conservators can often successfully identify the materials of which an object is composed, using these attributes.

Microscopy: Many materials are best identified and examined through microscopy which reveals unique visual aspects of their microstructure, enabling their characterization. Wood species (Schweingruber 1978), leather (British Leather Manufacturers Association 1957), vegetable-based fibres (Catling and Grayson 1982), animal-based fibres (Appleyard 1978), pollen (Moore *et al.* 1991), pigments (Feller 1997; Roy 1994), paint cross-sections (Byrne and Cook 1976), dust (McCrone and Delly 1973) and metals (Scott 1991) can all success-fully be identified by the conservator with suitable microscopy training. In many cases (e.g. metallography) aspects of the preparation and processing of the materials can also be identified.

There are also many small but important features detected through optical microscopy which relate to use and wear on an object. For example, microscopic examination of a series of Roman boxwood combs revealed the presence of nits, hair lice which infect the human scalp, thus graphically revealing the need for the use of the comb and problems of life in Roman Britain (Fell 1996). Some materials reveal their structure at higher magnifications and with greater depth of field; for these a scanning electron microscope is becoming a standard tool of investigation (see Figure 6.2). Mineral-replaced organic materials (Janaway 1984, see Case study 6A), the wear on tools (Olsen 1988) and the unique marks of tools such as punches (Larsen 1987) have all been effectively identified through this technique.

Identification of materials can enable us to recognize the beliefs of past peoples, the aesthetic considerations of human experience in a historic-object production sequence. Work by McGhee (1994) showed that the pre-Inuit, Thule Culture peoples of northern Canada, used harpoons and ice knives primarily made from ivory (seal or walrus) whilst their arrowheads were made from caribou antler. These materials were selected not for their physical properties, but for their magical sympathy with intended use. This belief system which correlated sea-mammal ivory with winter, women and the sea and antler with

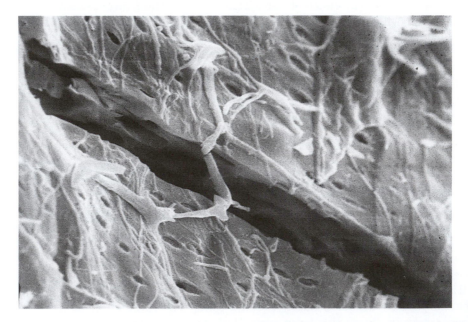

Figure 6.2 Scanning electron micrograph of the charcoal of the timber beams from the neolithic long barrow at Haddenham, Cambridgeshire, showing infestation with both neolithic and modern fungi (photograph by the author and Will Murray).

men, the land and the summer, also carried on into the verbal traditions of the later Inuit peoples.

Dating: The dating of an object is usually undertaken by:

- Typological comparison of its form or decoration with a known series of objects or artistic style or movement.

- The object coming from a known dated context.

- Identification of a material in the object which was introduced or abandoned by a given time period.

- A historic record of the object with either written or visual record; for example, its presence in an oil painting or recorded as the property of a known dated individual.

- Attribution to a known artist or craftsman.

Almost all objects have their date derived through comparison with examples of similar objects from a known culture and date, or they were retrieved from a specific cultural context. Occasionally objects are dated through scientific means. This usually applies to archaeological objects more than 400 years old. Where objects are composed of carbon they can be dated through radiocarbon-dating techniques, or if composed of ceramic or stone which has been heated they can be dated by thermoluminescence (Aitken 1990). Objects of wood, particularly oak, can if they have more than fifty growth rings be dated through dendrochronology (Baillie 1995).

Sampling: True non-destructive analytical techniques are extremely rare. The surface layers of most objects have reacted with the surrounding environment, fundamentally altering their composition; for example, water vapour and oxygen react with metal surfaces to produce an oxidized mineral layer (see Figure 6.3). This may not be detectable to the naked eye but non-destructive techniques, such as EDXRF and reflectance mode FTIR, only analyse the surface composition of the object and thus the result obtained is not necessarily representative of the body of the object. It is misleading to present it or regard it as such. If the conservator wishes to extract typical composition information about an object it will invariably need to be sampled. It is a matter of careful judgement as to the extent to which the visual and structural disruption of the object is acceptable in order to obtain the sample (Roy 1998). In some instances it is not appropriate to sample as the visual damage is not worth the information gained. For some 'low value' objects, of which there are numerous examples, it is worth sacrificing a whole object for the complete and accurate information which can be gained (e.g. the metallographic examination of some of the nails from the Roman fort of Inchtuthil since over 5 tons of nails were recovered). In several cases, such as the Leonardo cartoon (see Case study 13A), existing damage could be utilized to provide a microscopic sample for analysis, information essential to understand the structure of the object and ultimately to lead to its successful conservation. In most cases the samples removed are so small as not to be visually disruptive (e.g. the removal of a few fibres from a textile). Where there is visual disruption, such as when a sample is removed from a neolithic stone axe for petrographic identification, it is possible to restore the missing area.

Almost all major works of art, and even sacred objects such as the Turin Shroud have been sampled; small fragments sacrificed for analysis in order to increase our knowledge

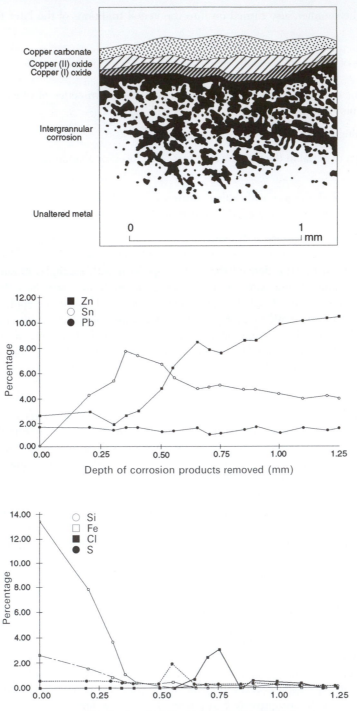

Figure 6.3 Cross-section through copper corrosion (redrawn by Y. Beadnell from Dungworth 1995). Over 1 mm of corrosion crust must be removed before the true copper alloy composition is detected.

about the object. When undertaken it is essential that such sampling is kept to a minimum to avoid any unnecessary damage to the object. All the information produced must be made available, usually in the form of a report, so as to minimize or eliminate the need for any further sampling. Samples should be carefully stored for potential future reanalysis. The samples and materials removed from an object remain the property of the owner of the object unless specific permission has been given for disposal of these samples and materials (Jaeschke 1996). Wherever possible samples should remain associated with the object or its record and they should always be clearly labelled.

Reporting: Any analytical or dating work which was undertaken as part of the conservation work should be reported to the curator/owner of the object. The report should:

- Describe the object and indicate from where the sample was removed.

- Describe the analytical method used, indicating the accuracy and precision of the method used. Any sample preparation techniques used should also be described as well as any data manipulation and standards used to obtain the analytical data.

- Present the data.

- Interpret the data with reference to comparative analyses.

- Present conclusions drawn from this analytical work.

Consideration should always be given to making the information available to a wider audience. This may mean direct publication or release of the information to individuals who could publish it with larger collections of data at a later date.

How far the conservator goes in recording and analysing an object is always a matter of judgement. Awareness of the nature and uses of the conservation record and balancing the limitations and cost of analytical techniques against the usefulness of the information which can be obtained should lead to justifiable decisions regarding recording and analysis.

6A Case study: Benwell Box (Keepax and Robson 1978)

During the excavation of the Roman villa of Benwell a corroded mass of iron fragments, which were the fittings of a chest or box of second-century-AD date was discovered. The archaeologists and conservators on the excavation judged that that there was considerable potential for gaining further information from this concreted mass and, therefore, decided to lift and carefully excavate it back in the laboratory. The mass of corroded iron and soil was carefully isolated from the surrounding soil, covered in aluminium foil and after a wooden crate had been inverted over this, the gap between the foil covered corroded mass and the crate was filled with expanding polyurethane foam. The corroded mass was detached from the soil beneath and carried away, safely held in its wooden crate, to the conservation laboratory. The soil and corroded iron mass was X-rayed and slowly excavated. No traces of the wood of which the box had originally been composed were recovered. Only the iron nails, corner clamps, straps and hinges remained.

When iron corrodes, it releases ferrous ions into solution. These subsequently oxidize to form ferric-oxyhydroxide minerals (rust). If iron corrodes quickly in

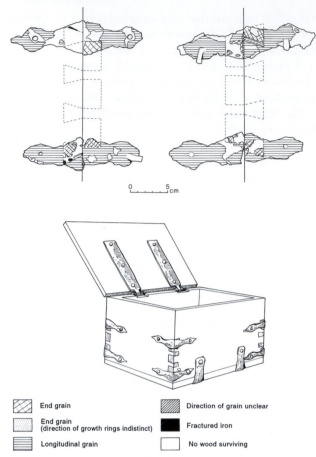

Figure 6.4 The Benwell Box (redrawn by Y. Beadnell from Keepax and Robson 1978). The evidence of the direction of the mineral-replaced wood permitted the original nature of the joints of the box to be deduced and thus an accurate reconstruction of the box to be created.

association with organic material the iron minerals which are formed can be deposited:

- Around the organic material forming a 'cast'. Eventually the organic material, such as wood, textile, leather, skin, horn or bone, will degrade leaving this impression of the decayed organic material and its structure.

- Inside the organic material replacing it as it degrades. This forms an exact copy or 'pseudomorph' of the organic material.

- In both 'cast' and 'pseudomorph' forms.

Such deposits are known as mineral-replaced organics or mineral-preserved organics and they can reproduce all the microscopic aspects of the structure of the organic material (Keepax 1975). This occurred on all the iron fittings of the Benwell Box.

As a result of not cleaning off the rust from the iron fittings of the box and by observing the traces of mineral-replaced organics present on the fittings it was possible to deduce information about the type of wood and the nature of the construction of the box. From the microscopic examination of the microstructure of the mineral it was possible to identify oak (genus *Quercus*) as the wood used for the whole box. By noting the depth of the wood grain on the nails and the length of the nail shank before the points were bent over it was clear that the base board of the box was 22 mm thick, whilst the sides were 25 mm thick, as was the lid. From noting the direction of the wood grain on the corner clamps it was possible to deduce that the four pieces of wood forming the sides of the box were held together with dovetail joints, which in size and shape conformed well to modern carpentry practice. These traces indicate the high level of expertise of the craftsman who constructed this object. The dovetail joints were only used for joining the lower half of the sides of the box; the upper half was a mitred joint. The careful lifting of the mass of soil and corroded iron fittings had preserved the iron straps which ran from the front of the box all the way to the top of the back of the box. These appear to have formed the hinges which ran beneath the lid of the box. The exact dimensions of these straps allowed the height and depth of the box to be established, whilst the positions of the corner clamps which had also been preserved through the careful lifting allowed the approximate width of the box to be established.

Careful examination and recording allowed the preservation and decipherment of the traces of mineral-replaced organics and allowed an accurate reconstruction of the original box to be created (see Figure 6.4). The crucial judgements were the recognition of the potential of the object to reveal information, the use of X-radiography and microscopy to examine and identify the mineralized fragments, the decision not to clean off the evidence, reference to the expertise of others in order to identify the nature of the carpentry techniques involved. The careful recording of this object has subsequently formed a useful reference point for examples of corroded iron fastenings which have been subsequently unearthed.

7 Cleaning

7.1 Cleaning

Cleaning describes the removal of soiling and decay products from the surface of an object:

- Soiling II: solid matter deposited during burial or storage.

- Soiling I: solid matter deposited during use – ethnic or ethnographical dirt (Oddy 1994).

- Decay products: the layer of material produced from reaction between primary or secondary materials of the object and water, light, oxygen or biological organisms.

- Secondary materials: layers of materials added to the object through its working life (e.g. paint layers).

- Primary materials: the substance of the original object.

Soiling in the form of soil from burial, dust from storage and as caked-on mud, grease, oil, dirt, sweat and blood from use, is detrimental to objects. Soiling associated with textiles, wood and paper acts as a food and moisture source for micro-organisms. Microbial activity, therefore, centres on the soiling resulting in subsequent attack of the substrate by micro-organisms such as moulds. Soiling particles and microbial growths adsorb water and retain it in close contact with the substrate thus acting as a source for corrosion of metals and hydrolysis of organic materials. Soiling is usually acidic; the rates of reaction for corrosion and hydrolysis increase as the pH decreases. Soluble materials are drawn from the soiling into the object leaving staining and discolouration (e.g. iron staining). Dirt and dust obscure the surface of the object from view, making the object appear duller and darker than it actually is and obscuring decorative detail and other features. The extent to which the conservator removes soiling and decay products is a matter of careful judgement, balancing the loss of information which the soiling and decay products can contain against the benefit of improving the stability of the object and revealing more of its original visual form.

7.2 Acting on aesthetic impulses

The impulse to clean, removing the dirt and dust which obscures an object, stems from the unconscious idea that cleanliness is the correct or appropriate state. This seems to be almost instinctive for many conservators as well as a large percentage of the population of Western

Europe and North America. It probably derives from deep in the human past, when human surroundings were old and dirty and all things clean and new were seen as desirable. This desirability and purity of a clean state was extolled through expressions such as 'cleanliness is next to godliness'. The virtue of cleanliness was reinforced in the nineteenth century as disease was linked to dirt and squalor. For most people a coating of dust was seen as a sign of neglect. An object which was clean demonstrated that the owner valued and cared for it.

The concept that the objects of the past were aesthetically pleasing derives from the Renaissance ideas regarding the beauty and proportion of classical images (see Chapter 4). That which obscured beauty – soil, metal corrosion or concretions and staining on stone – were cleaned, ground or chipped away (Cellini 1878). These ideas about dirt obscuring an object's image and its beauty and the correctness of cleaning continued and led to the fierce dusting and cleaning regimes of the Victorian era (Beeton 1859). This urge to clean off the dirt and decay which comes between the viewer and artist's image could, in conservation terms, be articulated by the concept of revealing the 'true nature' of the object. More than justifying cleaning an object, it demands it. However, this raised the question: 'What was the true nature of the object?' (see Section 5.4). When the evidence of an object's use is considered, it can be seen to lack any single point which can be defined as 'the' true nature of the object. A revised format of 'removing that which is clearly not part of the true nature of the object' may be a more realistic approach to describe cleaning.

When the Statue of Liberty was restored in the early 1980s there were suggestions that it should be cleaned down to the bare metal and made to shine 'penny bright'. This approach was not considered appropriate since it was clear that most people considered the statue 'correct' in its green patinated state. That was how they knew it and wished to retain it (Baboian *et al.* 1990, see Case study 3A). It is becoming apparent that because of the widespread availability of bright and shiny new products, age and originality are becoming more highly valued in present-day Western society. This valued 'aged' condition is, however, still a selectively applied aesthetic appreciation. Reproductions, distressed furniture and antiques sell well; other objects with less aesthetically pleasing ageing characteristics such as chipped and broken china and rusty iron objects do not. When one considers the changing fashion of what is considered 'aesthetically pleasing' in pictorial art, or how ideas of feminine and masculine beauty change with time, even over a period of a few decades, cleaning any object to fulfil the fashionable ideas of what is aesthetically pleasing in the current age would appear to be a short-term policy and unworthy as a conservation ideal. Consequently ideas of cleaning for aesthetic reasons, instinctive as they are, have to be recognized as subjective and more coherent objective reasoning for cleaning sought.

7.3 Soiling

It is possible to consider that all events, including damage, discard, burial and even the recovery and collecting of the object, are part of an object's life, part of the truth about the object. If this is correct then everything up to the present moment, even the deposits of museum dust which gently fall upon it (Soiling II), are part of the full history of the object, 'an object never ceases to accumulate history' (Jaeschke 1996). As such even removing the dust from museum objects could be considered an act of vandalism, if carried out without being fully recorded as part of an object's past. However, common sense must prevail. Whilst the museum career, even its coating of dust, can be regarded as part of the history of the object, it is not an important or informative part of the object's life. The object was collected for what it can tell us of the past, not to form a record of recent museum-storage conditions.

Dust should normally be removed since it obscures and can potentially discolour an object's surface. Any old museum numbers written on the object's surface relate to the use of the object as a museum exhibit and not to its use in the past, which was the reason for its collection and thus like the museum dust they could be removed. However, since they do carry specific information about the history of the object and they do not represent a threat to the continued stability of the object, whilst the object is in store, it appears sensible to leave them in place. Consideration should be given to recording and removing them, if they are visible when the object is put on display, since they can mislead the viewing public and detract from the purpose of the display. Many objects which have been in collections a long time bear considerable traces of their storage and display.

Many archaeological objects have corroded, discoloured and are covered in earth as a result of their long burial in the ground. It has usually been seen as appropriate to remove all traces of adhering soil (Soiling II) and soil staining from the object's surface. Some objects have been broken or crushed by the weight of soil above them as in the case of the Sutton Hoo Helmet (see Case study 9B). In such cases the pieces of the object have usually been readhered and restored to their original form (see Figure 7.1). Where there is some doubt about the exact nature or the original form, as in the case of the Bush Barrow Gold (Case study 12A), the extent of the cleaning and restoration has been questioned.

Where the burial environment has interacted with the object the matter is more sub-jective and the extent of cleaning can depend on the perception of the artistic merit of the object, as well as the date and pervading ethical climate when the decision to clean was made. The Vix crater is the most important example of Greek metalwork imported into North-West Europe in the pre-Roman Iron Age and demonstrates the contact between prehistoric Europe and the classical world. All traces of soil and degraded leather, which

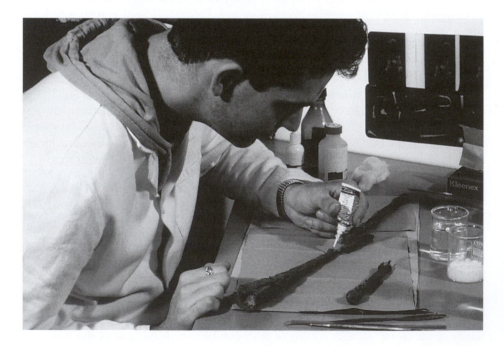

Figure 7.1 Conservator Matthew Simpkin re-adhering pieces of a mineralized iron object recovered from excavation (photograph by the author and Trevor Woods).

surrounded this object when found, were cleaned off as it was perceived that 'they harmed the beauty of the object' (France-Lanord 1996). In this case the aesthetic qualities of the crater and a specific aspect of its historic past, in this case the classical scenes depicted in the metalwork, were seen as more important than the evidence that, for burial, it was wrapped in a piece of leather. Thus the cleaning was judged to reveal the more 'important' truth. The interpretation of the object determines what aspects of the object are kept and what are sacrificed (Jedrzejewska 1976). In the case of objects such as the Benwell Box (see Case study 6A), the importance of the evidence which can still be recovered from such deposits is apparent (Janaway and Scott 1989) and is seen as the true nature of the object. Such deposits are now frequently retained on the object by archaeological conservators.

Where soiling relates to the use of the object (Soiling I), there is a more difficult balance to be struck between preservation of the object and preservation of the information about the use of the object. Acceptance of an enhanced rate of decay of the object because of the retention of dirt, dust, staining, body fluids, etc. is judged worthwhile if the information is crucial to the understanding of the object. This retention of soiling can become a matter of fairly subtle judgement. In the case of a 'biker's' leather jacket from the 1950s the textile conservator at the York Castle Museum judged that the jacket was deliberately kept and used in the stained and soiled state by its owner as part of the antisocial rebellious creed of the 'biker' subculture. Whilst the jacket undoubtedly had points within its history when it was clean, there was additional information and a message to be displayed in its dirty state (Eastop and Brooks 1996). In a similar case the hood worn by Robert Merrick, the Elephant Man, was not wet cleaned, since it was felt that future analytical techniques may be able to recover information from the body staining of this cloth, which could not be obtained at present. As conservators become more adept at identifying materials, even simple surface cleaning could remove evidence of the use of a garment, which we would now seek to retain. An example are the turn-ups of an agricultural worker's trousers which contained the wheat seeds and husks which provided the evidence for the occupation of the owner of the trousers (Eastop and Brooks 1996). In some cases more deliberate attempts have been made to keep this crucial evidence. At the Australian War Memorial Museum the uniform of a soldier who served at the Somme which was still caked in the mud of the battlefield had a consolidant applied in order to retain the caked-on mud, which was seen as a key element of the 'truth' about this object (Eastop and Brooks 1996). The greater awareness of preserving soiling on all forms of object, which is apparent in areas such as textile conservation, is not yet routinely practised in other areas of conservation, such as historic vehicle conservation

There has been, as yet, little research work to aid the conservator in distinguishing the ethnic dirt (Soiling I) which accumulates and is indicative of use, from the dirt acquired during storage or burial (Soiling II). There are clear differences in terms of information content, though often little physical or visual difference is observable. Too often the lack of time and skill available for cleaning and the lack of information or techniques for distinguishing between the two leads to the choice of retaining or removing all the soiling.

7.4 Original surface

The original surface of any object invariably contains valuable evidence of how it was manufactured, such as the marks of the tools which made it, even if these are only the scratches of the final polishing, evidence of pigments or other forms of surface decoration and marks from use (see Section 6.3). In some materials, such as glass, stone and some copper alloys, the decay occurs so slowly it does not disrupt the original surface, which is preserved on the exterior of the decay/corrosion products. In other materials, such as iron, the corrosion rate is a lot faster and the original surface is usually buried within the corrosion products (see Case study 9A, the Sutton Hoo Helmet). In the case of organic objects the original surface is degraded through interaction with light, water, oxygen, biological organisms or surface-dirt deposits so becoming discoloured and fragile. As stone decays it can form a crust above a fragile stone-powder layer. This crust is often blackened and is often considered visually disfiguring to the building. Unfortunately this original surface, now a crust, contains the tool marks, traces of pigment and other information on the surface of the original stone. Removal of this crust surface for considerations of the aesthetic beauty of the building eliminates all the information on the original shape and decoration of the stone. Durham Cathedral is built of a beautiful honey-coloured stone which had by the eighteenth century become blackened with soot and degraded by weathering. The cathedral architect, John Wooler, had stonemasons chisel 2–3 inches of stone off the whole of the outside of the cathedral (Roberts 1994). This changed every exterior architectural detail. All the windows were 4–6 inches wider whilst the pillars and all other decorative motifs were 2–4 inches thinner. This has considerably altered the proportions of all the much admired stonework features of this cathedral. A similar loss of surface evidence has occurred to many of the archaeological metal objects which were electrolytically stripped in the early twentieth century. Though this technique stabilized the object and halted any further decay, in removing all the corrosion layers it removed valuable surface evidence (Norman 1988).

Present-day conservators usually seek to preserve the original surface of every object. They will often consolidate fragile external surfaces of organic objects or those of glass and stone in order to preserve them. When cleaning metal objects they selectively remove the corrosion products in order to uncover the object's original surface (Cronyn 1990). Exceptions to this procedure are made where important information has become incorporated into the corrosion beyond the original surface such as that contained by mineral-replaced organics (see Case study 6A, the Benwell Box).

7.5 Cleaning: Where to stop

As described in Sections 2.3 and 5.2, objects have many truths, and every object bears traces of all these truths. Some relate to the creation of the object, others to the use, discard, burial, rediscovery and care of the object in a museum. When it is decided to display an object a conscious decision is taken regarding the point in its history at which it is to be displayed. If necessary it is cleaned or even restored to that point (e.g. the Vix crater). Though the owner/curator and conservator normally discuss this point, there will invariably be many instances where the conservator who works on the object will have to make decisions on their own about how that truth is achieved and where it lies within the object, its soiling and decay products.

In many instances oil paintings have been found to have earlier paintings beneath them. Usually the later more complete image is retained since it preserves both the original (even if unseen) and later image. In some instances where it is known that the image has only been partially altered, the earlier image is exposed since it was substantially intact and the 'true nature' of the original artist's work is revealed. This was certainly the case when Ian McClure conserved the painting *Henry Prince of Wales on Horseback* by Robert Peake the Elder painted circa 1610–12. Originally this was a picture of the young prince seated on a medieval warhorse, surrounded by the iconography of courtly love and jousting, similar to

Durer's 1513 engraving *The Knight, Death and the Devil*. After the restoration of the monarchy the painting was transformed into a young man on a dashing white horse in front of an arboreal Arcadian landscape similar to the later painting *Charles I on Horseback* by Anthony Van Dyck (1637). After consultation with the owner and art historians it was decided that the original painting was a complete vision of the artist; the later alterations simply indicated the fashions of a later age. The conservation of this painting, therefore, involved, after full recording, the removal of all the later alterations and the restoration of the original image (McClure 1992). The conservator, even when working in conjunction with an owner or curator, needs to have confidence and experience to make such decisions. Such aesthetic judgements are more commonly seen with pictures and buildings than in other areas of conservation.

The rooms in almost any historic house contain furniture and elements of decor from numerous styles and periods. Thus frequently there is no single point (coherent period) back to which rooms, buildings or even many artefacts can be restored without losing much important historical information (see Figure 7.2). In most cases, the room and buildings are retained in their present form with all the evidence of their past available for the discerning viewer. In the case of objects this equates to the 'last used' phase. The dirt and dust of storage are removed but no attempt is made to restore or take back the object to any earlier form.

In addition to the importance of the information retained or displayed, there is often a consideration of completeness. As in the case of the portrait of *Henry Prince of Wales on Horseback*, the state chosen for display is one which most completely remains, and where the most coherent image of the object, at some point in its past, can be displayed. The cleaned surface though referred to as 'the' or 'an' original surface is in reality an approximation. It will not have all its original characteristics; for example, an ancient bronze mirror will have

Figure 7.2 The medieval town wall of a French hilltop town showing almost continuous alterations to the wall from the time of its construction through to the present day. There is no single point in the history of this wall to which it could be restored without removing valuable evidence of the historic past (photograph by the author).

corroded and no longer possess its original highly reflective metal finish, an oil painting will not have its original varnish, and the dyes on the textile will have faded. Cleaning cannot turn back time. It can often reveal the original form but rarely completely and will always leave exposed some of the effects of time.

7.6 Cleaning paintings

Following the appointment of Charles Eastlake as Keeper of the National Gallery in 1844, a cleaning programme was begun, removing the golden hued varnish from many of the National Gallery's paintings (Kirby Talley 1998). In 1847 John Ruskin sent a letter to *The Times* in which he complained about the National Gallery's excessive cleaning of Ruben's *Peace and War* and Titian's *Bacchus*. These had recently had their brown aged varnish removed and their original vibrant colours revealed. There appears to have been much popular feeling in support of Ruskin's view, perhaps best expressed at an earlier date by Sir George Beamont (1753–1827): 'A good picture, like a good fiddle, should be brown' (Kirby Talley 1998). As a result of the critical debate which ensued throughout the late 1840s and early 1850s the National Gallery sent its pictures abroad for restoration before they were brought to the gallery for display. In this way the gallery retained control of the restoration process, avoiding the moral sensibilities and desires of some artists and sections of the public for 'toned down' pictures (Bomford 1994). However, in 1853 the outcry was renewed when a further nine paintings were shown in their cleaned condition. Though a subsequent government enquiry found that the charges of overcleaning were unfounded, it left the National Gallery sensitive to the issues of cleaning and restoration (Wilson 1977).

The controversy of cleaning of pictures flared up again in the late 1940s at the National Gallery when cleaned pictures were again presented to the public and again in the late 1980s with the cleaning of the Sistine Chapel ceiling frescoes (Beck and Daley 1993, see Case study 7A).

This subject of the distorting effect of yellowing varnish on the chromatic diversity of varnished oil paintings has recently been clarified by the work of Dauma and Henchman (1997). Photo-oxidation affects almost all organic materials and induces a noticeable yellowing of all picture varnishes over time. Using colour measurement, such as the CIE or L*a*b* system, the chromatic variation experienced by a viewer looking at an aged varnished picture can be shown to be limited to a narrow variation in the yellow–brown part of the spectrum. The only method of seeing something close to the original colours and the original intentions of the artist is to reduce or remove the varnish layer.

The often substantial visual alteration of pictures, when they have had their yellowed varnish and the dirt and grime of decades removed, is clearly shocking to some. Walden (1985) has criticized the 'complete cleaning' of oil paintings as practised principally in Britain and North America as overcleaning and seen the 'partial' or 'selective cleaning' practised in continental Europe as preferable. No objective evidence has yet been provided showing the loss of original paint during complete cleaning (Hedley 1986, 1990). Three possible approaches to the cleaning-off-varnish controversy can be discerned (Hedley 1986, 1990).

- Complete cleaning: removes all the yellowed varnish and subsequent restorations and exposes the original paint layer. This gets as close to the original colours as possible and enables a substantial amount of analysis to be undertaken so revealing much informa-tion about the artist, his technique and materials. No part of the original is lost, damaged or obscured. There is a responsibility to restore the visual integrity of the object where substantial restorations have been removed. However, the complete cleaning of Leonardo da Vinci's fresco *The Last Supper* has shown that this can involve very substantial areas of loss and a very delicate balance needs to be struck between the object as an historic document of da Vinci's work and the loss of the aesthetic impact of the image (Kemp 1990).

- Partial cleaning: removes most of the varnish retaining just a thin surface layer. This retains the tonal harmony and the aged appearance of the picture which have built up over the years. The result is usually seen as aesthetically pleasing, though it fails to go as far as revealing the original colours of the picture and retaining the varnish invariably limits the level of investigation which is done to the picture.

- Selective cleaning: removes the varnish in some areas and not in others. It aims to create an aesthetically desirable unity to the picture. It seeks to get as close as possible to the artist's original intention whilst maintaining the aged appearance of the picture. It recognizes that pictures do not age evenly and is perhaps the most subtle and subjective of the cleaning processes.

Walden has drawn a correlation between the clarity and brightness of completely cleaned pictures and the art, advertising, television and photography of the late twentieth century. This she suggests is the distinctive visual style of the late twentieth century to which modern-day conservators, who completely clean, unconsciously transform the pictures upon which they work. The belief of Walden, Gombrich, Beck and others is that the darkened pictures of the past possess great subtlety and harmony. This may, however, be largely attributed to the tonal harmony induced by the yellowing varnish (Hedley 1986, 1990). A preference for looking old can be just as subjective and unconsciously desirable as looking bright and new. As Hedley (1986, 1990) has described, the present-day image presented by any picture is not quite that intended by the artist; the pigments have differentially aged and have reacted with the binder and covering varnish to permanently alter the chromatic and tonal balance of the picture. This means that no matter how it is cleaned the artist's intentions cannot be fully recovered and a new 'relativity' between the artist and the viewer must be established. The three methods of cleaning works of art on canvas which are currently used present equally valid but different 'relativities' to the viewer.

7.7 Damage during cleaning

Just because it is possible to clean an object, does not mean that it should be cleaned. A conscious decision is required as to what the conserved state of the object should be, and reasons for it being in that state need to be given. There needs to be awareness that any cleaning activity will unintentionally remove evidence of the object's past. This is balanced against the further harm that the dirt and corrosion layer may inflict on the object. Examples of a clear perception of this balance can be seen in the removal of iron stains from textiles. The disfiguring red stains and the continuing damage to the textile fibres must be balanced against the damage to the textile fibres which any chemical used to remove the stain will cause. Similarly the bleaching of paper may improve the aesthetic appearance of paper but this must be set against the potential damage of the bleaching chemicals to the paper fibres. For a badly stained print the balance, given the importance of the object's aesthetic properties, may lie with the 'cleaning' action which bleaching represents. For an important historic document the balance may lie with preservation and against bleaching.

Cleaning is an irreversible process, it is undertaken if the benefits outweigh the risks of damage to the object. Leaving dust in place obscures the object from view and acts as a potential centre for corrosion. However, removing dust simply by wiping it off can microscopically damage an object since hard gritty particles are dragged across the surface so scratching it. Almost all mechanical polishing processes are mildly abrasive and mechanical removal with scalpels, wire wool, jeweller's rouge or air abrasive can potentially damage the layers beneath the dirt or corrosion. Earlier this century soldiers were set to work, using brickearth and oil, cleaning the armour at the Tower of London. The abrasion removed almost all traces of gilding and inlay from a number of pieces of armour (Corfield, personal communication). However, in the hands of a skilled conservator such damage is minimal. Once the decision to clean is taken then the risk of minor damage to the object is accepted and judged to be acceptable. Similar risks and damage are encountered with chemical cleaning methods (Merk 1978) and though quicker than physical cleaning they are usually less controllable.

The highly reflective polished state of metals such as silver are part of the aesthetic intention. Such artefacts were deliberately kept in this state. Polishing whilst in use was an abrasive process and slowly wore away the object. If continued by the conservator, the object would eventually lose definition of all raised and incised decoration. For such objects conservators seek to maintain the polished state by lengthening the periods between cleaning (e.g. through the use of protective lacquers and controlling the display case environment). Objects not required for display can be allowed to retain patinas which act as a protective layer slowing the rate of corrosion.

Examples of overcleaning are rarely published so conservation students are often unaware of the fact that all experienced conservators have occasionally done such things (Smith 1990). It is in the very nature of judgement that practitioners occasionally 'get it wrong', and all conservators have, at one time or another, found themselves unintentionally overcleaning objects. At this point it is difficult and embarrassing to admit the mistake and stop. This is where the question of an ethical approach becomes crucial. It is unethical to damage an object intentionally, continuation is not an option for a conservator. It is the willingness of the conservator to stop their overcleaning, where appropriate, record the damage they have unintentionally done and modify their cleaning method, which demonstrates commitment to the ethics of conservation. Upon discovering that an object is being over-cleaned there is often an urge to 'cover up' the mistake. It may indeed be appropriate to restore the visual integrity of the object. This should, however, clearly be seen as restoration work and should be treated in the same way as any other piece of restoration work; for example, only undertaking it when the object will be viewed, recording the extent of the restoration work and seeking to use reversible (retreatable) restoration media and techniques (see Chapter 9).

In other examples the need for complete cleaning can be questioned. The large number of pieces of archaeological ironwork and the voluminous nature of the corrosion product make complete cleaning expensive. The use of partial cleaning and investigation using X-rays, described in Chapter 12, is a cost-effective alternative (Cronyn 1990). The development of new techniques, such as laser cleaning, brings the zone of surface interaction down to a very small layer. Using lasers the soiled crusts of stone can be cleaned with minimal risk of crust removal, even pen and pencil marks can be removed from paper (Cooper 1998). As interventive conservation techniques, technology and expertise improve there should be much less damage caused to objects, as a result of cleaning, in the future.

7.8 Cleaning: The decision

Evidence is gathered at the start of the conservation process in the form of full recording of an object and any context to which it relates. Considering both the state and nature of the object, the intended use of the object (display, study or storage) a decision is reached by the conservator and curator/owner (using RIP balance) regarding the conservation work required. In particular a judgement is reached on the desirability of the nature and extent of cleaning of the object. Though conservation-cleaning work may then commence, conservation is an iterative process, and further evidence is usually recovered during the conservation process. The original judgement often needs to be re-evaluated in light of the new information. This has been described by Berducou (1996) as a 'dialectical relationship' between study of the object and the cleaning and conservation of the object. In some cases this may mean starting the cleaning all over again, using a more aggressive cleaning method in order to remove further dirt and decay deposits. When viewed in these terms the final cleaned, conserved form of the object can be described as 'the concrete expression of a critical judgement' (Berducou 1996).

The process of cleaning imposes a view upon the object, a conscious decision is taken to remove some things and not others; thus cleaning is not 'an interpretively neutral treatment' (Orlofsky and Trupin 1993; Eastop and Brooks 1996). The conservator has, together with curatorial colleagues or the owner of the object, the responsibility for deciding what is the most important truth about an object and then, through cleaning, revealing that truth which can then be displayed. For inexperienced conservators this can be a difficult decision, and it is important to remember:

- It is not possible to preserve everything. The archaeologist when excavating a site accepts the responsibility of destroying 100s or 1,000s of years of information as the layers of earth and occupation debris are removed. The curator accepts the responsibility of only revealing one of an object's many truths when displaying it with a single brief label. No museum visitor will read an essay.

- The present surface of an object is an arbitrary effect of man and nature. The present dusty, damaged, rusted, dirty surface has occurred as a result of neglect by previous owners, the attentions and deprivations of nineteenth-century servants, the variable effects of burial in the soil or the primitive cleaning of an archaeologist. It is frequently not a deliberate or meaningful surface. Inevitably when the conservator has researched and investigated the object a clearer picture of the object and its history is established and far more meaningful surfaces can be identified and recovered. Though concerns can be raised about the alteration of the surface appearance of objects and associated loss of evidence as a result of surface cleaning, these must be set against the visually important 'truth' of the surface which is uncovered.

- No one is likely to be in a better position to make the decision than the conservator. They will usually know most about the object, and consequently they have the greatest chance of successfully revealing the desired surface. If nothing is done, other less well-informed and skilled individuals may make the decision and do the work. The recording work and careful approach of the conservator will not be used. The conservator should consider the consequences of their inactions as carefully as they would their actions. Simply leaving the decision to nature or the less well qualified, is a waste of the education and experience the conservator has acquired.

- The object should not be excessively or needlessly damaged. A paper or textile object would not be subject to an aqueous cleaning treatment (washing) if it were: too weak and might disintegrate, contained a water-soluble adhesive or dye or if the relaxation in the water would remove important folds or embossed patterns. The more extensive the cleaning the greater the risk.

- If it is decided not to clean, the reasons for not cleaning should be clearly stated in order to inform subsequent conservators. It is important to distinguish between those objects where cleaning is not carried out because of a desire to preserve the soiling and information associated with the object and those objects where it is felt that cleaning work with the present facilities, expertise or methods risks unacceptable damage to the object.

- Cleaning should not be undertaken simply because similar objects have previously been cleaned or are always cleaned in this manner. A case needs to be made for each object as a separate entity and, even if a process is repeated on one object after another, it is because it can be justified in each separate case.

- It is important to remember that all the aspects of an object's past are important. For every object a conscious decision is made regarding the balance of revelation (display), investigation and preservation. This decision takes into account the loss of information upon cleaning balanced against the truth of the object revealed.

It takes time and practice before any conservator is confident about cleaning an object and can accept that the benefits, for the purposes of gaining information and transmitting information through display, are judged to be worth possibly removing some of the traces of evidence about an object's past.

7A Case study: The Sistine Chapel (Brandt 1987; Colalucci 1991; Mancinelli 1991, 1992; Ekserdjian 1987; Beck and Daley 1993)

The Sistine Chapel was created for the papal court of the Vatican in 1477–80 by Pope Sixtus IV della Rovere. The chapel was extensively decorated with frescoes by Tuscan and Umbrian artists including Sandro Botticelli in 1481–3. In the early Renaissance frescoes were primarily executed in the true or *buon* fresco technique in which finely ground inorganic pigments in water were painted on to fresh lime-based plaster. In 1508 Pope Julius II della Rovere commissioned Michelangelo to replace the initial ceiling frescoes of a starry firmament, resulting in the nine scenes from The Book of Genesis flanked by figures of youths, prophets and sibyls which are seen covering the ceiling today. Michelangelo also undertook the decoration of the lunettes above the windows with depictions of the ancestors of Christ, completed in 1512. Subsequently in 1536–42 Michelangelo depicted *The Last Judgement* on the altar wall replacing the earlier damaged fresco of the 1480s by Perugino.

As early as 1543 the office of 'mundator' (cleaner) was created to keep the frescoes of the Sistine Chapel clean from dust, smoke from lamps and other filth. In accessible areas cleaning probably occurred annually. There are sixteenth-century written references (Johannes Fichardus) to the blackening of the ceiling by the smoke of candles and to the presence of salts and cracking (Paolo Giovio). While a number of artists and writers such as Clovio, Piccinni, Rados and Conca still find the frescos visible and exciting works of art well into the nineteenth century, others such as Milanesi and Charles Heath Wilson comment on the obscured darkened and blackened form. A substantial cleaning operation is recorded in 1625; Simane Lagi, who cleaned the wall and possibly the ceiling frescoes, initially dusting them with a linen cloth then scrubbing them with slices of coarse bread, occasionally moistened with water. In 1710–12 Annibale Mazzuoli cleaned the frescoes with Greek wine and sponges.

More substantial 'restoration' work was also carried out. Between 1565 and 1572 Matteo da Lecce and Hendrick van der Broeck repainted the frescoes on the entrance wall following subsidence damage sustained in the early sixteenth century. In the late sixteenth century Domenico Carnevali restored the ceiling, reworking several of the scenes and figures. Where these additions and restorations sought to match the colour of the earlier Michelangelo frescos the artists used much darker colours since the original frescoes had become discoloured with soot. Though all these events were recorded in the Vatican's records, other interventions such as the overpainting of details on *The Last Judgement* in 1762 and the regilding around some the ceiling figures in 1814 were not. Thus the historic records of the cleaning and restoration of the frescoes of the Sistine Chapel are far from complete. The fact that cleaning and restoration work started in the sixteenth century indicates that there has been extensive soiling and some damage to the original frescoes and consequently what was seen by the mid-twentieth century was not what the artist had originally intended.

In the twentieth century conservation work on the frescoes in the Chapel by Seitz in 1904 undertook sealing and consolidation of the plaster as well as limited cleaning tests. In the 1920s and 1930s Biagetti also undertook consolidation work. A more thorough cleaning programme for the frescoes commenced in 1964, directed by Deoclecio Redig de Campos until 1979 and thereafter by Carlo Pietrangeli. Between 1964–74 the frescoes of the side walls were cleaned, principally removing the accumulation of surface soiling. Following work in 1975 to prevent rainwater reaching and damaging the ceiling, the frescoes of van der Broeck and da Lecce on the entrance wall were cleaned in 1979. These frescoes had been subject to numerous previous cleanings and restorations, and the 1979 removal of the surface dirt, leaving all later restorations in place and intact, left a very patchy image. It was suggested by the Vatican conservators that a more complete and thorough cleaning and restoration programme was clearly required to give visual integrity to this wall and it was this regime which was ultimately extended to the ceiling.

The conservation work of the 1930s and the 1970s indicated the presence of a thick even layer of glue over much of the surface of the ceiling frescoes. It has been shown by Dauma and Henchman (1996) that this glue layer heavily distorted the chromatic range of the fresco colours. In various places there were several layers of glue with deposits of dust and soot present between them and on the surface. With evidence that the glue was causing some flaking of the paint it was decided to remove this glue, which the Vatican restorers regarded as a later protective coating applied by Mazzuoli as part of his eighteenth-century restoration. It is important to note that there is no mention in the historic records of any cleaner/restorer putting glue/varnish on to the ceiling, though clearly they did so. This emphasizes the poverty of the historical record in regard to cleaning and restoration for a building which is otherwise regarded as having a well-documented history. The question raised by

Beck, and others who are critics of the Sistine Chapel fresco cleaning, is whether this glue layer is, at least in part, the *a secco* work of Michelangelo and thus part of the original fresco. In *a secco* work pigment is held in a binder added to the dry plaster wall and is often used to add details and apply fugitive pigments to true or *buon* fresco images. On the basis of what was revealed during the cleaning the Vatican conservators have indicated that there is virtually no *a secco* work by Michelangelo on the ceiling. Beck and others, who have lost confidence in the statements of the restorers working on the project, claim that it is extensive. Other conservators and art historians such as Brandt who have seen the work being undertaken have written statements in support of the restoration work. Paint cross-sections show slight dirt layers beneath the glue and in one place part of the original fresco covered by the restoration of the 1560–70s does not have a glue covering. This evidence supports the suggestion that the original fresco was completed almost entirely in pure fresco techniques.

The conservation work on Michelangelo's ceiling frescos commenced in 1975 by making the vault above the frescoes waterproof in order to stop the ingress of water, which had caused problems of salt efflorescence and cracking and delaminating of the *intonaco* (the thin surface layer of plaster containing the pigment). The cleaning and conservation work of Michelangelo's frescoes was undertaken in three stages: the images of the Popes and the lunettes 1980–4, the ceiling 1985–9, and *The Last Judgement* 1990–3. The cleaning and conservation was completed by April 1994. The conservation work was sponsored by Nippon TV who have, in return, gained the visual rights to the Sistine Chapel images for the period of the restoration plus 3 years. Access has been maintained to the Sistine Chapel throughout the conservation period for visitors, and many tens of thousands of people have consequently seen this conservation process 'in action'. The cleaning of the ceiling was principally undertaken using AB57. This is a solution of ammonium bicarbonate, sodium bicarbonate and Desogen (a fungicide, bactericide and mild sequestering agent) in a paste of carboxymethyl cellulose applied for 3 minutes and removed with a repeat application 24 hours later followed by thorough washing in distilled water. This cleaning agent primarily assists in solubilizing the glue and dirt layers, though, like ammonium carbonate treatments, it may have some action on the calcium sulphate crusts which can form on the very outer skin of marble, limestone, lime plaster and mortar surfaces, holding dirt at the surface. The limited application time and gel formulation restricts penetration of this agent into the plaster ensuring it only has a surface effect. After the use of the cleaning agent the fresco surface was rinsed with distilled water until no trace of glue or AB57 is detected. Any areas of *a secco* work which were identified were consolidated with Paraloid B72 (an acrylic copolymer) whilst cleaning occurred around them. They were then separately treated with appropriate organic solvents. Substantial areas of the *intonaco* were found to be delaminating from the underlying *arriccio* (the substantial plaster backing of the wall), as a result of the infiltration of rainwater over the centuries. This necessitated readhesion of the *intonaco* through the injection of Vinnapas (PVA–PVC terpolymer of ethylene) and, where necessary, grouting the voids with La Farge desalinated hydraulic mortars. The overall effect, in terms of removing the dirt and darkened glue-covered surface, has been a dramatic heightening of the colours of the ceiling frescoes (see Figure 7.3). Despite concerns raised by Beck regarding the loss of shading, there remains considerable evidence of shading and modelling on the images. Differences, particularly in the extent of shadows and shading, have been observed between the photographic images taken prior to the restoration and those taken after it. It has been suggested by Brandt (1987) that photographic evidence is often a poor guide to the visual improvements in the frescoes since the pre-cleaning photographic images minimized the effect of the dirt layer because of the penetrating depth of the photographic lights and some of the post-treatment images appear flat and thin since

Figure 7.3 Partially cleaned image from the ceiling of the Sistine Chapel (photograph courtesy of the Vatican Museum).

the rougher surface of the fresco now deflects a large amount of the strong photographic light. Statements by writers, art historians and others from the Renaissance to the present day regarding Michelangelo's use of shading, modelling and colour are entirely subjective and unreliable in determining the truth of this matter. The cleaned images appear, with their heightened colouring, similar to other Renaissance frescoes, and Michelangelo's use of pigment and technique is consistent with the Tuscan tradition of fresco artists.

The later cleaning of *The Last Judgement* fresco has been achieved using a slightly different conservation regime. Michelangelo completed substantial areas of this fresco *a secco* as the pigments used included Naples yellow and lake pigments which must be retained in a binding medium and not applied directly to the alkaline plaster which degrades the colour. The cleaning regime used on *The Last Judgement* was initial washing with distilled water then treatment with ammonium carbonate solution and nitro thinner. A second application 24 hours later used the same solution applied through Japanese paper and then washed off with distilled water. For *The Last Judgement* and the ceiling frescoes weak and powdering areas have been consolidated with Paraloid B72 or Primal (an acrylic colloidal dispersion). The few damaged or missing areas on the fresco have been gap filled with lime and marble dust and then coloured using watercolours in a cross-hatching technique to give the visual continuity of the image, whilst allowing all such restored areas to be readily identified upon close inspection.

In addition to the interventive cleaning work, preventive conservation work has also been undertaken. Following the study of the chapel's microclimate, a new cold-lighting system, with shades to reduce updrafts has been introduced, an anti-dust carpet was laid on the steps to the chapel in order to reduce dust levels, the windows were sealed to prevent the polluted Roman air entering the building and air conditioning was installed to help maintain stable temperature and humidity despite the large numbers of visitors to the chapel.

The glue layer which contained the history of the cleaning and restorations has now been removed. The lack of precise dating techniques for this type of material limits the certainty over the date of application, but it appears likely that a substantial application of glue to stabilize the plaster, obscure the salts which were forming and increase the depth of colour of the frescos was applied at a date well after the frescos had been completed. There were a number of different applications producing a complex indivisible sequence. Any traces of black outlines and shadows present within this glue layer are seen as the work of later restorers either enhancing the outlines of Michelangelo's figures which were becoming indistinct as a result of the accumulating glue and dirt layers or creating additional modelling and shading *chiaroscuro*. The dates and creators of these effects are unknown and must, at best, be deduced from comparison of stratigraphy or comparison of minute details. This level of detail can only be done by the conservators working on the image who have a duty to inform their colleagues and ultimately the public of their findings.

In Italy decisions regarding the release of information are, like all major decisions on conservation projects, made by the art historians, scientists and owners/curators of the object, who are in overall charge of the project (Cather, personal communication). It is this hierarchical structure of wallpainting conservation projects in Italy and the natural reserve of the Vatican which has led to only slow and limited response to the criticisms by Beck and others over the cleaning of the Sistine Chapel frescoes. The media thrive on controversy (e.g. Lister 1991) and thus opinions about the cleaning, voiced principally by art historians, have overshadowed the truth of this conservation project. Conservators need to be aware of the responsibility to bring public opinion with them, especially when cleaning well-known works of art, where the visual appearance of the work will be greatly changed by the cleaning and conservation process.

8   Stabilization

8.1 The nature of stabilization

Stabilization is the act of preservation by causing the cessation (or slowing to a minimal rate) of the decay processes. This requires the identification of the cause of decay and its mitigation, which can be achieved through preventive or interventive conservation. Any stabilization treatment normally seeks to retain the object's present visual form. Decay and stabilization processes occur in three categories: biological, chemical and physical.

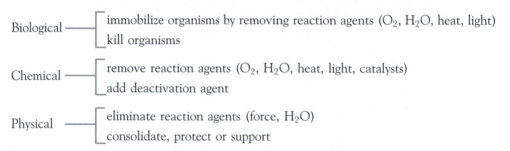

Biological ——— immobilize organisms by removing reaction agents (O_2, H_2O, heat, light)
kill organisms

Chemical ——— remove reaction agents (O_2, H_2O, heat, light, catalysts)
add deactivation agent

Physical ——— eliminate reaction agents (force, H_2O)
consolidate, protect or support

In many cases the decay of an object is composed of several different decay processes linked together. Thus the decay of waterlogged wood occurs through chemical decay, hydrolysis of cellulose, and consumption of cellulose by micro-organisms (fungi or bacteria depending on the environment) leading to a weakened structure which is then supported by water. The loss of the water (drying) causes physical damage in the form of cell collapse and shrinkage of the cell walls (Cronyn 1990).

Stabilization of biological decay processes can be achieved through the denial of reaction agents essential for sustaining biological organisms. This includes such processes as placing an insect-infested object in a freezer to deny the insects heat, so killing them (Blyth and Hillyer 1993), or an oxygen-free environment such as fumigating with nitrogen (Gilberg 1991) or killing mould or fungal growth by drying out a damp-infested object. These denial mechanisms are preferred in modern-day conservation work to the addition of toxic agents which kill micro-organisms, such as fumigants like methyl bromide, insecticides such as paradichlorobenzene, or biocides such as 'Panacide' (dichlorophen), on the grounds of improving health and safety and with the aim of using minimum intervention to stabilize an object.

Chemical decay such as the corrosion of metals can be stifled by removing one or more of the agents of decay (e.g. removing water from the corrosion reaction with de-watering agents). The problem of maintaining that state, so corrosion is not restarted, can be difficult to achieve with such a ubiquitous substance as water. The storage of archaeological metalwork with a desiccating agent, such as silica gel, continues to deny water to the corrosion reaction. Paintings, textiles, paper and other organic materials are stored in the dark to avoid the damaging effect of light (see Figure 8.1). Early twentieth-century plastics and important documents, such as the American 'Declaration of Independence', which are subject to degradation through oxidation are stored in oxygen-free environments (Shashoua and Thomsen 1993). Almost all chemical reactions can be stifled by removing heat, no chemical reactions proceed at absolute zero, though this temperature is expensive and

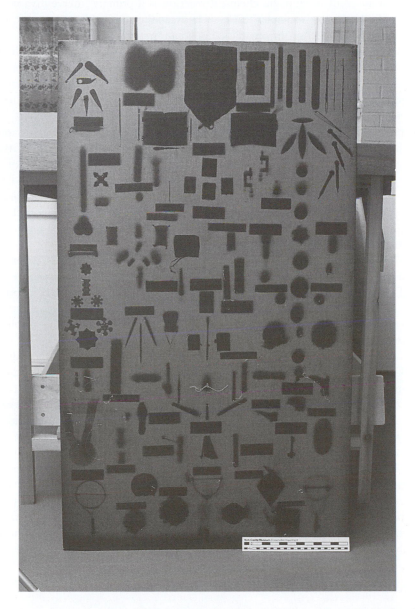

Figure 8.1 Light-damaged museum textile which covered a museum display board at the York Castle Museum for over 30 years (photograph by the author).

difficult to maintain. As all chemical reactions virtually halve their rate of reaction with every drop of 10°C simply lowering the temperature will considerably slow reactions. Where chemical decay is the primary decay mechanism, as with photographs, negatives and film, storage at temperatures of +5 to −10°C aids preservation. Corrosion promoters such as chloride ions have proved difficult to remove from metal-corrosion crusts (Watkinson 1996a), though their reduction can increase the stability of the object. In many instances objects are given coatings to reduce or slow down the ingress of the agents of chemical or biological decay.

The addition of an agent to stop the chemical reaction is a primary interventive conservation approach. Numerous examples exist such as adding antioxidants to soak up radicals and prevent their reaction in organic-consolidant systems (Bilz *et al.* 1993), the addition of alkaline-buffering agents through mass gaseous or individual aqueous washing processes to stop the acidic hydrolysis of the cellulose in paper (Smith 1987), the addition of benzotriazole to stifle the copper-corrosion process (Brostoff 1995), or the use of ammonia gas to react with sulphuric acid so stifling the pyrite disease of geological specimens of iron sulphide (Howie 1978).

In physical processes the elimination of reaction agents, such as water denied to a damp building, can halt soluble-salt damage to stone, or background heating can prevent the freezing and ice-formation decay of some building stones. Similarly the creation of a suitable box or storage container with an appropriate physical support cut to accommodate the exact shape of the object can prevent gravitational forces from slowly pulling a fragile object to pieces. Physical support can include lining for oil paintings, sewing on support cloth for fragile textiles, mounting fragile paper prints on to a new paper backing or replacing dowels and parts of joints in antique furniture.

To prevent the physical disintegration of fragile objects, or their decay products, different types of consolidant have proved to be highly effective. Consolidants invariably penetrate an object in liquid (or gaseous) form and convert to solid form to provide cohesion and support. All consolidants whether solidifying by cooling (wax or solder), solvent evaporation (polymer solvent or aqueous systems) are difficult to reverse; those solidifying through chemical reaction (epoxy resins or silanes) are impossible to reverse.

Stabilization can sometimes alter the visual form of an object (e.g. darkening of a surface when consolidated). There is a balance to be struck between gaining a physically stable robust object and the change in visual appearance. Where the greater need is to preserve the object because of its importance as an historic document or the subtlety of its colouring, then consolidation may be not be appropriate, though the object remains at greater risk of physical damage. Where the greater need is to preserve the whole form of the object for information or aesthetic purposes then it may be appropriate to consolidate.

It can often be helpful to combine a number of different approaches to stabilization; for example, treating a copper-alloy object with benzotriazole to chemically deactivate the corrosion process, coating and consolidation of the patina with 'Incralac' (an acrylic copolymer) which reduces the rate of ingress of water and oxygen and storing with a silica-gel desiccant to reduce water-vapour levels. This may ensure the object's continued stability though it does not represent a minimum intervention approach.

8.2 The nature of stability

Decay and corrosion is the natural order of things as the entropy of the universe increases. Remains of the past have survived to the present through two mechanisms:

Unconscious Preservation: an artefact (object, image, building) is left out of sight and out of mind, in a place where no one will disturb it. The level of decay continues unmonitored, but often quite slowly. Undisturbed an object will often reach an equilibrium with its surroundings which results in a minimal decay rate. The nature of the object and the nature of its burial environment are the crucial factors in determining the decay rate. Such conditions lead to the preservation of objects in their historic context (i.e. *in situ*, see Section 11.6).

Conscious Preservation: an artefact (object, image, building) of the past is deliberately preserved. Money, time and energy is poured into shielding the artefact from potential threats: human beings, insects, wind, oxygen and water. To prevent dispersal, decay and destruction, preservation is required and this requires the input of energy and effort. The reasons for putting in this costly energy and effort were outlined in Chapter 2, and such efforts are only normally made to protect the most 'important' parts of the past.

Stable is not an absolute state. An object is stable with respect to a given time-frame and within a specified environment. At absolute zero all things are stable and no decay processes, chemical or biological, can occur. In a good storage environment (e.g. dark, oxygenless, airtight conditions), most objects are relatively stable and most materials only decay very slowly. The more aggressive the conditions the less stable any object will be and thus any stabilization treatment must be more extreme. Conservators usually assess an object's stability as its ability not to decay in normal museum storage and display conditions: 45–65 per cent relative humidity (RH), 20–25°C, at atmospheric pressure and normal oxygen and lighting levels (MGC 1992, 1993a, 1993b, 1994, 1995a, 1996, 1998a).

Thus to preserve an object in a stable condition the conservator can choose either to make the object more stable or improve the storage (or display) conditions or both. The approach of preventive conservation is to improve the storage conditions so minimizing the extent to which interventive stabilization is required. If an object is to be stored in the open air, it will be susceptible to extreme chemical, physical and biological attack; the conservator stabilizes objects for their envisaged environment. In such cases the stabilization treatment would be extreme. Any metal object or metal parts of an object stored in the open will need a protective layer (e.g. paint), and since almost all applied coatings break down after a few years a maintenance programme (e.g. regular repainting) will be required. In some cases, such as The Statue of Liberty (see Case study 3A), a natural partially protective patina of corrosion is maintained. Open-display objects are frequently touched by the public, consequently all small, loose, detachable elements of the object are removed or fastened down to ensure that they are not lost or do not harm the inquisitive visitor. Better that this work is done carefully with full recording and consideration for the loss of historic evidence by a conservator than without such care by an untrained member of staff.

The stability of an object will not only vary depending on the environment but will change over time within a given environment. Thus in the case of an object buried undisturbed in the soil, the rate of decay will initially be quite fast, although it usually slows with time as it comes to equilibrium with its environment (Dowman 1970). If the object is disturbed (e.g. through excavation), the rate of decay will suddenly increase until it eventually slows as it

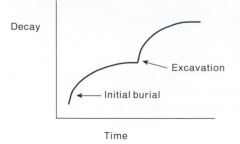

Figure 8.2 Decay rate for an object buried, excavated and stored (from Dowman 1970).

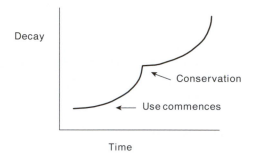

Figure 8.3 Decay rate for an object in continual use (e.g. working machinery).

comes to equilibrium with its new storage environment (see Figure 8.2). If, however, the object is in an environment when it is in constant use, it will initially be stable but as time passes and the object degrades, the rate of degradation will increase as small-scale damage is enlarged until there is either a catastrophic failure, or the object is conserved and the rates of decay are back to low levels to again climb slowly with time (see Figure 8.3). Similar decay curves have been suggested for the decay of buildings by Brand (1994: 112), who showed limited decay and limited costs were achieved with regular maintenance, occasional maintenance led to higher decay rates and higher costs, whilst no maintenance led to extremely high decay rates and the high costs of total refurbishment. This is because buildings are not initially stable structures and are under constant attack from the weather, which is an aggressive continual-use environment. Eventually buildings become ruins slowly reaching equilibrium with the environment.

8.3 Stability of materials

As described in Section 5.3, there is an ethical requirement that the materials which conservators use are stable, so that they do not alter over time and affect the object on which they have been used.

   The concept of stability of materials has changed over time. Initially conservation used a wide variety of polymers as adhesives, coatings and consolidants, since these were commercially available. Concepts of chemical stability such as long-term polymer degradation and cross-linking had not been fully appreciated. As problems became apparent with materials such as soluble nylon (Bockhoff et al. 1984) and PVC, there was a realization that the requirements of modern industry and conservation were very different. The industry concept of stable refers to a working life of a few years, and not the decades which conservation envisages.

In 1978 Robert Feller (Feller 1978) defined a number of common conservation polymers by a system of stability to light degradation based on the ISO R105 and BS 1006:1971 'Blue Wool' standards. He used a simplified classification system to define their stability:

Class A: Excellent stability with a stable working life of >100 years (e.g. Paraloid B72) (A1 > 500 years, A2 > 100 years).

Class B: Intermediate stability with a stable working life of 20–100 years (e.g. Elvacite 2044).

Class C: Unstable or fugitive with a stable working life <20 years.

Class T: Materials which should only be in temporary contact with an object having a stable working life <6 months.

There has, however, been limited testing and classification of products because:

- There is no well-funded central agency to undertake the testing.

- The range of parameters for which stability could be tested is enormous.

- Many commercial products contain additives such as detergents and plasticisers (Down 1995) which make potentially stable products unstable.

- The commercial nature of many products means that manufacturers may vary the exact formulation of the product (Down 1995).

- There are problems with the traditionally used method of testing for shorter times at higher temperatures. Both Bilz and Grattan (1996) and Down (1995) have found problems using the Arrhenius equation to extrapolate back to normal storage and display temperatures.

The increased appreciation of the need for the use of stable materials for conservation and archival work has seen the rejection of many materials as unstable and the emergence of 'improved' materials designed for conservation and archival use. The correlation of lignin and acidity with accelerated decay in paper has led to the use of paper free from acidity and lignin for many archival and storage functions. The use of unbleached washed cotton and linen cloth has become accepted, as the deleterious effects of bleaching agents have become recognized. The use of detergents in emulsions (e.g. PVAc emulsions) has been linked to degradation or yellowing of the polymer (Horie 1987) and led to increased use of cellulose-based adhesives. Another approach to creating 'safe' materials for conservation and archival use has been the addition of chemical compounds which specifically inhibit decay. Plenderleith and Werner had the 1971 edition of their book *Conservation of Antiquities and Works of Art* printed on a loaded paper, one containing $CaCO_3$ which would neutralize any acidity which was created in the paper as it aged and thus provide a more long-lived stable material. Manufacturers have added UV absorbers to coating materials, such as 'Incralac', in order to increase their stability, and Grattan has urged the use of anti-oxidants in PEG (polyethylene glycol) in order to combat oxidative degradation of the PEG molecules (Bilz *et al.* 1993: 196). The use of antioxidants and radical absorbers is likely to become commonplace in many conservation polymers over the next few decades. Awareness of the most likely degradation route permits judicious use of additives to increase the lifespan of the material. For example, Horie added $CaCO_3$ to the PVB adhesive, used in the conservation of St Cuthbert's Coffin, since the most likely breakdown route for this polymer in this situation is acid hydrolysis (Cronyn and Horie 1985).

The breakdown of a material is not a single event, but a gradual one. There are numerous different breakdown stages in a polymer.

- The onset of ageing. An epoxy resin may yellow with age, though it may still adhere strongly, thus the critical factor may not be the onset of ageing.

- The critical point when the polymer or other material fails to perform the function for which it was intended. Whilst it may no longer support or shelter the object, it may not actually harm or damage it. Thus a protective coating may fail, which though it may not help the object survive, does not of necessity directly harm the object.

- The point at which the breakdown products actually react with the object to degrade or accelerate degradation.

Hanssen-Bauer (1996) has emphasized the need to be more aware of these stages. Some materials may be better as conservation materials since their failure does not harm the object, whilst other materials, initially resistant to breakdown, do have damaging breakdown products, such as the hydrochloric acid gas given off by degrading PVC. Thus a profile of the breakdown of every material is ideally needed in order to assess their use in conservation. Since the way in which a conservation material is used can affect its stability, there are numerous different breakdown routes to be considered.

This problem of product stability is most clearly manifest in the use of commercial products by those involved in redisplaying, building and decorating exhibition cases and galleries. A series of simple tests, 'The Oddy Test', was developed by Andrew Oddy (Oddy 1973, 1975) which have been subsequently developed, refined and expanded (Blackshaw and Daniels 1979; Green 1991; Green and Thickett 1993; Lee and Thickett 1996), to test the effect of gases given off during the breakdown of paints, fabrics, woods, boards, sealants, varnishes, mounting and display materials. Additional tests, such as the Azide, Beilstein, Iodide–Iodate, Chromotropic, Surface and Aqueous Extract pH (BS 2924 : 1983) tests, can be added to the basic Oddy Test to provide a more comprehensive series of tests for material stability (Lee and Thickett 1996). Though many products have been tested the frequent reformulation of products by commercial companies demands constant retesting. Such testing is an integral part of the working lives of many conservators and every conservator has the responsibility to ensure that materials in use for conservation, as well as for the display and storage of objects, are stable and will not alter over time to the detriment of the object (Ganiaris and Sully 1998).

8.4 Recording versus stabilization

There are a number of circumstances where it is difficult to effect stabilization:

- Where you cannot control the environment; for example, buildings or monuments which are exposed to the weather or objects which are too large to enclose and which are consequently on 'open display' either inside or outside the museum building.

- There is insufficient money to fund stabilization. This is especially true for large objects, buildings, machines or even landscapes.

- Where the object is inherently unstable. This is particularly true for polymer materials of the twentieth century.

In such circumstances, whilst one may attempt to minimize the rate of decay through issuing guidelines on the use of the object or providing some form of shelter or a regular cleaning regime, it is often not possible to preserve the object. It is then most appropriate to make a copy or replica of the object.

Numerous possible methods for replication exist (Larsen 1981, 1984). Two general approaches can be taken:

- Making a copy of the object, for replacement of the original on display, as in the case of the Durham Cathedral Knocker (Geddes 1982).

- Making a copy of the object, for retention in storage for reference and research purposes whilst the original object continues to be slowly eroded away as in the case of the Pillar of Eliseg (Watkinson 1982).

Most copying is through a 2-D visual recording, such as a drawing or photograph, and is seen as part of the recording process; though in instances where the object is discovered to be inherently unstable, or too large or technically difficult to stabilize, recording is as far as the conservation process goes.

Many recordings of transient events, or objects, much of our recent past as well as many modern creative processes are carried out on film, photography, video and sound recording, using materials which are not chemically stable (Westheimer 1994). The best mechanism for preserving photographic emulsions, film negatives, computer, video and sound recording tapes, is storage at reduced temperatures which slows all the chemical degradation reactions (MGC 1996). Sub- or near zero storage, which is that normally used, prohibits the instant use of the object as it will take some time to be slowly warmed, without detriment, from storage temperature back up to room temperature. For example, The Royal Commission for Historic Monuments of England maintains the National Monument Record store in Swindon at 9°C and constant RH, with a 24-hour acclimatization required before stored records can be used (Corfield, personal communication). It is both costly to maintain such cold-room facilities and to keep retrieving and replacing material into the cold store. There is also a delay in obtaining material. Therefore, copies of the information contained on these media are usually created prior to storage, so that the information is instantly available for use (Wilson 1999). This raises the question of why preserve such objects? Is the original carrier material of interest or is it the images and information contained which are of interest? Invariably it is the latter so a substantial amount of this material can simply be copied and discarded when it degrades. Large numbers of early cinema films, which were on unstable cellulose-nitrate film stock, have been copied onto modern safety film and the combustible cellulose-nitrate film discarded. As storage is a costly business such schemes often depend on the ability to realize money through selling the images. In such circumstances the costs of storage, the value of original images and the costs of copying and conveying the image determine how many objects are preserved.

It is inaccurate to say that an object is preserved through recording since creating a record is not an act of preservation but a form of replication, though it may realistically be the best that can be done. In such instances recording is an alternative to stabilization and the conservator and owner/curator or archaeologist must judge when it is more appropriate and cost effective to record rather than attempt to preserve. Many things are known not through direct experience but through visual or written record (e.g. events such as the Battle of Hastings exist primarily through the record of the Bayeux Tapestry). It is likely that much of the unstable ephemera of the twentieth century will be known through record rather than actual objects.

8.5 Health and safety

More than any other area of conservation, stabilization with its use of biological toxins, chemical deactivation agents and physical consolidants dissolved in organic solvents has involved the use of potentially hazardous chemicals. In using these substances the conservator should consider both the risks of damage to the object and the risks to the health and safety of the conservator (Howie 1987). People are more cautious now than in the past about chemical treatments. There remains a constant requirement to judge the effectiveness of a treatment against financial cost and potential health hazard of using the treatment chemical.

In the past, the effects of insect damage were considerable. They could, and did, eat their way through substantial numbers of beautiful and important objects. Natural-history specimens, such as stuffed animals, were particularly prone to attack. The need to protect such artefacts became paramount and a variety of methods were used. In the nineteenth and early twentieth century infected specimens were dusted with insecticides such as arsenic. In later years chlorinated hydrocarbons such as DDT and 'Lindane' were preferred, whilst more recently permethrins and pyrethroids have come into use. These chemicals have decreasing levels of mammalian toxicity whilst maintaining their potency against insects. However, the long-term damage to biological systems of all these chemicals has now become apparent and their use has almost ceased. At the time of their use, a judgement was made to use them; the choice appeared to be either treat with a toxic chemical or lose the object. Nowadays considerably more information on the harmful effects of toxic chemicals is available, consequently a great deal more effort is made to monitor pest levels (Child and Pinniger 1994) and, through good 'housekeeping', the use of quarantine facilities and control of the environment, reduced the risk of insect infestation to minimal levels. Where infestations do occur they are usually small scale, localized and can be dealt with by freezing or heating individual items (Child and Pinniger 1987). More widespread outbreaks require the use of anoxia fumigation. This is a high-cost solution, taking more time and effort than using toxic powders; however, the chances of infestation should be theoretically receding as museums become more active places with good housekeeping throughout the building.

It is important to develop a balanced view about chemicals and avoid either an irrational fear about chemicals or become overly confident and cavalier in their use. The perception of the risk to health of using such chemicals has increased, though the risk, as a result of greater awareness and use of safety equipment, has reduced. This is emphasized by the UK's COSHH (Control of Substances Hazardous to Health) legislation, where it is not just the toxic (mutagenic, carcinogenic) or other hazardous properties of the substance which are considered, but the volume of material being used, the form in which it is presented and the nature of the exposure, which constitutes the risk (Health and Safety Executive 1993). The biggest risk is ignorance. The move away from the use of chemicals has resulted in a loss of knowledge, and thus although the procedures for dealing with the material are potentially better the base level of knowledge is not.

8A Case study: Lindow Man (Stead *et al*. 1986; Turner and Scaife 1995; Omar *et al*. 1989)

Lindow Moss is a peat deposit of 30 hectares located near Wilmslow in Cheshire. On 1 August 1984 two men working on the peat-processing machinery discovered a severed human foot. This occurred barely a year after a woman's head (Lindow I) had been found and, despite confusion with a modern police investigation, was radiocarbon dated to the Roman period. Investigation, by the Cheshire county archaeologist Rick Turner, of the vicinity from which the peat had been cut, several months earlier, indicated that further human remains still lay buried. The remains of a body were located and partially uncovered through archaeological excavation. They were removed intact on a block of peat which was crated up and sent to Macclesfield District Hospital. Following the removal of samples for radiocarbon dating and further careful excavation and packing the peat block was placed in a smaller, more secure box which was placed in the hospital mortuary cold store.

Following confirmation from the radiocarbon dates that this body probably came from the Roman period, it was removed to the British Museum for excavation and investigation. The body was retained in its box, stored in a larger container and kept at 4°C in order to prevent microbial growth. The body was X-rayed to aid the excavation, which commenced gently removing the peat from the body using water jets, brushes, plastic and wood tools to ensure that no sharp hard implements could damage the fragile skin. It was regularly sprayed with distilled water to keep it damp and the temperature monitored. Every time the body temperature rose to 10–12°C excavation was stopped and the body cooled. To minimize the temperature the number of people around the area of the excavation was kept to a minimum and the filming of the process for television was undertaken using 'cold lights'. The body, which had originally been found in a slumped head-down position, had been packed with peat and turned on its back during the lifting and boxing process. Consequently the front was now visible and was fully exposed and cleaned (see Figure 8.4). An exact mould was made of the front using cling film followed by a layer of water-activated fibreglass tape (which set hard) and layers of fibreglass and resin. This enabled the body to be turned and the back cleaned. Subsequently a mould of the back was made again using the fibreglass and, with the two pieces of rigid mould bolted together, Lindow Man could be moved safely for further investigation. Computer Aided Tomography, X-radiography and Nuclear Magnetic Resonance Imaging were used to gain images of the internal features of the body. The body also underwent endoscopic examination and samples were removed from the body for a variety of different forms of analysis.

Figure 8.4 Lindow Man, recovered from Lindow Moss, Cheshire (photograph courtesy of the British Museum).

The excavation and analysis revealed:

- As a result of the damage from peat cutting, only the upper half of the body was present together with the left foot. There was considerable damage to the hands and lower arms.

- The body was naked apart from a small band of fox fur on the upper arm.

- The body was that of a man around 25 years old, 5′ 6″ tall, strong and well built. His beard and moustache had been carefully trimmed with shears (stepped pattern on the cuts) and the smooth ends of his fingernails suggested he did not do manual labour. This would suggest that he was a member of a religious or secular elite.

- The stomach contents indicated a last meal of unleavened bread (e.g. a griddle cake containing heather-charcoal fragments from the cooking). He drank water with traces of 'sphagnum' suggesting that his last meal was prepared and eaten near a bog or moss such as the one in which he was sacrificed. The presence of small amounts of mistletoe pollen, the sacred plant of the Druid cult, may suggest some religious rite associated with the last meal.

- He had several wounds :
  - Two blows from a blunt axe on the crown of the head, probably administered when the victim was in the kneeling position. These would have rendered him unconscious.
  - A blow from a blunt instrument to the occipital region of the skull.
  - A broken rib consistent with a blow to the chest.

- A sharp deep cut to the throat which severed the jugular vein.
- A short two-strand ligature was found around his neck. The ligature, made of animal sinew, was knotted at both ends and had an overhand knot securing the ligature tightly around the victim's neck. Though the ends of the ligature were quite short and thus would have been difficult to use to strangle the victim, it could have acted as a garrotte where the ligature is tightened with a stick. This pressure both constricts the windpipe and can break the neck. Damage to the third and fourth cervical vertebrae were consistent with this form of execution.
- From this evidence it appears likely the victim was killed with blows to the head intended to render him unconscious, garrotted breaking his neck, probably breaking a rib in the effort, and then had his jugular vein cut to induce a spurt or stream of blood.

- From the excavation it is clear that after being killed Lindow Man was dumped into the pool of boggy water in the middle of Lindow Moss.

- Radiocarbon dating of parts of the body by different laboratories gave dates of first century AD or fourth to fifth century AD. The cult of killing and depositing bodies in bogs appears to have been most prevalent in North-West Europe circa 800 BC to 200 AD. The fact that a number of bodies have similar strangulation and stab wounds suggests that many were ritually killed.

The body was preserved through being quickly adsorbed into the anoxic (oxygenless) waterlogged deposits of the bog. It is probable that chemicals such as sphagnan (5-keto-D-mannuronic acid) present in the sphagnum moss of the bog will have a variety of preservative, antiseptic, collagen-stabilizing actions (Painter 1995).

Where bog bodies or any waterlogged skin or leather is allowed to dry out naturally, it goes hard, shrinks, cracks, loses all strength and often falls apart. Consequently it is necessary to conserve (stabilize) such bodies if they are to be retained for future research and display. No bog bodies have been conserved in recent decades, though bog bodies recovered earlier in the century have received a variety of treatments:

- Graubaelle Man (Denmark) discovered in 1952 (Glob 1969) was conserved by tanning through immersion in a slurry of oak bark which was refreshed three times during the 18-month immersion. This was followed by immersion in Turkey red oil and gradual drying and impregnation with a mixture of glycerol, lanolin and cod-liver oil. Some areas were additionally consolidated using cellulose nitrate dissolved in ethanol and diethyl ether.

- Tollund Man (Denmark) discovered in 1950 (Glob 1969) was soaked in a solution of formaldehyde and acetic acid for 6 months, then in a solution of 30 per cent ethanol followed by 99 per cent pure ethanol with toluene, pure toluene and then toluene containing increasingly high concentrations of wax.

To conserve Lindow Man experimentation was undertaken using freeze drying, a modern conservation technique frequently used for preserving waterlogged archaeological leather and wood, which was practised on pieces of pigskin which had been packed in peat for several months. The best results were obtained by pretreating the pigskin in a solution of polyethylene glycol (molecular weight 400) (PEG 400) and then freeze dried. Accordingly, Lindow Man was attached to a Perspex support, immersed in 15 per cent PEG 400 for 10 weeks then frozen to $-28°C$ and freeze dried. After slowly acclimatizing to room temperature and humidities it was clear that Lindow Man had been successfully conserved with only slight shrinkage of 5 per cent and a slight lightening and stiffening of the skin, though it still remained flexible. The body was otherwise quite stable with no hardening, cracking or odour. To increase the long-term stability of Lindow Man's remains, they were placed in a sealed case which helps ensure stable humidity and are displayed at reduced light levels. Since going on exhibition Lindow man has remained one of the British Museum's most popular exhibits.

In 1987 seventy pieces of another male body (Lindow III), again dating to the Roman period, were uncovered from Lindow Moss. In 1988 the buttocks and left leg of a male body were also recovered, very close to the site where Lindow Man was recovered and they are believed to be the missing parts of Lindow Man. It is now clear that at least three individuals were ritually killed and deposited in Lindow Moss in the Roman period. This appears to be part of a long-lived cult of human sacrifice in watery places, of which only those deposited in the preservative environment of bogs have survived.

The lack of oxygen (anoxia), reducing conditions (Caple *et al.* 1997) and chemicals such as sphagnan (Painter 1995) which develop in the waterlogged conditions of a peat bog all contributed to the preservation of this body. The conservation process had an emphasis on investigation of the body since, as a rare historic document, it provided us with a glimpse into the beliefs, rituals, lifestyles and even diet of the past. Information on personal grooming, hygiene, diseases, diet and methods of execution can only be gained from studying human remains. The preservation of the remains is achieved through a stabilization process replacing and removing the water from the degraded flesh without inducing cellular collapse and shrinkage. Though there are always concerns when dealing with human remains, which are always treated with respect, the need for information, which only human bodies can provide, means that it remains important for modern conservation to investigate and preserve a few appropriate ancient bodies. Judgement is exercised in the bodies chosen; factors such as the period from which they derive, the nature of their death and deposition, their association with living people and their importance as historic documents are considered (see Section 13.4).

9 Restoration

9.1 Restoration as a philosophy

Since human beings recognize objects, designs or parts of objects by comparison with existing images from memories (see Chapter 1), it is the elements of difference between the viewed object and the remembered object which are automatically highlighted in the mind. This accounts for Brandi's observation that it is the unexpected, such as damage, breaks, and losses in any object, which always stand out. The loss of part of the image of a wallpainting or oil painting immediately draws the eye and the image cannot be viewed without first seeing the loss (Vaccaro 1996a). It is the urge to remove this visual impediment to see the whole image that leads to the aspiration to restore the object to its whole, true, original appearance.

Restoration can be seen to comprise:

Reassembly of the broken pieces of an object. In all cases as much of the original object as possible is stabilized, reassembled and incorporated into the restoration.

Reintegration, filling in the loss and in-painting the missing area seeking to create the illusion of the original complete image and reintegrate the area of loss into the visual image of the whole (see Figure 9.1). This can be achieved on a number of levels:

- Functional: Where the area is restored in order to make the object stable. This may mean the replacement of a working part of a machine (e.g. a new cog), or the use of a gap fill in a ceramic to ensure that the reassembled vessel will not readily break apart, or infilling tessera in a mosaic so that other tessera on the broken edge are not levered up and the damage increased.

- Background: Where the filled area is given a colour and texture to blend with the base or background colour and texture of the object. This makes it less visible, but does not suggest any decorative scheme, often because information on the exact nature of the original decorative scheme is not available. This is usually a cost-effective option for restoring the loss, without spending much time or money on the reintegration.

- Similar: The filled area is pigmented to give a crude approximation to what was originally present, though no detail is included and exact colouration is deliberately not achieved.

Figure 9.1 The Sundial from Nendrum, Northern Ireland (photograph by the author). The parts of the sundial were recovered from the excavation of this Dark Age monastic site and restored using cement mortar. This restoration allowed the object to be returned to the site, where it continues to function as a sundial, a working object. Aspects such as the height and location of the original pieces of stone within the restored sundial are conjectural.

- Exact: The filled area is restored to its original appearance with all elements of the design included and correctly coloured. As for all restoration, 'exact' reintegration must still be detectable upon close examination in order to avoid faking and deception. To undertake this level of reintegration there must be clear detailed information about the design and pigmentation originally present in the area of loss.

The level of integration used will depend on the object, the restorer, the information available, the time available, materials and expertise available and what is appropriate for each individual loss. Different levels of integration may be appropriate on the same object.

Restoration must aim to re-establish the potential unity of the work of art, as long as this is possible without producing an artistic or historical forgery and without erasing every trace of the passage of time left on the work of art.

(Brandi 1996)

Reshaping an object can be seen as a form of exact re-integration; for example, the metal bent back to its original form which is difficult to distinguish from undistorted metal.

At the 1994 British Museum Conference 'Restoration: Is it Acceptable?', a clear majority of the speakers articulated this present-day Westernized view, defining conservation as the means by which the object was preserved and restoration in terms of recreating the visual or physical form of the object to a former or original state. Conservation and restoration were depicted as opposite ends of a continuum with most actions, such as cleaning, lying between both extremes and containing some elements of both. Oddy (1994) suggested that restoration could involve:

- Joining existing fragments.

- Filling in missing areas (lacunae).

- Reshaping.

- Visual integration (e.g. in-painting areas such as fills).

Such actions are seen as important to restore the visual form of the object and accurately convey its purpose or meaning to the viewing public. Such actions form part of the museum's mission to 'interpret' the past (Child 1994) and 'explain how things work' (Mann 1994). In all instances, the original object forms the basis of the restoration and should not be harmed by the restoration work. The restored work should be detectable, upon careful examination, so that the truth of the past is clear to future generations.

In some more ancient traditional 'native' and 'Eastern' cultures the original material of the object is not considered essential, it is what the object symbolizes and what it embodies which is important, as in the case of the 'intangible cultural properties' of Japanese cultural heritage (Yagihashi 1988). In such a culture the act of restoring or copying an old object is seen as preserving it (Kitamura 1988). It is a 'modern Western' approach to distinguish between 'preservation' and 'restoration' and to place value in the original physical material. Japanese temples are constructed primarily of wood and over the hundreds of years of their existence have traditionally be restored by replacing the original wood with new. For them the spirit, the purpose and the past associations of the place were important and not the physical material itself. This is true of many societies which have extensive traditions using organic materials; they have an acceptance of decay and renewal as an integral part of their culture. It is, perhaps, those societies which build in stone which often see decay as associated with loss and destruction. It can be suggested that the retention of the spirit and purpose of the place, using a regime of continual replacement to maintain the physical beauty, is crucial in preserving that which is important to us as human beings. Fixating on the degraded physical remains of a couple of original battered stumps of wood fails to recognize the crucial role of the human spirit, the 'genius' within our past.

It can be argued that to perceive the 'true nature' of an ancient artefact, it is necessary not only to have the original visual form, but to have the 'eyes' of the past to perceive it as the peoples of the past did. Simply revealing or restoring the original appearance gives us a hybrid experience, the twenty-first century looking at the ancient past. Thus a modern tourist will see Hadrian's Wall as a long garden wall; they do not see it as the Roman aristocracy did, 'the end of the civilized world' and 'a bulwark against barbarity'. Those societies which emphasize the spirit, the purpose and the past associations of a place, make considerable effort to preserve the context or setting in which it occurs as well as the philosophical basis for its construction. When the viewer enters the context, a complete temple rather than a ruin, they understand to a greater extent what they are seeing, and have an experience and enjoy feelings which are much closer to those experienced by the original user of the building. This is, perhaps, far more profound and makes a deeper impact on the viewer than simply observing the truthfully preserved surviving fragmentary original traces of the past. There are increasing efforts to create more substantial all-enveloping museums within modern Western cultures which both preserve original physical evidence and seek to develop a context in which the physical remains are meaningfully experienced. For example, Beamish Museum in North-East England where the recreated sights, sounds and smells of the past provide a context for understanding the late nineteenth and early twentieth-century remains of social, domestic, agricultural and industrial life of one of Europe's largest coalfields.

The experience of restoration in Western Europe and Britain in particular (see Section 9.3) has shown that enthusiastic 'over-restoration' in the eighteenth and nineteenth centuries has led to an awareness of the value of original physical form of the object or structure. This value is now enshrined in the ethical codes of conservators and the 'modern Western' approach to conservation which seeks to retain the original material at all costs, and sees restoration as impermanent.

9.2 Definition of terms

Numerous distinctive terms are used to describe the different types of restoration which are used in the various areas of conservation. Dictionary definitions are invariably too broad and self-referencing to provide any useful distinction between the terms. Therefore, the definitions offered below are derived from the reading and understanding of 11 years of conservation students at Durham University. In these definitions the term 'original state' refers to a significant earlier state:

Restoration – Returning an object or building to its original visual form or condition. It implies use of some material from the original and a resultant visual form which is very close to the original. 'All action taken to modify the existing materials and structure of cultural property to represent a known earlier state. The aim of restoration is to preserve and reveal the aesthetic and historical value of a cultural property. Restoration is based on respect for the remaining original material and clear evidence of the earlier state' (MGC 1994).

Reconstruction – Bringing to a form very similar to the whole original, where there is evidence or material from the original. Thus historical events are reconstructed from the existing documentary evidence; crime scenes are reconstructed from the remaining physical evidence. 'All actions taken to recreate, in whole or in part, a cultural property, based upon historical, literary, graphic, pictorial, archaeological and scientific evidence. Reconstruction is aimed at promoting an understanding of cultural property and is based on little or no original material but clear evidence of a former state' (MGC 1994).

Recreation – Similar to reconstruction, but implies starting with nothing of the original. It is undertaken using new materials and usually involves a certain amount of imagination.

Re-enactment – Similar to reconstruction, but is usually applied to historic events. It implies starting with nothing of the original, is undertaken using new materials and usually involves a certain amount of imagination. Usually relates to events such as historic battles which are re-enacted by modern-day enthusiasts.

Renovation – Bring back to working order usually using some parts of the original object. There is an implication of subsequent use of the building or object.

Rehabilitation – Used principally in North America in reference to buildings. 'The process of returning a property to a state of utility through repair or alteration, which makes possible an effective contemporary use, while preserving those portions and features of the property which are significant to its historic, architectural and cultural values' – US Park Service (Brand 1994).

Refurbishment – As rehabilitation but is used to refer to objects as well as buildings.

Replacement – Construction of a new part or whole object to perform the function of an original. Usually used in conjunction with the creation of a part in a new material to take the place of an old, damaged or worn part. The function is more important than the form, thus when one painting may replace another it is the fact that there is a painting in place which is important rather than the need for there to be any similarities in the visual depiction in the painting. Damaged parts of a machine are replaced in order to keep it running.

Repair – Make good and return to working order. Thus a watch has been repaired when it is working again.

Reused – Brought back into use, previously dormant and unused it again performs a function. As with reused timber it does not have to perform its original function, though it often does.

Revived – Brought back into use after a period of dormancy and neglect. It performs its original function and implies life, worth and vigour.

Renewed – Made functional or valid again.

Replication – Manufacture using new materials to exactly resemble an original visual form. Often a specific object is exactly copied.

Reproduction – Manufacture using new materials to resemble an original visual form. It usually implies a generic style from the past (e.g. reproduction furniture) rather than a specific copy of an object.

All these terms have a useful role in trying to accurately define work which is being done to an object, building or event from the past.

9.3 The development of restoration

Perhaps the earliest recorded example of restoration is by King Nabonidus of Babylon who, in the sixth century BC, appears to have excavated, recorded and then restored (or perhaps more accurately reconstructed) the original form of the temple of Ebabbor, which had been founded by King Hammurabi 1,200 years earlier (Berducou 1996). This exemplifies the value and prestige which is often associated with collecting and restoring things of the past (see Chapters 2 and 4).

The restoration work of the Renaissance has been described as 'repristination' (Giusti 1994) returning an object to its pristine 'as new' state. This clearly places the aesthetic beauty of the object above all other things. This work was undertaken by the artists of the period such as Cellini. Some of these artists readily amended the work of the sculptors and artists of antiquity, others would not. In the eighteenth century Canova refused to restore the figures by Phidias, which Lord Elgin had brought back from the Parthenon, claiming that it would be sacrilege to touch them (Podany 1994). There were, however, some extremely able pieces of restoration. Many of the classical marble statues of ancient Greece and Rome were restored by eighteenth-century carver/restorers – such as Albacini who probably worked on *The Lansdowne Herakles* circa 1790, squaring up much of the damaged original first/second century AD Roman statue (a copy of the fourth century BC Greek original) and cutting in additional pieces to match, especially limbs and a base which were adhered with metal dowels on to the original. If necessary the original statue was shaped to ensure a better fit of the new pieces, the aim was undoubtedly to create a statue 'in the classical style' as demanded by the English aristocracy. It was felt that the damage evident on classical statues was an act of barbarism and that restoration removed evidence of that barbarity (Yourcenar 1996).

The concept of aesthetic restoration continued into the nineteenth century and was the mainspring of the arguments of architects such as Eugene Emmanuel Viollet-le-Duc and his mid-nineteenth-century colleagues who sought to restore buildings 'in the style of'. This required them to strip away much poor quality later material and restore substantial amounts in the style of the original building. 'To restore an edifice means to re-establish in a fundamental state, which may in fact never have actually existed at any given time' (Viollet-le-Duc 1996). Such assertive restoration was based on detailed initial recording of the building, knowledge of building styles (including regional variants) and of the construction process itself. Viollet-le-Duc recognized that buildings did contain differing periods of construction and where important, substantial or aesthetic, was in favour of their retention. His approach epitomized the confidence of the Victorian age and the improved scholarship over previous generations. It is, however, questionable how many of Viollet-le-Duc's adherents possessed the levels of knowledge he espoused. It was Viollet-le-Duc's belief that a building's well-being stemmed from its continued use, which led to his determination to keep buildings functional and an enthusiasm for renewing or restoring roofs, windows and doors. Had his 'adaptive restoration for use' not occurred it is likely that many present-day churches and other buildings would be in ruins.

Opposing this view was William Morris and colleagues who, in 1877, founded the Society for the Protection of Ancient Buildings (SPAB) and described themselves as an anti-restoration movement.

Restoration of ancient buildings ... which by its very name implies that it is possible to strip from a building this, that, and the other part of its history – of its life that is – and then to stay the hand at some arbitrary point and leave it still historical, living and even as it once was.

(Morris 1996: 319–320)

But those who make changes ... under the name of restoration ... have no guide but each his own individual whim to point out to them what is admirable and what contemptible.

(ibid. 1996: 320)

The fashion of the period for Gothic architecture led to the removal of substantial amounts of fifteenth to eighteenth-century architectural features and the incorporation of many 'Gothic' features into restored buildings for which there was no evidence. The problem of deciding what to remove and what not led to questions of what was good, important or aesthetically pleasing of the past. Morris and John Ruskin recognized the importance of all of a building's history, anything 'artistic, picturesque, historical, antique or substantial' is considered worthy of salvation (Morris 1996). The past was not simply the buildings which survived, as Morris noted; the architecture of churches was part of the complete social, cultural experience which comprised the religion of the past. The loss of many of the social customs and religious practices meant that simply 'restoring' the architecture still did not provide the experience of the past, thus he questioned the whole purpose of restoring the building.

Though Morris and Ruskin were prepared 'to treat our ancient buildings as monuments' (Morris 1996), they also emphasized the need to continue to preserve the building 'bind it together with iron where it loosens', 'stay it with timber where it declines' (Ruskin 1996). In doing such preservation work they sought to make their interventive conservation measures obvious and of their period. Both Morris and Ruskin suggest that there was a constant need to 'stave off decay with daily care' (Morris 1996). 'Take proper care of your monuments and you will not need to restore them' (Ruskin 1996). This effectively stated the philosophy of preventive conservation in the mid-nineteenth century. In similar words to the UKIC 1996 Code of Ethics (UKIC 1996), there was a clear perception of preserving for the future generations – 'they belong partly to those who built them and partly to the generations of mankind who are to follow us' (Ruskin 1996). Modern conservation philosophy has clearly adopted elements of the philosophy from both camps, the realistic functionalism of Viollet-le-Duc and the preventive conservation, and respect for all aspects of a building's history, from SPAB.

The collecting of prints and drawings had begun in the sixteenth century with Archduke Ferdinand of Tyrol collecting an album of the works of Durer. The collections of later eighteenth-century collectors show early examples of simple repairs to torn pages and removal of stains (Kosek 1994). As early as 1846 Alfred Bonnardot had produced a book on the restoration of paper *Essai sur L'Art Restaurer les Estampes et les Livres, ou Traité sur les Meilleurs Procédés pour Blanchir, Détacher, Décolourier, Réparer, et Conserver les Estampes, Livres, et Dessins*, which clearly warns against the removal of historical evidence as part of the restoration process (Kosek 1994). It is clear that there was an appreciation of objects as important records of the past in their own right, prior to Morris and Ruskin. This sensitivity to the restoration process for works of art is also evinced by the Italian painter/restorer Secco-Suardo who, in 1866, was advocating the avoidance of excessive retouching, and using tempera or watercolour for retouching since they do not darken upon ageing (Bomford 1994). It appears, however, to have been the rise of the Society for the Protection of Ancient Buildings which generated a more widespread sympathetic approach to the value of original work and the value of objects such as buildings as historic documents. This issue is, however, partially obscured by what may be seen as a late nineteenth-century change in fashion, a preference for the old, aged and venerable rather than the bright, gaudy and new.

By the mid-nineteenth century, in addition to the idea of restoring art for aesthetic reasons, there was also a renewed fashion for 'restoration' of art for a moral purpose (see Section 2.3). This manifested itself in the addition of fig leaves and loin cloths to cover genitalia on both statues and paintings. This can be seen as an extension of aesthetic restoration, the imposition of the taste of the period. Some artists, such as Molteni, kept records of his activities, additions which can now accurately be removed with no lasting damage done to the original object. In other instances the moral sensitivities of the age have resulted in permanent and substantial changes to objects. This is evidenced by the Brussels tapestry of *Anthony and Cleopatra* owned by the Worshipful Company of Goldsmiths (Brooks *et al.* 1994), in which Cleopatra's leg, which was indecorously draped over the seated Anthony, was cut out and the gap woven in red to replicate part of Anthony's cloak. The differential fading of dyes has now resulted in Cleopatra possessing an amorously draped bright orange leg. Present-day conservators are uncomfortable about restoring the leg since they know nothing of the detail of eighteenth-century original and thus the distracting orange leg remains a highly visible reminder of nineteenth-century moral sensitivities.

By the 1920s the public had largely accepted the ideas of the historic importance of the paintings, notions of overpainting them for public decency were long gone, and for the more important paintings even in-painting of restored sections was becoming more measured (Bomford 1994). The restoration debate of the nineteenth-century architects was to some extent moved into the twentieth-century art world, with two approaches being evident.

- Exact restoration, only in-painting losses in the picture for which there was clear evidence.

- The 'in the style of' restoration where it was felt that the importance still lay in the image as a whole and restoration of lost areas of the painting in the appropriate style. Losses, including a lack of depicted detail, ruined the aesthetic experience.

The developments in technology which followed World War II allowed greater analysis and more detailed information about objects to be obtained. This enabled the 'exact' school of restoration to have far more detail and confidence in their restorations from this period onwards. This trend continued into the 1960s with more strident demands by some art historians to distinguish the original material, leading to developments such as visible in-painting (Bomford 1994). This could be achieved at numerous different levels, from using a neutral monotone of the infilled area, to copying the colours and shapes exactly as in the painting but not imitating the natural *crinquelure* of an aged paint film. This subject was influenced by Cesare Brandi, director of the Istituto Centrale del Restauro in Rome, who balanced ideas regarding the importance of the object as a historical document against those of the importance of the aesthetic impact of the object and its importance as a whole object. His ideas were published in 1963 in the book *Teoria del restauro*. At the Rome centre, in collaboration with Paolo Mora, the most well known of the 'visible' techniques of in-painting, known as *tratteggio* or *rigatini*, was developed. This technique uses discrete vertical brush strokes in the colours of the missing elements of the picture, which allow the original colours in the missing area to be reproduced but the vertical strokes remain visible and thus the in-painting is obvious upon careful inspection. Adaptations of this technique by the Florentine School in the 1970s and 1980s, such as chromatic selection, allowed the brush strokes to follow the forms of the elements in the image, but involved separate lines of primary and secondary colours, which merge optically to provide the correct colour to the infilled areas. In large areas techniques such as 'chromatic abstraction' were used, where a mesh of brushstrokes in black and the primary colours relied upon the relative proportions and positions of the brush strokes to give a generally appropriate colour balance to the missing area. Paolo Mora has used the *tratteggio* technique to good effect on many wall-painting restorations (Mora, Mora and Philippot 1996), though the main use of these techniques has been for infilled areas in oil paintings. These techniques have met with variable levels of success, depending on the nature of the painting and the skill of the restorer as it is not easy to achieve the required chromatic balances (Vaccaro 1996a).

Possibly as a result of living in an age where endless, colourful, exact copies are available there has been a growing appreciation of the authentic and the aged in the late twentieth century, so that even small pieces of the past, almost devoid of meaning, are valued. It has also been suggested that the public of this century have become more comfortable with abstract art than their nineteenth-century counterparts, so find no problem viewing damaged statues. No longer obscured by the barbarity of their desecration, they became abstract depictions of parts of bodies, beautiful for the craft of their sculpted form (Yourcenar 1996). This led to the de-restoration of a number of statues, and other works of art, from the 1960s to 1990s. An example of this was *The Lansdowne Herakles* which had eighteenth-century restorations undone in 1979, largely to remove the corroding iron dowels which threatened to push it apart. When re-restored, any infills which were non-structural were left out and modern epoxy on a polyurethane foam base was used to fill many cracks and crevices. This was painted a monotone and the original marble was left standing proud. This restoration, rather than celebrate the original, emphasized the 'squared off' edges of the statue during its eighteenth-century restoration and by the 1990s the statue was re-restored when the eighteenth-century marble restorations were reinserted (Podany 1994). There is a growing interest in the history of conservation/restoration and it is suggested that all earlier restorations, especially those which were not recorded when they were created, should be fully recorded. Any restorations of the nineteenth century or earlier may be of importance.

The quality and care of restoration work has increased in this century, such that Oddy could, by 1994, call attention to the inappropriate practices of the British Museum in its restorations of the past. In the restoration of the Portland Vase in 1845 there was evidence that the pieces of the original object had been filed down to fit the restoration (see Case study 4A, Oddy 1994). It is this tempting practice, where aesthetic considerations have overcome respect for original material, which ethical codes are intended to clearly signal as unacceptable.

9.4 The purpose, acceptability and extent of restoration

The arguments regarding restoration have frequently acquired the air of religious creeds rather than scholarly debate. In such an atmosphere intemperate analogies are made, such as comparison of the desire to restore to a single period as 'a purity of thought and purpose' and thus 'Protestant', whilst an approach which retained the accumulated history of the object regarded as 'Catholic' (Philippot 1996a). Similarly Brandi (1996) suggested 'Restoration is generally understood as any kind of intervention that permits a product of human activity to recover its function'. This cannot be regarded as literally true, as a restored ceramic does not resume its function as a wine container. However, it demonstrates how overstated views are likely to lead to extreme positions within a debate on restoration. Restoration can be seen as 'covering the scars and damage of the past, and thus distorting the past by beautifying it', and 'denying part of the history of the object'. Equally, avoiding restoration leaves every object looking broken and damaged gives the impression that all the objects of the past were broken and damaged. For almost all objects restoration lies somewhere between a beautiful fiction and a barbarous truth.

In the past it has been possible to accuse restorers, especially those of the aesthetic 'in the style of' school of restoration, of creating subjective restoration work. Howard in 1990 described such restoration work as, like the Rorschach ink blots, 'images into which the perceiver projects his fantasy, intelligence, faith, understanding, desires, expectations, intent, meaning, preoccupations etc., thereby revealing as much or more of himself and his world as of the object of contemplation' (Podany 1994). The present-day ethics on this subject demand that the restored image only be of a form and contain decoration for which there is clear evidence. Thus symmetrical vessels can accurately be restored, and patterned objects redecorated (Smith 1994, plate 5), or where the nature of the depicted image is known, as in the case of the wall paintings of the Map Gallery of the Archbishop's Palace in Salzburg, which townscapes were copied from Braun and Hoggenburg's (1572–1617) *Civitas orbis terrarum* (Leitner and Paine 1994). In instances where there is no information, vague generalized shapes may be used to convey the impression of the work and avoid visual disharmony – such as the use of featureless faces for the unidentified saints depicted in the reconstruction of the thirteenth-century glass mosaic from the Baptistery of Florence (Giusti 1994).

Simple rules – such as restoration work being undetectable at a distance of 6 feet, but detectable at 6 inches, the '6 foot 6 inch rule' – have been advocated as a simple articulation of the desire to maintain the visual continuity of objects, such as ceramics, though allowing restoration to be detectable (Buys and Oakley 1993; Hodges 1975a).

The ethical position on restoration, or 'compensation for loss', has become more consistent in the more recent ethical conservation codes. It is referred to, not in the ethical codes for conservation since it is not normally considered as conservation, but the associated codes of practice. The AIC (1994) Code sees compensation for loss as acceptable provided:

- It is fully recorded.

- It is reversible.

- It is detectable by common examination methods.

- It does not falsify the aesthetic, conceptual or physical characteristics of the object.

- It does not remove or obscure original material (respect for the traces of time).

The UKIC (1996) Code has similar requirements, though it accepts that they could be overridden for clearly defined 'structural or physical reasons' with the owner's consent. The diverse ethical and practical arguments regarding restoration were raised in the pre-prints of the conference *Restoration: Is It Acceptable?* (Oddy 1994).

One of the areas of greatest controversy is the reshaping of metal (Hodges 1975b; Oddy 1994; Corfield 1988b, see Case study 12A). Oddy (1994) has pointed out that textiles, paper and basketry are routinely reshaped through humidification, without any similar level of discussion. In modern-day conservation and restoration work, metal is normally never reshaped if it has been bent out of shape during its working life. Many objects, such as swords, were deliberately broken or bent as part of the burial or deposition burial ritual and so the break is part of the important history of the object. In the cases of metal objects damaged during their finding, such as the Coppergate helmet, which was damaged by the mechanical excavator which found it (Tweddle 1992), or through burial when the object can be crushed by the weight of soil above it, such as the Anastasius Dish from Sutton Hoo, then reshaping could be considered ethical (Corfield 1988b).

The question of damage or alteration of the object in order to facilitate its restoration is usually considered unacceptable (Brooks 1998), though it is normal practice where conservators are assembling a stone statue to drill into extant stone in order to affix a dowel so that a broken piece of the original statue can be securely adhered.

9.5 Variations in approach

When dealing with the past, especially with archaeological finds, fragments of objects (e.g. sherds of ceramic) are usually recovered rather than whole objects or vessels. The fragments are often quite stable, and can survive well if simply and carefully packed away. There is, however, a tremendous human urge to reassemble any object one finds in fragments. This is presumably related to early responses learnt in childhood that objects were supposed to be whole and not in fragments. However, the reassembly of whole objects takes up time that could often be better spent preserving other objects, and the reassembled vessels or objects are often less stable and more prone to damage than as a bag of separate sherds. Therefore, there must be a good reason for spending the time and posing increased risk to the well-being of the object to justify reassembling an object. Archaeological objects are normally only reassembled when:

- It is necessary to identify what the object is in order to ascertain its function, and determine its date or culture.

- It is necessary to draw, photograph or describe the object (e.g. for an archaeological report).

- The reassembled vessel or object will be used for display purposes, so people may learn what the object originally looked like and what it was used for, etc.

- The object would be more stable and better preserved and cared for when reassembled than it would be in individual fragments.

The differing approaches to restoration which stem from perceptions of different relative values of aesthetic and historic content are exemplified by the British Museum approach to conserving ceramics (Smith 1994). The older and more functional the object the more likely the conservators are to leave it as a historic document than a restored item; thus the Egyptian ceramics are left assembled with gaps unfilled, whereas the post-medieval majolica wares and porcelain are fully restored. Where objects become important pieces of art, such as the Greek 'red and black' figure-ware vessels, the emphasis is again on aesthetic restoration. The extent to which the colours are matched exactly or simply of similar tone will vary with the extent to which the object is intended for exhibition. The ease with which one should be able to detect such restorations varies from conservator to conservator and institution to institution.

A similar variation in approach to restoration based on factors including age, original function, rarity and conservation tradition is seen in the case of textiles. Ecclesiastical vestments, or trade-union banners, are very symbolic visual images and would normally be restored, whereas archaeological textiles, such as the Fifth Dynasty shirt recovered by Petrie from his excavations at Deshasheh, are preserved for its historic value (Brooks *et al.* 1994).

Variations in restoration approach depending on tradition and practice in that area of conservation are most readily seen in mixed collections, such as those of the V&A Museum. Losses in paintings are infilled and in-painted though polychrome sculpture losses are not restored. In furniture conservation missing veneer is replaced with matching new veneer, though textile conservators do not reweave losses in tapestries (Ashley-Smith 1994). There is, as yet, no single consistent approach to restoration through the various areas of conservation, though they are becoming more aware of each other. Until the relative importance of aesthetic and historic attributes in different types of object are brought into balance there will continue to be different approaches to the extent and nature of restoration.

Objects which are intensely privately collected, such as paintings, porcelain, arms and armour (Edge 1994), are more drastically and extensively restored than other areas such as archaeological, ethnographic or natural-history specimens which are usually held in public collections. This is because:

- Many objects, such as arms and armour or historic vehicles, are not collected for their historic value but because of their associations or the thrill of driving or using them. For many of these objects, their owners consider that the evidence of age and originality is not of sufficient importance to warrant retention. Their view of the past being more important to them than the truth of the past. Consequently such objects are little more than 'toys for boys' and with the machismo of competitive collecting such objects are often required in pristine, working or 'authentic' (as new) condition. This leads to excessive cleaning as well as excessive restoration. Such excessive actions are also often cheaper than more careful and measured conservation work; for example, removing tattered rags attached to a breastplate and shining it up is simpler, quicker and cheaper than worrying about preserving the traces of attached textile and traces of paint on the metal surface.

- Many collectors acquire objects, such as prints and drawings, paintings, fine furniture and china, because of the aesthetic or financial value of the objects. In both categories undetectable restoration for any missing part or blemish on the original would enhance the value. Thus there is pressure on conservators of privately owned objects to engage in more complete, exact or invisible restoration. Prott (1995) quotes the example of an American indian headdress 'Northern Kwakiutl thunderbird head-dress' which was originally valued at Can $45,000; however, after conservation/restoration its value rose to Can $75,000, a price which it duly obtained. This is one of many examples where restoration has considerably increased the value of an item.

Conservators working on privately owned objects are generally in private practice. As commercial enterprises they lose considerable time and money in going to conferences, writing articles and books, etc.; therefore, their views are rarely expressed in the conservation literature. Such conservators may endeavour to stay inside the existing ethical codes, though they often spend minimal time recording the object and there is frequently no funding for analytical work (Manitta 1994). These commercial considerations do influence judgement so it is important that all conservators keep in mind that society only values and pays for conservation, because it values the past. The ways in which it values the past (see Chapter 2) determine what conservation it wishes to fund. Consequently restoration for aesthetic purposes often has a greater importance in the eyes of the public, than in the eyes of the 'heritage professionals', such as conservators.

When considering restoration it is often appropriate to consider the collection as a whole and not just every single object. Restoration of one exemplary object may be judged far more appropriate when there are several similar objects in poor condition (Child 1994). Consideration of the bigger picture might also lead to the replacement of a single cog in a wheel so allowing the waterwheel to turn and a mill to run. The educational value of understanding the process of milling and its role in transforming natural forces to harnessed rotary motion may outweigh the historic importance of a single damaged cog. Where such additions are not readily detected and, even if they are, it is advisable to date all restoration work, particularly new pieces of working objects and additions to stonework, metalwork and furniture, so avoiding any element of deception.

Early building restorers, such as Viollet-le-Duc, had advocated the use of new improved building materials which became available during the nineteenth and twentieth centuries. Unthinking use of such modern materials led to visually intrusive restorations. The 1964 UNESCO Venice Charter extended ideas, first promoted by the 1931 Athens Charter, of placing some clear ethical guidelines/constraints on the restorers of historic buildings. They emphasized respect for the materials and aesthetic ideals of the past requiring that: 'repairs to historic buildings should be done using original materials'. Though well intentioned, using traditional materials can make it difficult to distinguish between original and restoration work, making it impossible to accurately remove restoration work and reconserve the building. This indicates the limitation of the simple dos and don'ts of charters. Ethical consciousness needs to develop well beyond simple concepts of traditional and modern materials, before restoration work is undertaken, to a careful juxtaposition of the various competing requirements of conservation (Philippot 1996b). The use of stable materials (see Section 8.3), which will not harm the original object and which do not degrade any more quickly (or slowly) than the original object are appropriate. The differential ageing of the restoration, as exemplified by the nineteenth-century alterations to the tapestry of *Anthony and Cleopatra* (see Section 9.3), can ruin the aesthetic appreciation of the object.

Where localized replacement of stone, regilding or other highly visual repair or restoration has taken place, there can be a marked difference between the visual appearance of the aged and patinated surface and the newly restored area, as seen in the recently restored stonework of Westminster Abbey. In 20–30 years the restored area will have weathered to match the rest, though other areas will no doubt have further decayed and require restoration, thus the object or building will possess an almost constantly mottled appearance. The alternative is to amend the new material to match the aged surface; for example, the addition of *crinquelure* to a reintegrated loss in an oil painting, the addition of a tinted glaze to dull and darken fresh gilding, or the roughening and dirtying of stone surface. The toning down of new gilding (Jenner 1994) and similar practices is seen as an acceptable ethical practice, provided the condition of the original object is not altered and that the restoration remains detectable by careful inspection. In the case of stone replacement careful consideration must be given to the overall visual appearance of the weathering of the building over future years and not overly shortening the life of the costly replacement stone. Clearly this only becomes an issue where the restoration is visible.

There is a fine but clear line to be drawn between the creation of an aged surface for the purpose of restoring visual integrity and that of faking or forgery. This may often be one of intent but it should be mirrored in the level of execution. Restoration should always be discernible to close inspection.

9.6 Where to stop

The act of restoration, when it involves replacing parts, can lead to objects which, after a number of acts of restoration, are so altered that their similarity to the original is questionable. This can lead to problems in terms of how they should be described; for example, 'If I replace the handle of the axe and my father had already replaced the head, is it still my grandfather's axe?' Such arguments depend on whether the description relates to the material truth of modern Western cultures, or the meaning and symbolism of more traditional cultures.

In the sixteenth century the Hellenistic statue known as *Laocoon* was uncovered and later restored by Montorsoli on the 'in the style of' principles, with many new pieces carved for missing evidence, with no information regarding the form of the original save a general appreciation of the themes and style of classical statuary. This restored form became famous. However, the subsequent discovery of an arm from the statue left a difficult series of judgements for the conservators of the period. Whether to reunite the arm with the statue and do away with part or all of the restoration, or leave it as it was with the real arm separately displayed. All had some ethical advantages and some disadvantages. The restored statue had become an important nineteenth-century icon, and it was difficult to deliberately destroy such an important image. Eventually a cast of the complete Montorsoli restored statue was made and displayed, the original subsequently had the Montorsoli restoration removed, the original arm added without any further restoration (Philippot 1996a).

The past is invariably used to provide justification for our present political and social views (see Chapter 2). In presenting the past we project, often unconsciously, our present ideas into the past, selecting the facts we consider relevant and important so shaping history to the form which we currently think it ought to have. In restoring an object we unconsciously mould the physical form of objects to fit our perception of the past. Thus restoration says as much about the present day as it does about the past. The colour and texture of the materials used, the examples copied, the knowledge exhibited and the extent and nature of the restoration, all betray the age and aesthetic tradition to which the restoration belongs.

9A Case study: Sutton Hoo Helmet (Maryon 1947; Williams 1992)

The Sutton Hoo Helmet was discovered as numerous pieces of mineralized iron corrosion and a number of gilded-bronze castings, part of the grave goods of a hugely rich Saxon burial in a completely degraded 90-foot-long boat buried beneath a substantial burial mound at Sutton Hoo in East Anglia. This burial was excavated in

1939 (Bruce-Mitford 1978; Evans 1986) and stored throughout World War II. Analysis of the contents of the grave suggested that it was that of Raedwald the Anglo-Saxon king of East Anglia who died around AD 625. Conservation and reconstruction of the helmet was initially undertaken in 1946 by Herbert Maryon of the British Museum Research Laboratory. His initial reconstruction was subsequently taken down and reconstructed in 1968–9 by Nigel Williams and the staff of the British Museum.

X-Radiographic examination and physical cleaning of the helmet fragments, together with some elemental analysis, revealed that the helmet was composed of iron plates decorated with thin tinned-bronze foils which were stamped with a series of complex figurative and decorative designs. A number of decorative gilded-bronze castings, inlaid with silver wires, niello and garnets formed, a nose-piece with moustache and mouth, eyebrows, and crest terminals. Careful observation indicated that the thin tinned stamped-bronze foils were affixed to the exterior of the iron plates using fluted bronze strips which overlay the foils and were riveted to the helmet. The corrosion processes had fused the iron and thin bronze foils and strips together as brown mineralized crusts.

There were no records of the original positions of the pieces when they were uncovered upon excavation, thus the only guide was to try and piece together the helmet from the corroded iron pieces using actual joins between the pieces, the patterns of the decorative foils and the lines of fluted strip visible on the surface of many of the pieces. From comparison with the decorative and stylistic features of a series of similar helmets from Vendel culture graves in Sweden it was clear that the helmet was composed of a skullcap to which a face mask, neck guard and ear flaps were attached.

Since the 500 separate fragments of mineralized iron and associated bronze gave little information to the museum visitor, it was judged that restoration was appropriate for this object. The images and information which have been generated as a result of this restoration have indicated how informative restoration can be. The restored helmet has been pictured in almost every book on the Anglo-Saxon period produced since World War II.

Herbert Maryon's original restoration was heavily based on the existing information on Vendel helmets, though relatively little information had been published by 1946. After months of piecing together mineralized helmet fragments they were mounted on to a preformed head shape made from plaster of Paris with wire mesh and plaster backing for the ear flaps. Any remaining gaps between the helmet fragments were filled with more plaster which was coloured with brown umber to match the corroded iron. The principal lines of the fluted strip and decorative plates were incised into the plaster to give the viewer a clear impression of the helmet as a whole (see Figure 9.2).

Subsequently, as both greater knowledge about Saxon and Vendel helmets became available, and certain practical limitations of using a helmet of the reconstructed form became apparent, a new restoration was required. It was only because there was a first restoration that could be constructively criticized, that there was the impetus and improved ideas available for a second restoration.

It is uncertain to what extent Maryon was conscious of using reversible materials when he made his first reconstruction. In practice it was not a simple task to locate and remove the corroded pieces from the plaster backing. Because of the density

Figure 9.2 Sutton Hoo Helmet, the 1946 original reconstruction (photograph courtesy of the British Museum).

difference between corroded iron and plaster, the original reconstruction could be X-rayed and the original helmet fragments and restorative plaster distinguished. The X-ray images and the brittle nature of the plaster made it possible to locate and remove the plaster from around the corroded iron leaving the pieces of the original helmet largely intact. Thus the first reconstruction proved to be physically reversible, though it did require considerable effort.

The limited extent of the cleaning of the mineralized iron fragments prior to the first restoration ensured that much evidence remained. It revealed that there were variations in thickness and corrosion patterns on the inside of the helmet and traces of gilding on the bronze strips near the helmet's crest. This information, together with a clearer understanding of the nature and arrangement of the tinned-bronze plaques on the helmet exterior, allowed the second restoration to reposition many more fragments in their original locations. After the location of as many of the fragments as possible had been determined, they were adhered together and the missing areas

Figure 9.3 Sutton Hoo Helmet, the 1968–9 reconstruction (photograph courtesy of the British Museum).

infilled with a jute textile stiffened with adhesive which was heat softened to form the curved shape of the missing areas and covered with pigmented plaster of Paris in order to recreate the full visual appearance of the helmet. This second restoration was larger than the original, had a clear pattern to the punched decorated bronze plaques, a location for all the cast dragon's-head terminals which had not been included in the original reconstruction and far more effective defensive ear flaps, neck guard and face mask. It is clear that this second restoration is more accurate than the first (see Figure 9.3).

An exact replica of the second reconstruction of the Sutton Hoo helmet was created by the Tower of London armouries, and is currently displayed beside the original. This enables museum visitors to appreciate how this highly polished metal helmet originally appeared. The information for both the restoration and the replica helmet have been derived from careful study and analysis of the original fragments and information and experience gained during the two restoration processes.

9B Case study: Hans Holbein's painting *The Ambassadors* (Wyld 1998)

The Ambassadors is an oil painting executed on a wooden panel, of oak planks, painted by Hans Holbein in 1533. The picture was acquired in 1890 by the National Gallery and, after an initial restoration in 1890–1, the picture was again restored in the mid-1990s in time for the 500th anniversary of Holbein's birth, 1997. The picture depicts Jean Dinteville, French Ambassador to England, and Georges de Selve, Bishop of Lavaur, standing on an intricately inlaid marble floor, with a rich green patterned curtain in the background. Between the two men is a stand covered with a carpet on which lie a globe, lute, hymn book and many other objects which describe the interests and ideas of the men. In the foreground is an anamorphic depiction of a skull, an image depicted as if seen through a distorting lens or at an extreme angle.

The picture, which is regarded as one of Holbein's finest surviving works, was probably passed down through the Dinteville family and after a brief period in the south of France it was sold in Paris and again in England, eventually being acquired by the Earl of Radnor in 1808–9 who hung it in Longford Castle until he subsequently bequeathed it to the National Gallery in 1890. Examination of the picture in 1890–1 and in the 1990s revealed that it had suffered some damage during its earlier history. A substantial crack in the centre of the picture has led to suggestions that the picture was at some time split into two and subsequently rejoined. The left-hand side of the picture has suffered from damp over a number of years and consequently has numerous small paint losses. The flexing and warping of the oak planks, which were initially butt-joined together using small wooden dowels, has led to lines of slight paint loss at the junction between the planks. There is evidence of several earlier campaigns of restoration. The most substantial of which probably occurred in France prior to 1787 when it was still in the possession of the Dinteville family, since the restored depiction of the medal which hangs around Dinteville's neck, the obscure order of St Michael of Basel, was accurately depicted. The extensive restoration at this time obscured some of the original Holbein paintwork, sections of the hymn book, the green curtains and areas of the costume of the two men were overpainted.

In 1891 the painting was restored by William Morril who worked on the wood of the panel and William Dyer who worked on the painted surface. To counter the concave warping across the width of the planks, they were planed down from the back to a thickness of 5 mm and then subject to heavy pressure which flattened the plank panel. A 'cradle' backing of vertical and horizontal bars was then attached to the back of the panel in order to provide a stable backing to the panel. The worst of the earlier restorations were removed and replaced with more careful work by William Dyer. The old highly discoloured varnish was removed and replaced. This substantially improved the visual quality of the painting, made it more stable and exposed more of Holbein's original work. Little further work was done to *The Ambassadors*. Splits in the painting were noted in 1892, 1895, 1940 and 1952 which necessitated some strengthening and replacement of part of the cradle backing. Repairs to blistering paint occurred in 1929 and 1939.

During World War II much of the National Gallery's collection was stored in the carefully controlled conditions achieved in buildings constructed in the caverns of the slate quarries at Manod in North Wales. The stability of the paintings in this store contrasted with the problems which arose upon their return to London where, as a result of the low Relative Humidity (RH) experienced in the bitter winter of 1946–7, the panel painting, *Landscape with Het Steen* by Rubens, split (Saunders 1997). Subsequent control of the humidity, through the use of air conditioning, in the National Gallery has eliminated the risk of splitting wooden-panel paintings.

The 1990s' restoration was intended to utilize the greater technical competence now available to conduct a much more extensive analytical investigation into the nature of Holbein's painting and, following evidence obtained from X-radiographs of *The Ambassadors* taken in 1984, improve the restoration work of the 1890s. The structure of the painting was, upon analysis, revealed to be composed of a panel constructed from ten vertical straight-grained planks of oak, derived from the Baltic/Polish region, butt-joined with dowels to give a panel just over 2 m square. This panel was covered with two layers of ground (natural chalk and animal glue) followed by a mid-grey priming layer (lead white and lamp black). Infra-red reflectance imaging suggested that it was on to this surface that the cartoon for the painting was sketched, probably in charcoal. Visual analysis, and a small number of cross-sections through minute fragments of paint, revealed that Holbein painted most of the areas of the painting directly and simply on to this sketched outline using ground pigments in a linseed-oil binder. In places this binder was thickened through partial heating, in other areas its gloss was increased using an addition of pine resin. In some areas, such as Dinteville's pink satin doublet and the green curtain background, the rich visual effect was achieved through building up a number of paint layers.

The stability of the panel since 1952 indicated that no conservation work was required on the existing support which was adequate in conditions of stable relative humidity. The ageing and darkening of the 1890s' varnish now obscured areas of the Holbein image and some of the 1890s' restorations were discolouring. The X-radiographs taken in 1984 gave a clear indication of the extent of the damage and infill to Holbein's original paintwork, some of which was still clearly obscured. Therefore the 1890s' varnish was removed; this was undertaken following tests which revealed the most effective solvent (ethanol, propan-2-ol and white spirit in a 1 : 1 : 3 mixture) and tests confirmed that this solvent altered neither the microstructure nor composition of the paint layer beneath the varnish. Subsequently most repainted areas were removed using solvent and mechanical cleaning. The restoration filling of cracks and losses was removed only if it was weak, damaged or inappropriate. Flakes of original paint were held in place using isinglass (an adhesive made from the swim-bladders of the sturgeon). Any cracks or losses were filled with an easily reversed mixture of polyvinyl acetate (PVAc), polyvinyl alcohol (PVAl) and chalk to ensure the continued stability of the paint layers and avoid further flaking.

The removal of the 1890s' varnish and some earlier restorations revealed even more of the Holbein original than had been expected. Details of the original form of the dagger hilt, the original notes and words of the hymn score and aspects of the clothing, particularly of Jean de Dinteville were revealed. The extent of Holbein's original work was fully recorded. The National Gallery has a policy of wishing its public to enjoy 'an image uninterrupted by damage, loss, panel joins etc.' and thus it usually chooses exact (deceptive) retouching, restoring paintings to their original image. However, the gallery recognizes a need to balance legibility and authenticity

Figure 9.4 Hans Holbein's painting, *The Ambassadors*, following restoration (photograph courtesy of the National Gallery).

and will only restore images where it has a clear indication as to the colour and form of the original image. In most cases, the losses on *The Ambassadors* were so small that the missing areas could be clearly extrapolated from the colour and form of the surrounding areas. In some areas, such as the floor and carpet, the symmetry of the image clearly indicated what was missing. In one or two areas, though the general nature of what was missing was apparent, the exact nature of the original could not be discerned. In these areas difficult decisions (judgements) had to be made balancing the need to achieve the true aesthetic experience of the picture, but to avoid falsehood. In all cases the range of possible outcomes was discussed between the conservators and curators and the approach which best achieved the desired aims selected. In one example it could be suggested, from the folds of the drapery, the figure of Jean de Dinteville originally wore a codpiece. However, it was judged that insufficient information existed to indicate the form or extent of such a garment and so the existing dark folds of the garment, seen in earlier restorations, were replaced with no distinct form specified. Similarly areas on the globe, which were restored, were painted so as to have the approximate outlines of the missing continents taking information from existing globes of the period, though all lettering and any other specific information was omitted. Extensive research was undertaken using digital imaging to reproduce the exact distorted form of the anamorphic depiction of a skull. The development of the ability to distort a skull into the exact form used in the image allowed the principal components of the skull to be accurately restored. Subsequently the picture was varnished, as it would have been when it was originally painted. This was done using dammar resin which, though it yellows slightly on ageing, was found after testing to be preferable to modern varnish alternatives, which did not saturate the colours of the picture properly unless applied in thick heavy coatings which were inappropriate to the period of this picture. The picture was then given a frame suitable for the period and displayed (see Figure 9.4).

Considerable publicity in the form of information panels, publications and television programmes explained to the general public the process of conservation which the picture had undergone and the judgements which the conservators had made. The reaction both to the restored image and to the careful conservation work which was undertaken was generally very positive.

10 In working condition

10.1 Preserving the sounds, smells and movements of the past

It is the educated elites of modern Western civilizations who are primarily concerned with preserving the physical form of the material culture of the past; other cultures hold 'folkways' – such as song, dance, meetings, festivals, rituals, food – more important than the physical reality (Lowenthal 1996). It is not the instruments or masks used which are important, but the festival celebration itself. Lowenthal quotes the example of the offspring of a family of poor Tennessee homesteaders who gather each year for a barbecue and get together at the old family homestead, even though it is now ruined, overgrown and no longer worked (Lowenthal 1996). It appears likely that many prehistoric rituals were similarly celebrated on the sites of much older burial mounds or monuments. The Japanese celebrate 'Living Cultural Treasures' – master craftsmen such as papermakers, swordmakers, calligraphers – whose work is so venerated that the attitude, approach and actions of their work are seen as an art to be celebrated and encouraged every bit as much as the physical product they produce. The distinction between the physical form of an object and the care and love and skill (genius) which go into its creation are separated only in modern western societies; they remain bonded in many native and traditional cultures (see Section 13.4). Since the past is composed of such folkways, are they not as worthy of preservation as the physical realities of the past? Is not the tune played on a musical instrument as worthy of preservation as the instrument on which it is played?

Though we tend to always refer to and recognize the past in its visual form, it can also be defined in terms of our other senses. It is possible to define a past in terms of the changing sounds or smells. Sound, smell, taste and touch are highly evocative senses and they add greatly both to the intensity and apparent 'reality' of any experience and to gaining a more comprehensive understanding of what the past was like. A steam train is a far more involving experience when you smell it, hear it and feel it thundering past. You also understand much better what it was for, how it worked, how people felt about it, when you see it motion. Working historic objects (objects performing their original function, usually moving mechanical objects) attempt to provide both this feeling and a greater level of understanding though intensifying the sensation by more fully informing the range of human senses. Working objects, rather than being just aesthetic entities, create an evocation of the past which provides an 'informative activity' for those experiencing (viewing, smelling or hearing) it. As described in Section 9.1, to appreciate the true meaning of an object it is important to be aware of the spirit and purpose of an object. For many objects which were designed to be working objects the 'context' of an object is to be active (e.g. in motion). Similarly, for working objects, the 'true nature' of the object only becomes fully evident when it is working, thus the activity is informative. It is impossible to fully appreciate the nature of any musical instrument until it has been heard. The music (activity) is not random or meaningless, but it informs the viewer in an aesthetic sense, as well as making the purpose and form of the object more understandable. Therefore, working objects are not purely historic documents and aesthetic entities, but also 'informative activity' providers. This capacity does not relate to the physical structure of the object either as a historic document or an aesthetic entity, it only relates to the object in operation as it transforms from one state to another, thus it is definable as a third characteristic of an object, related purely to its activity as a working object.

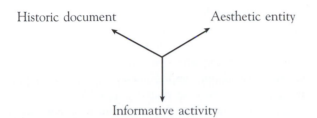

Working objects are conserved, not purely to retain the historic object itself, but to provide the sights, sounds, smells and motions of the past. Whilst the conservation of the object which enables the motion to be made is one element of preserving the experience of the past, it is also necessary to preserve the expertise of operating or playing the object. The 'expertise' (operation, playing) and the 'product' (movement, music, etc.) of an object were identified in Section 6.3 as essential aspects of that object requiring identification and characterization. 'Expertise' and non-physical 'products' such as sound and motion have been difficult to capture and study. This became easier with nineteenth and twentieth-century advances in technology. Methods included:

- Oral tradition – expertise in creating the phenomena handed down from parent to child, master to apprentice, teacher to pupil.

- Written record, where instructions or descriptions of the phenomena enable actions to be copied or descriptions appreciated.

- Visual or audio recording. Initially single-frame static images (e.g. photographs or drawings) conveyed limited information, but the advent of film and audio recordings permitted phenomena, such as movement and sound, to be fully appreciated. Knowledge on the operation of machines and their consequent movement could accurately be recorded.

The developing technology of the twentieth century made many crafts and processes redundant but also provided the means by which the process could be accurately recorded.

Evidence on record, such as film, audiotape, videotape, photographs, written description, of the use of objects and the outcome of using the object's 'expertise' and 'product' are of primary importance for working-object collections and are, in many cases, as important as the physical object. The specialist storage standards for paper archives BS 5454 and photographs BS 5687 should be achieved for all such material. Specialist stores for magnetic media and film records (see Section 8.4) exist in very few museums (MGC 1994; Ball and Winsor

1997). The conservator should be as concerned for the preservation of these primary records as for the well-being of the physical objects.

10.2 Museums of working objects

Individuals or institutions who collect, display, restore and work these objects do so in the hope that, through experiencing the full aesthetic sensation of, say, a steam train, visitors will both see and feel the need to preserve (and so repeat?) this experience. Thus they come to believe, as the collector and institution does (see Chapter 2), that these steam engines are valuable and worth preserving.

In museums of archaeology, the theory of what happened in the past stems from the objects. The artefacts and their associated contextual information recovered through archaeological excavation are grouped using aspects of their form, decoration, function and their associations with other objects to form sequences of evolving material cultures. Through these material-culture sequences we identify and define the past. Museums of archaeology retain the objects of the past as evidence so that it is possible for us to re-examine, reorder and recalibrate the past, as occurred after the development of radiocarbon dating (Renfrew 1973). For this reason objects are primarily important as historic documents which help define the past. Similar claims for the role of specimens can be made for subjects such as ethnography and natural history.

Museums of science and technology, folklife, agriculture, industry and social history focus on the recent historical period for which there are written and pictorial records. Consequently there is a greater perception of already knowing what happened; the history of events has already been written and this will not be rewritten. Therefore, the objects in the collection primarily illustrate rather than define the past. Consequently they are seen primarily as having an aesthetic and educational role.

If we initially examine working objects in terms of those which are capable of movement, working objects can be seen to include vehicles from cars to traction engines, industrial machinery, musical instruments, clocks, some electrical equipment, boats, aircraft, toys from merry-go-rounds (carousels) to spinning tops. The reasons for the assembly of these collections, identified by Mann (1994), correspond to the generic categories for collecting defined in Section 2.2:

- A wish to remember and commemorate a technical achievement (value).

- A love of the working object (aesthetic).

- As trophies or specimens. Often seen as the biggest, best, fastest, etc. (value).

- To show how things work (understanding).

- To show how things were (belief).

- Demonstration of technical superiority (control).

There is an element of nostalgia running through almost all such collecting which leads to the enthusiastic use of the objects. There is also an element of trophyism often manifest in the display of the objects always seen 'looking their best' This has resulted in many such objects being restored to mint condition (see Section 9.5). A tradition for extensive restoration has grown up for restoring mechanical devices, based largely on the craft skills of the manufacture of such items. The craft tradition of object manufacture is always towards objects in their best condition, and the museum ethos for 'the truth' has yet to overcome this desire for visual 'perfection' which is derived from the commercial basis of needing to sell the object to a potential buyer.

This concept of restoring an object to working condition is justified in modern museum terms as being the 'true nature' of the object and has become the expected norm by both the museum visitors and staff. 'In science and technology museums the point of the object is often what it does or did' (Keene 1994).

Though working objects occur in many museums, they usually form a significant part of the collections of four different types of museum.

- Science-and-technology museums, which had their origins in the late nineteenth century, and whose purpose was to make the masses aware of scientific and technical principles and achievements. This was an extension of national pride which generated most national museums of the nineteenth century.

- The folk museums, which record a vanishing way of life and started with Artur Hazelius and his museum at Skansen outside Stockholm in 1891 (Kavanagh 1990), now boast numerous large museums (e.g. Ironbridge Gorge, The National Museum of Wales Folk Museum at St Fagans, Beamish, etc.). Part of the *raison d'être* behind these museums was the desire to preserve craft skills and this necessitated working objects.

- Private collections of working objects such as The National Motor Museum at Beaulieu and the Tank Museum at Bovington. Often based on old industries or other organizations these collections specialize in collecting, displaying and working a single type of mechanical device – aircraft, motorbikes, cars, tanks, etc. Many of the visiting public come to worship objects they hold dear, or learn about the technical advances and development of one particular type of machine.

- Local museums who collected objects, including machines and other working objects, important to the town or local industries.

These museums, all of whom are working with objects of the recent past, often have very large collections, substantial buildings and many large objects. There has been limited funding for the establishment and maintenance of large collections since most of the central and local-government museum funding was allocated in the late nineteenth and early twentieth century. Therefore, these museums and their collections, with a few exceptions of national museums such as the Science Museum or the National Folk Museums of Wales and Ulster, have had to generate their own funding. This has led to a much greater interest and awareness in what the public want from a museum, and the consequent creation of a far more holistic and involving experience of the past. This has meant recreating shops, factories and streets, actors in costume explaining the past. Working objects which recreate the movement, sounds and smells of the past are an essential element of this recreation. From Colonial Williamsburg in Virginia, USA to Beamish Museum in County Durham visitors pay for the experience. Dependent upon the income from the public to stay open these museums have, through restoration and recreation of the past, found a way of generating the income which is essential if they are to engage in any conservation and preservation of artefacts.

It is probable that museum exhibits which use working objects are popular with visitors because movement subconsciously attracts our attention, our eyes are designed to catch and study movement. This is presumed to derive from our prehistoric hunting past, but it leads to a fascination with machines and their movement; thus a working object is an arresting sight and there is an obvious fascination for restoring these machines to working order. There is also a perception of movement being equated with life and making a machine work is often described as bringing it back to life.

10.3 Museum objects with differing function and status

The physical objects in museums may be seen as having three states of existence:

- A museum object – an object which has ceased to be used and which exists primarily to illustrate the functional and aesthetic preferences of a particular social group or individual of a given period in the past. The worm-eaten leg of a chair in this category would be retained as a record of the original in its functioning life. It may be conserved, strengthened (e.g. through consolidation) in order to ensure that it survives and that the rest of the object's safety is not imperilled. Objects in this category are primarily historic documents or both historic documents and aesthetic entities.

- A living object (Oddy 1996) – an object which still performs its function and retains its visual form. An object designed to be seen and visually appreciated which if repaired is both functional and aesthetic. Thus the worm-eaten leg of a chair might be cut away and a new leg created and securely fastened in its place. The chair leg would be carved of the same wood as the original and stained to resemble the other chair legs purely for aesthetic reasons. Objects in this category are historic documents, aesthetic entities and informative activities (see Figure 10.1).

- A functional object in use in a museum – an object which is present in a museum and is used in educational activities fulfils essential functions, or fulfils an essential function such as transport, and is part of creating the impression of the past. Reproduction or replica objects, objects not formally accessioned to the museum's collection, or objects which are frequently worn, damaged or replaced all fall into this category. Many of the objects which are used in living museums, especially objects which are working exhibits, are of this type. It is not the object which is the primary entity being preserved, but the sight, sound, feel, emotion generated by the object. Objects in this category are aesthetic entities and informative activities.

In additional to the above some objects are retained in order to be 'cannibalized' in order to support the functional or living-object categories.

Though the term 'working object' is frequently reserved for objects such as vehicles, machines and musical instruments, it can, however, be applied to a far wider range of objects or constructions, as it is applicable to any object which is performing its intended function. By this definition almost all buildings, which continue to withstand the attritional effects of weather and shelter their contents, are working objects. All works of art on public view, withstanding the constant assault of light in order to delight a viewing public, are performing their original function and thus are in the broadest sense working objects. Following this logic it would appear reasonable that similar approaches to conservation should be adopted for objects as diverse as castles, old masters and steam engines

Figure 10.1 The Electric Posser on display at York Castle Museum, restored to working order (photograph courtesy of the author and Richard Stansfield). An electric posser is an electric-motor-driven revolving dollytub, oscillating dolly peg and mangle with resolving rollers, of early twentieth-century date. This machine is the 'missing link' between the hand washing of the Victorian age and the washing machines of the 1930s and 1940s. When this machine was restored to working order the galvanized steel guards, which had been added late in its working life, were replaced with Perspex covers so that the simple cog-and-screw mechanisms could be seen by the public. The electrical wiring and switch were replaced to meet modern safety standards but retained in their original housing to preserve the sense of period.

(Michalski 1994). If the regular replacement of an oil painting's varnish, when it yellows, is equated with the replacement of a worn cog in a machine, there is surprisingly little difference between fine art and working-object conservation. For working objects it is the interface between the object and the outside world, whether it be the varnish of a picture, the teeth of a cog or the paint on the exterior of a building which will wear away and have to be replaced. It is essential that this layer is replaced in order to protect the object beneath (see Section 8.3), and to preserve the object and maintain its working function. The replacement respects the artist/craftsman's original intention, as these layers were designed for wear and replacement.

It is unfortunate that given the financial necessity of attracting visitors, the present preoccupation of many industrial, social history and folk museums, containing working objects, is with presenting the 'informative activity', and there is only minimal interest in preserving working objects as historical documents. Mann (1994) highlighted this in the regret he expressed that the original fragments of Stephenson's 'Rocket' had not been treated like valued archaeological objects, but had been incorporated into various reconstructions. The Science Museum and a number of the other major science and technology museums are starting to take note of the emerging problem of the lack of unrestored originals, and are starting to 'preserve' many of their objects retaining their original paintwork rather than 'restoring' them. It is unfortunate to report that much of this effort may come to late. There is more chance of seeing original Roman armour preserved and visible in British museums than seeing a 'Spitfire' in its original paintwork. All such planes have now been rebuilt and restored by enthusiasts, so that these, like many other high-profile working objects, are being smothered with affection and their 'truth' is being lost for ever.

Whilst many fine art and archaeological objects are, through careful cleaning, exact filling and reintegration of losses, conserved as an aesthetic entity and historic document, working objects, vehicles, machines and instruments are invariably restored to working condition (i.e. as an aesthetic entity and for informative activity), so losing much of the essential evidence which would make them historic documents. In such cases a museum appears to require two objects; one to remain preserved, unrestored as an historical document and a second to be restored to provide the informative activity of the object. It is important, not simply to consider each individual item but the collection as a whole (Child 1988) and all the objects of that type retained within museums. Thus if there is more than one specimen, it is frequently appropriate that one is preserved untouched to save the historical information, ideally the most complete and informative specimen, whilst one or more of the others can be restored for the interpretation processes.

10.4 Objects in working order

There are numerous types of working object. The most common are vehicles from carts to aircraft and various forms of manufacturing machinery, from spinning wheels, early washing machines (see Figure 10.1) to conveyor belts, clocks and musical instruments. The requirements for collecting and running larger and working objects have been detailed elsewhere (MGC 1994; Ball and Winsor 1997) as have those for musical instruments (Barclay 1997) and clocks and watches (Brodie 1994). There are both advantages and disadvantages in keeping the object in running order and periodically using them. Advantages include:

- Use of an object can prevent damage which derives from static display and lack of use. Examples include: periodic playing of wooden musical instruments prevents them from drying out and cracking as a result of the higher RH (relative humidity) generated during playing; mechanical devices which receive benefit from lubrication during use; regular movement adjusts the loads in a structure, preventing distortion of stressed or loaded components such as wheels and tensioning wires.

- Enhanced ability of the object to be used as a visitor attraction and educational exhibit.

Disadvantages include:

- The potential risk of a dramatic failure. Components are invariably stressed during use (e.g. the strings of musical instruments), leading to increased risk of failure during use. No matter how carefully you drive, if you drive a car often enough you will eventually have an accident. The risk of dramatic failure is increased with use. This argues for taking measures for reducing the risk of dramatic failure; for example, running steam engines at reduced boiler pressures, running engines on compressed air rather than steam (as at Bradford Industrial Museum), running vehicles on private roads without other users, limiting the number of users and the lengths of journeys, using gradual warm-up procedures, suspending operation when trained personnel who know that particular object well are not present, regular maintenance and planned disaster procedures.

- Working objects must meet the modern safety standards and it is difficult to achieve this without making significant additions or modifications to the objects; for example, installing guard rails, fitting a tachograph to commercial vehicles, adding covers to hide exposed machinery, installing cut-out switches, even replacing old boilers with new, safe and legally certifiable ones. Such measures can create a false impression of the past and damage the object as a historic document.

- In almost all cases the wearing and heating action of running degrades the condition of the object, even if at a barely perceptible level – such as the increased oxidation and eventual breakdown of the polymer sheathing of the electrical wiring. Similarly running a gearbox or similar mechanical device, even with an oil-filled sump to keep it lubricated, will still lead to wear of the teeth on the gear cogs. No working object can operate without wear. The wear and tear of use leads to the need for a maintenance regime for replacement of worn parts.

- In addition to the normal museum and conservation record working objects require an operating manual in which all aspects of safe operation of the object (e.g. running-up times, fuel, lubricants, operating temperatures and pressures) are indicated, and an operation log which records every use of the object. These help ensure safe operation of the object, limiting the risk of catastrophic failure and ensuring all minor faults are reported and checked.

- It is costly to run working objects. Costs include:
  - Operators who must be properly trained and certified (e.g. having a current driving or pilot's licence).
  - Training staff and retaining skilled staff.
  - The requirement for regular safety checks. This is particularly the case for machines such a vehicles which take passengers such as members of the public. Thus any road-

going vehicle must have a current MOT certificate and any aircraft flying in the UK must pass their AID inspection.

The need to modify the object to meet modern safety standards or to preserve as many original aspects of the historic object as possible can lead to a wide variety of approaches to the restoration. Therefore, the nature and extent of any planned working of the object should be established prior to conservation and restoration work commencing.

There are a number of strategies for achieving working order, or simulating it. Several of these options were explored by Keene (1994) who, juggling the desire to preserve examples of early computers as historic documents and giving the museum visitor the experience of an early computer, identified four possible approaches:

- Run the original computer hardware and wear it out. Repair the system using rare historic parts such as valves, thus giving a finite operational life.

- Run the original computer hardware and wear it out. Repair the system using new parts such as microchips or transistors, which will give it a far longer life though it will continue to emulate its original operational mode. With each passing year it is less and less the original computer which you initially sought to preserve.

- Do not run the computer, preserve it intact as a static exhibit.

- Preserve it intact and run an emulation programme such that the system appears to be operational, with visual output on a monitor which mimics what the original output used to look like.

This final category of emulation is used with modern video or CD players and monitors present within the carcass of an historic object. Thus you can apparently show 1950s' TV programmes on a 1950s' television set. In a similar manner you can use audio cassette or CD of recorded music or radio programmes of any appropriate period with the sound coming out of a modern speaker located in the carcass of a radio of the relevant period. In all cases the removed working mechanisms are valuable and should be retained; saved by modern technology taking their place, they are preserved intact. Provided no damage is done to the object carcass being used or the removed parts, this appears an ethical approach both preserving the historic object without damage or wear, and giving the aesthetic experience of the working object. It is essential that good records of the dismantling and the location of the different parts of the object are made. This technique could be extended to putting modern engines in old car bodies or modern movements inside old clock cases. However, in most cases it is extremely difficult to get modern mechanical devices to accurately mimic the exact sound and movement of their historic counterparts. The alternative is to make a complete replica.

In order to keep working objects working, worn or damaged parts are frequently replaced. The extent and nature of any replacement will be governed by the nature of the restoration, the object, time, facilities, available expertise, historical importance of the piece. Since many working objects are frequently repaired or restored, small amounts of replacement add up and the total volume of replaced material in frequently restored objects can be large – leading to the 'Grandfather's axe' conundrum (see Section 9.6). At what point does it cease to be the original object? Some restored cars have frequently had very little original material in them, some little more than the original chassis number. It remains important to distinguish any replacement piece as a replacement and not an original. This may be achieved through marking the replacement pieces, usually with the date of restoration, or using an unambiguously modern material that equates with the use of deliberate restoration techniques such as *tratteggio* in oil and wall painting (see Section 9.3).

In numerous working objects it is important to identify that there are two specific areas of the object. The exterior surface which is largely a decorative device (e.g. the face of a clock or the bodywork of a car) and the inner mechanism. Whilst a case can be made for an element of restoration to working order of the mechanism, in order that the 'true nature' of the machine, its movement, can be appreciated, the exterior decorative surface is in effect a polychrome sculpture. The numerous layers of paint on the object represent a unique and unbiased record of the object's history and wherever possible such paint should be retained. It could be preserved as a work of art with careful cleaning and infilling of losses to preserve its present aged beauty, an accurate reflection of the period from which it comes. Unfortunately it is rarely treated in this manner and the same enthusiastic restoration as occurs for the mechanism is applied to the exterior decorative zone, which is restored 'in the style of'. Resprayed to a present-day view of how the past should be and repeating the overconfidence of the nineteenth-century restoration architects.

It is important for all working objects that conscious considered judgements are made about the use of the object and the extent and nature of any conservation. Initially a judgement must be made as to whether the object could or should be restored to working condition. Has the truth of the past, the object as a historic document, been safeguarded as well as having the object available as an aesthetic entity and active experience? If it is to be worked, bearing in mind the damage from use and risk of catastrophic damage, what level of use is appropriate. Safety must be assured for any working object but if the object is consequently not accurate in appearance or as an experience, what is the purpose of running it? Can the costs of restoration, operation and maintenance be justified? It is important to ensure that documentation has been secured to show the object in operation demonstrating how it worked and what it produced.

10A Case study: The Forth Bridge (Paxton 1990)

In the 1880s the North British Railway needed to bridge the Firth of Forth in order to complete the railway link between Edinburgh and Dundee. Sir Benjamin Baker designed a revolutionary bridge comprising three huge cantilevers with viaducts at each end, the whole edifice spanning 1.5 miles with a central span of 1,710 ft. This was only the second cantilevered bridge in Europe, the previous one at Hassfurt, Germany having a central span of only 426 ft. This construction form necessitated the use of steel to withstand the stresses, rather than cast iron, the normal material for metal-bridge construction of this period. The construction of the bridge, between 1882 and 1890, cost approximately £3 million and was undertaken by a consortium led by William Arral of Glasgow. It consumed 740,000 cubic ft. of granite, 48,000 cubic yards of stone, 64,300 cubic yards of concrete and 54,160 tons of steel held together with 6.5 million rivets (*The Sunday Times* 1995). This monumental structure was deliberately created in such a sturdy form to withstand the ferocious North Sea gales, which had collapsed the Tay Railway Bridge in December 1879. The Forth Railway Bridge opened as a functioning railway bridge on 4 March 1890 and continues to have up to 200 trains a day use it (Prescott 1995; see Figure 10.2).

Figure 10.2 The Forth Railway Bridge (photograph by the author). This bridge is an object whose size and exposed position demand a continuous maintenance programme which is funded through the continued use of the bridge as a functioning railway bridge.

It was appreciated from the outset that it was essential to maintain this bridge, in particular its 145 acres of steel surface, by a regular routine of repainting. This Herculean task involved the rubbing down of the metalwork with wire brushes followed by painting with several coats of the distinctive red lead-based 'Forth Bridge Red' paint manufactured by Craig & Rose of Leith Walk. By 1993 the maintenance programme consumed 1,000 gallons of paint, employed sixteen painters as part of a forty-strong workforce and cost £600,000 per annum (Bowditch 1993). The idea that the painters started at one end and worked their way to the other end, only to restart at the beginning is a modern myth. They actually tackle those areas which are in most urgent need of repainting. The painting of the Forth Railway Bridge has, however, passed into everyday usage as a metaphor for any unending task.

From 1989 onwards the regime of wire brushing was replaced with the more effective shot-blasting to remove the old paint and the coating of the exposed metal, within 4 hours, with primer followed by two undercoats and finally two topcoats of the distinctive 'Forth Bridge Red' paint. The original lead-based paint was replaced with an iron-oxide-based primer and undercoat, and vinyl-alkyl-based topcoat. Where possible the undercoats and topcoats are normally sprayed on to ensure even coverage. In 1993, in an effort to save money, the owners of the bridge Railtrack were reported in *The Times* as suspending the maintenance programme for a year (Bowditch 1993). However, in 1994, £3 million was spent strengthening and renewing the railway line running over the bridge thus allowing trains to traverse the bridge at 50 rather than the previous 20 mph. In 1995 there continued to be concerns expressed about the state of repair of the bridge (Linklater 1995; Jowitt 1995) and in 1996 *The*

Times reported that Railtrack had been ordered by the Health and Safety Executive to start an emergency maintenance programme or risk prosecution (*The Times* 1996). The impression given was that the owners Railtrack had cut the maintenance schedule to a minimum, and that consequently much of the steelwork was not being repainted for long periods, a measure which Railtrack were quoted as suggesting was 'a cosmetic job' (Linklater 1995). This was clearly not an accurate description of a steel structure in a marine environment. Following a review in 1996–7 Railtrack announced a £40 million programme of repairs and repainting for the bridge running up to the year 2001, followed by an annual maintenance and repainting programme (Railtrack 1997).

Though described by William Morris as 'the supremest specimen of all ugliness' (*The Sunday Times* 1995), its designer and more recent art critics have seen it as a structure of beauty and merit (Black 1997). Historic Scotland have recognized its prominence in the national psyche of Scotland and listed the structure. Although listing as an ancient monument gives only minimal protection, it is a recognition that this bridge is a significant element of Scottish history and as such the original nature of the structure is important and should be retained in its present form and colour. This was clearly understood by Railtrack who retained the original paint colouring in the final coat of their revised 1989 repainting regime.

Once people start to treasure any particular part of the past, it ceases to be retained purely for its functionality, it is also retained for its meaning, its aesthetic impact and its value as an historic document. This raises the question: 'To what extent is the repainting of the Forth Railway Bridge an act of conservation?' The functionality of the structure is not a significant issue. The Sistine Chapel, subject of one of the most extensive conservation programmes of recent decades, is also still a functioning building fulfilling its original role as a chapel. Scale is not relevant, as ancient monuments of the scale of Hadrian's Wall and the Great Wall of China indicate. The constant repainting of the structure undoubtedly preserves the Forth Railway Bridge, and though the original paint is lost in the shot-blasting, the steelwork is retained through this process and the original colour and finish of the object is clearly restored through the cleaning and repainting process. It would appear that every effort is being made to preserve the aesthetic entity and the informative activity of the bridge, conserving it as a working object.

In the case of the Forth Railway Bridge the maintenance bill is huge and at present can only be met whilst this bridge is part of a functioning railway. No heritage agency can fund the cost of sixteen full-time painters working on a single monument. Smaller bridges, such as the iron bridge at Ironbridge Gorge, have been seen as ancient monuments of a scale which can be successfully conserved purely as monuments. Only when the Forth Railway Bridge ceases to be a functioning railway bridge will we find out if the public of Scotland treasure it sufficiently to see it conserved and are prepared to meet the full cost of preservation.

11 Preventive conservation
Storage, environment and legal protection

11.1 Preventive conservation

Preventive conservation includes all measures taken to preserve an object short of specific interaction with the physical form of the object. Thus preventive conservation includes:

- Managing object risk: assessing the risks posed to objects by display, movement, storage, loan, and limiting those risks (Keene 1996). Techniques such as building assessments, condition assessments, disaster plans, loan agreements, handling policies and limiting the use of working objects may be used to manage and minimize risk to objects.

- Environmental control: all procedures to place the object in a secure location surrounded by a benign environment, which includes using stable materials to confer physical support and protection to the object. Seeking to minimize the interaction with the surrounding environment (e.g. through preserving objects *in situ* within their burial environment). Limiting the temperature fluctuation, light levels and the access to harmful gases and insects in museum environments.

- Legal protection: the creation and implementation of laws which protect objects, whether buried or in collections, from theft and despoliation.

Interventive conservation involves cleaning an object (see Chapter 7), and this imposes a view upon the object. Preventive conservation imposes no view seeking only to preserve the object in its present chemical and physical form.

11.2 Storage

As part of a museum collection, objects gain a value beyond their financial worth. As museum objects they are intended to be preserved for ever – for study, display or loan – and have information permanently associated with them. The term value is used, hereafter, to refer to the value of the object to the museum in terms of evidence of the past, a potential object for display and educative use.

The purpose of storage is to retain objects as a source of information, education and display, by preserving them in as near as possible their present condition. This can be seen at its simplest as putting a broken chair away in an attic to prevent further damage. If the chair is not valuable, the risk of loss or damage (stacking, dust, insects) in the attic may be seen as

Collection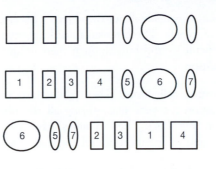

Catalogued collection

Categorized collections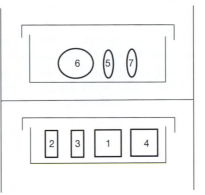

Stored collections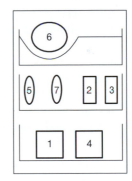

Well-stored collections

Figure 11.1 Levels of storage.

acceptable. As the object rises in value then it becomes more important to store it carefully and safely ensuring that it is both well preserved and readily retrievable.

A series of increasingly protective and useful levels of storage can be defined (see Figure 11.1):

- Collection: Initially objects are collected. This prevents their loss, deliberate damage or disposal. There remains risk of environmental and physical damage to the objects, objects are difficult to find and they have little purpose or meaning.

- Catalogued collection: Every object is uniquely identified and a written record of information is made about the object. This enables the collection to be of use to a wide range of people. There remains a risk of environmental and physical damage. Objects are difficult to find but, through their unique identifier, can be correlated with their information.

- Categorized collections: These collections are categorized to aid storage, object or information recovery (e.g. storing all the objects of a similar type, or from a single location, together). There remains a risk of environmental and physical damage, but objects and information are relatively easy to find.

- Stored collections: These collections are given some protection against physical and environmental damage. Large objects are draped with dust sheets to prevent dust and light raining down on the object; smaller objects are boxed. Such measures reduce handling and physical damage to objects, insulate the object against changes in temperature and humidity and reduce accessibility for insect pests and unnecessary human inspection. Objects are placed on shelves or on pallets to lift them above the floor surface and the risk of flood damage. Improved security reduces the risk of theft. Storage locations are numbered (building, room, aisle, bay, shelf, box) and a summary of the contents of the box, aisle, room, etc. is marked on the outside of the container.

- Well-stored collections: These collections will have their environment monitored and modified to meet the recommended conditions for storage. There will be an even density of objects through the storage space to maximize the modified storage environment. Storage materials used are inert and pose no threat to the collection. Often the object is stored with regard to the material of which it is composed in specialized conditions (e.g. archaeological ironwork stored at low humidities to prevent further corrosion). Many objects will sit in specifically made or shaped support to provide the highest level of protection, which results in objects only being stored in a specific location. Such 'specific-location storage' is most appropriate for high-value objects, so that if an object is missing the loss is quickly noticed, or fragile items where specifically designed and constructed storage is crucial to the continued well-being of the object. All storage locations are marked on object records and the contents of every box, shelf, bay, aisle and room are summarized on the exterior of the container.

The construction of a special storage support and container is always an important element in the conservation process. It provides a strong visual cue, emphasizing to the curator or owner how valuable the object is and indicating the need to care for the object. Only through using the specifically shaped storage support and container will the object be stored 'in the approved manner'. If it is more difficult or awkward to store the object in other ways, the simple correct method will be used.

Costs

Bringing objects into a museum collection, cataloguing them and providing storage materials and facilities gives rise to costs. The higher the level of storage the greater the cost. In practice a cost–benefit analysis is unconsciously performed for every object which goes into store: benefit from storing the object being considered greater than the cost of storing it. Storage costs are composed of:

- Building: rent, rates (local taxes), services, security, maintenance, heating, cleaning, environmental monitoring and control.

- Materials: storage boxes, acid-free tissue, shelving, purpose-made supports, computers or cards for recording.

- Time: curator to catalogue; museum assistant, volunteer or conservator to store; curator or museum assistant to retrieve object when required.

The higher the object's value the greater the extent to which the benefits of storage outweigh the costs. Thus high levels of storage costs are seen as justifiable for valuable objects such as 'old-master' paintings.

The costs of collecting and storage are appreciable (Lord *et al.* 1989) This has led to recording rather than collection and storage for some large objects. There has also been the experimental practice of reburying waterlogged archaeological wooden objects in naturally occurring waterlogged conditions (Fry 1996; Jesperson 1985).

Condition assessment

With limited resources it is important to have information so that judgements can be made on how the limited resources can be used most effectively. Questions such as:

- Are the objects stable in the present environment?

- What objects or type of objects are degrading fastest, or under greatest threat of decay, in this environment?

- Should a small number of objects be stored well or a larger number of objects be stored at a more basic level.

Such decisions, when consciously made, arise from object-condition assessments for the collection. Which objects in a large collection should receive conservation or have improved storage is a difficult judgement to make. Since the human brain can only consider up to seven variables efficiently (see Chapter 1), there is a natural tendency to coalesce or 'chunk' information, leading to stereotyping and inaccurate assessment when faced with thousands of objects. The condition assessment aids judgement by breaking the process down into a series of small steps, each with a limited number of variables (so encouraging accurate assessment) which is given a numerical score. Then comparison of the numerical scores permits the accurate selection of the objects needing the required action (conservation, re-storage, etc.). Keene (1996) has summarized the approaches which formal condition assessments or collection audits can take. In such audits the nature of the collection, its level of decay, its need for conservation and storage are assessed, usually through an appropriate sampling. From such audits the requirements of the collection can be prioritized and limited resources appropriately allocated.

Dollery (1994) has shown how, in the National Museum of Wales, condition assessment and curatorial assessment (grading of the object in terms of research importance and display potential) of the collection is combined to derive a comprehensive assessment factor for determining prioritization of conservation and storage resources. This ensures that an object which is seen as likely to degrade and has high archaeological value is given conservation treatment first, whilst stable objects of little archaeological value are treated last. Such audits give a prioritized order for storage or conservation treatment. Financial resources usually limit the speed at which the collection moves towards good storage conditions and being fully conserved.

Both Keene and Dollery have demonstrated the importance of only collecting useful information (e.g. through carefully defining the purpose of the condition survey/collection audit prior to collecting the information). Every condition survey is thus uniquely adapted or designed for its purpose. It is important to seek high levels of objectivity in condition surveys, through standardizing and defining terms, ensuring that a limited number of trained assessors carry out the process. All assessors should be initially trained or calibrated on a control group of objects so that they all record the same objects in the same condition in the same way. It is also important to retain detachment and avoid becoming distracted into improving object-storage conditions during the survey process.

Use and risk

The level of use of objects within stores can vary tremendously. A small number of objects are frequently used for display and are favourite subjects for researchers and curatorial interest. Most objects are researched or displayed on a very occasional basis, whilst others are virtually never seen, requested for research or put on display. Many paper archives, archaeological finds (particularly ceramic sherds and bone), fossils and other natural-history-specimen collections fall into this final category. These objects remain crucially important evidence for the way in which the past is interpreted and understood, though their level of use is very limited. Careful storage of this material has allowed present-day researchers to reanalyse objects (e.g. DNA information to be retrieved from ancient bones and organic residues to be extracted from ancient cooking pots), which has enabled us to reassess our interpretations of the past. In practice, however, the level of use is often the most significant factor in determining the level of storage an object receives, rather than any collection condition assessment or curatorial assessment.

Where the risk of damage to an object may increase (e.g. through going on loan, becoming part of a travelling exhibition, or being a frequently researched object), then the need to reduce that risk through improving storage conditions is apparent. Consequently higher levels of storage (e.g. shaped supports for the object and environmental monitoring and control) are used for objects which travel or go out on loan. Such specialized storage is often paid for by the institution receiving the loan or mounting the exhibition.

11.3 Black-box standard

The theoretical ideal for storing any object is in a black box. Such a theoretical box represents secure storage, insulation against temperature and RH (relative humidity) fluctuation, a barrier against harmful gases, light, insect pests and a barrier to being handled by human beings (Frost 1994). The box is labelled so the contents are known and can be retrieved. It represents the ideal environment for whatever it contains and every object's black-box standard is potentially different. Any actual object-storage environment can be compared with the black-box standard. Though, theoretically, storage approaching absolute zero $-273°C$, at which all chemical reactions cease, may be seen as the black-box standard, such conditions are costly and not practical (see Section 8.4), and less extreme conditions are more usefully considered as a workable black-box standard.

The need for human beings to interact with objects and the requirements for display has resulted in work to define modified ideal storage and display conditions where rates of decay are low enough to be barely perceptible. Probably the nearest to such environments were those created for storing Britain's national collections of art and artefacts during the World War II. After initial storage in the Aldwych Underground tunnels the British Museum collections were moved to the Bath stone quarry at Westwood. It had taken many months to achieve a stable RH because of the porous limestone of the Westwood quarry which had to be sealed and a refrigeration dehumidification system installed. Finally, when stable conditions had been established, the collections were moved during 1941–2. The National Gallery stored their collections in buildings specially constructed in the huge caverns of the slate quarry at Manod in North Wales. These buildings used heated air to control RH and managed to achieve a near constant 58 per cent RH and 63°F. These conditions were very stable and regarded as far better than those at the National Gallery (Haynes 1993, see Case study 9B).

The clearest attempt to define such standards in scientific terms and bring them together into a coherent form was the work of Gary Thomson of the National Gallery in London who published *The Museum Environment* in 1978. He proposed the first series of environmental conditions for objects, identifying that incorrect levels of humidity, light, temperature, pollutant gases, etc. would damage objects. His recommendations have been widely adopted throughout the museum world (see Figure 11.2). As a result of increased understanding of the nature of decay processes and advances in technology, research and management techniques, conservators should now be able to use their judgement to achieve better or more cost-effective environmental conditions for objects.

- Though the concept of specification of environmental standards gained acceptance in the 1980s, concern for the welfare of objects often led to absurdly narrow levels being specified. These could not even be accurately monitored, let alone achieved (Ashley-Smith *et al.* 1994). In the early 1990s work by Michalski and colleagues at CCI (Canadian Conservation Institute) (Michalski 1993) and Erhardt at The Smithsonian Institution (Erhardt and Mecklenburg 1994) demonstrated that cycling of RH in the mid-range does not damage most objects. Only extremely high or low RH will lead to direct damage of objects and materials especially stressed, jointed or composite objects.

- Work on environmental standards has led to the establishment of UK national standards for the storage and care of a range of types of museum object (MGC 1992, 1993a, 1993b, 1994, 1995a, 1996, 1998a, 1998b) as well as for the contents of archives BS 5454.

- It is the total dosage of light which determines the level of light damage to an object. There is increasing use of the concept of annual light dosage (annual exposure limit) and lifetime light dosages, rather than merely using light levels. There is no need for objects to be illuminated when not on public display. A 50-lux light level for the viewing public's 7-hour day (10.00 a.m.–5.00 p.m.) translates to 350 lux hours which, over a 6-day week and a 52-week year gives an annual dose of 109,200 lux hours, normally expressed as 100 klux hours. For more robust objects, annual exposure limits of 450 klux hours equate to display light levels of circa 200 lux (Cassar 1995). Though Saunders (1997) suggests that 200 lux can lead to annual exposure limits of 600 klux hours.

Figure 11.2 Conservator Alice Thompson monitoring the environment of the Hatton Gallery, University of Newcastle upon Tyne using a thermohygrograph (photograph by the author).

- Thomson's initial limits for UV radiation: 75 microwatts per lumen (Thomson 1978) were set to try and achieve a workable standard for museums in the 1970s. However, modern UV filters, lighting systems and monitoring devices mean that much lower levels of 20 microwatts per lumen or lower are often readily achievable.

- The testing of materials used in museum display and storage, see Section 8.3, has become routine and has indicated a wide range of problems exist. In addition to the inorganic pollutant gases such as sulphur dioxide, nitrogen oxides and ozone, volatile organic compounds (VOC) given off by many modern materials (e.g. through off-gassing as materials dry, harden and set, loss of plasticizer, degradation of polymers and emissions from wood, fibre and particle boards such as MDF (Thickett 1998)), are posing an increasing threat to objects. The need for greater accuracy and a more rigorous approach by conservators using materials-testing procedures such as the 'Oddy Tests' has been demonstrated (Blackshaw and Daniels 1979; Lee and Thickett 1996).

- Appreciation of the degradative effect of oxygen has led to the development of special-ized oxygen-free storage (Lambert *et al.* 1992; Gilberg and Grattan 1994). Creating such conditions is expensive and is thus reserved for valuable objects and those, such as degrading polymers, for which it is the only solution.

- Insect pests are now monitored and managed through housekeeping regimes and quarantines rather than periodic mass extermination. This reduces risks to the collec-tion and the risk, through fumigant and insecticide toxicity, to the conservator and others (Child and Pinniger 1994, 1987).

- As the detrimental effects of human beings on objects becomes more clearly appre-ciated (i.e. 'we are bad for objects'), the level of contact between objects and humans is increasingly managed and limited. Boxing, bagging and covering objects kept in dark stores discourages unnecessary contact. Creating easily accessible and informative records provides an alternative to examining objects. Ensuring the labelling of boxes, shelves, bays, aisles and rooms, the use of handling protocols, such as using gloves, limits human–object contact. Preventing any curator obtaining access to the objects needed for research or display purposes would negate the purpose of storing the object in the first place and is thus unacceptable. However, the suppression of casual, un-necessary and unspecified use of objects greatly enhances their chances of survival.

- Appreciation of the damage caused to objects during disasters such as fires and floods has led to the development of 'disaster plans' for almost all UK museums and historic houses. After an initial assessment of the likelihood of the museum and its collection to suffer a disaster and the implementation of mitigation measures to minimize such an occurrence, a 'disaster plan' is created. This details the procedures to be followed in the event of a disaster together with appropriate plans, information, suppliers' addresses, etc. A 'disaster team', the individuals who will enact the disaster plan, is assembled and trained and a stockpile of appropriate equipment created (Keene 1996).

- Maximizing the best storage and display conditions for the objects, which can be achieved for minimal cost, can be achieved through techniques such as:

  - Zonation of buildings – distributing objects through a building so they are in the most appropriate conditions which that building has to offer and improving the building's environments to offer an enhanced and extended range of storage and display environments (Cassar 1995).
  - Building envelopes – giving increased environmental protection to objects through increasing the number of barriers: building, room, case, box between the object and the exterior (Cassar 1995).

Loss rates: All the environmental factors mentioned above, such as light and polluting gases taken over a long time period (e.g. 100 years), lead to the loss of objects. This can be expressed as an annual loss rate (see Section 12.4). However, as Waller (1994) indicated in addition to the category of 'gradual damage' (large-scale minor damage through agencies such as light and RH), objects are also lost through 'severe sporadic loss' (insect infestations, loss of objects and water leaks which can badly damage small numbers of objects) and 'occasional catastrophe' (flood and fire damaging large numbers of objects). All these categories can express loss of objects through annual loss rate, giving a single factor which can be used for assessing the greatest threat to the collections and the most cost-effective use of limited resources (see Section 12.4). It can even be used to compare the loss rate of objects in museums with those buried (or reburied) in the ground.

11.4 Preservation through legislation: Buried objects

Archaeological objects buried in the ground have two values, both as individual objects and as part of a picture of the past in association with all the other objects in the ground and the stratigraphy which interrelates them. Any object removed from the ground without being properly excavated and recorded loses all the associated information. Most countries had, by the late twentieth century, realized that the archaeological past is finite and that archaeological excavation is expensive. Therefore they have sought to protect objects in the ground by passing legislation which protects archaeological sites and their precious contents. The appreciation of the need for such measures increased through the nineteenth and twentieth centuries, though it occurred at slightly different rates throughout the world. A summary of legislation to protect the archaeological heritage has been compiled by Cleere (Cleere 1984).

The earliest protection for archaeological sites and their contents emerged in the developing nationalism of the nineteenth century. The first such protection was created in Denmark, where a royal decree in 1807 set up protection for over 200 designated ancient monuments and recognized the need to preserve medieval churches and other public buildings from being destroyed (Kristiansen 1984). In Britain the Ancient Monuments Protection Act was passed in 1882 giving powers to take ancient monuments into 'guardianship' and creating the post of Inspector of Ancient Monuments. This bill gave very limited powers since all agreements for guardianship required the land owner's permission.

Up to the early twentieth century Britain gave less protection to its ancient monuments than any other country in Europe. The sale in 1911 of Tatershall Castle to an American who proposed demolishing it and re-erect it brick by brick in the USA enhanced moves in the UK for further protection for archaeological sites. This resulted in the 1913 Ancient Monuments Consolidation and Amendment Act (Champion 1996). This act created an Ancient Monuments Board to; advise the Commissioners, issue preservation orders to prevent destruction of important ancient sites and create a list (schedule) of important ancient monuments, which required an owner to give notice of any intention to demolish (Champion 1996). By 1931 over 3,000 sites had been scheduled, but it was not until the 1979 Ancient Monument and Archaeological Areas Act that preservation orders were scrapped and the concept of an owner requiring consent to alter or demolish a scheduled ancient monument was instituted. This change to 'a presumption to preserve' also made it an offence to use a metal detector or disturb the ground of a scheduled ancient monument. In 1932 the Town and Country Planning Act created protection for historic buildings. These provisions were strengthened in the 1944 and 1947 Town and Country Planning Acts which introduced the concept of 'listing' large numbers of important historic properties and, if necessary, preserving buildings against the owner's wishes (Cleere 1984). The concept of listing established the presumption of historic buildings remaining *in situ*. By 1997 legislation has protected 16,918 ancient monuments in England through scheduling and 363,788 buildings through listing.

The realization of the importance of context has prompted a more profound approach to the preservation of the nation's past by national-heritage agencies. The primary approach is now to leave the evidence of the past *in situ* (English Heritage 1991). Consequently research is now directed at detecting archaeological sites and protecting them, through scheduling or local-management agreements, and preserving the burial environment, through monitoring water-tables (Corfield 1993) and subsurface chemistry (Caple *et al.* 1997). Following the 'presumption of (the retention of) archaeological deposits *in situ*' as the norm (English Heritage 1991), the concept of 'the polluter pays' entered the area of cultural heritage in the UK with the introduction of Planning Policy Guidance Note 16 (PPG 16) issued in 1990. This requires developers to meet the full cost of archaeological assessment and, if destruction cannot be avoided, the costs of archaeological excavation. Thus whilst the owner of the land may continue to own the objects recovered from the ground, as a result of PPG 16, the knowledge about the past (information derived from excavation) must enter the public domain and is public property.

Elsewhere in the world the 1956 UNESCO Recommendations on International Principles Applicable to Archaeological Excavations resulted in many countries adopting two forms of protection:

- Declaring that all objects buried in the soil were the property of the state.

- Declaring that licences were required to undertake archaeological excavation and any excavation without a licence was illegal.

Though potentially more powerful than British laws on protection of archaeological sites, the problems with such severe legislation is in effective implementation and policing.

11.5 Preservation through legislation: Historic objects

In the UK, unlike many other countries, there is no law giving protection either to objects of national importance or archaeological artefacts (Tubb 1995; Tubb and Sease 1996). In Greece, Italy, Turkey, Cyprus, Tunisia, Belize and Kenya for example all archaeological artefacts recovered from the soil are legally the property of the state (O'Keefe 1995). In these countries illegal excavation and removal of objects from the ground automatically constitutes theft of state property. There are also laws in some countries, such as Spain or Australia, to prevent export of items of 'cultural property' – objects which are seen as important in the history of the country and part of the nation's heritage. Attempts to export such objects without proper licences and authorization constitutes a crime and results in the property automatically reverting to the state (O'Keefe 1995). The only limitations on the export of antiquities or objects of cultural heritage such as paintings from the United Kingdom come from The Waverley Rules which dictate that export licences are required for historic objects over a certain value (£39,600 in 1993–4) and which have been in the UK for over 50 years or antiquities recovered from British soil or territorial waters (Morrison 1995). Those objects which have important cultural, historic or archaeological value will normally be denied an export licence provided a British museum or gallery can match the sale price.

There have been international attempts to halt the looting of ancient sites and the illegal export of antiquities. In the 1970 UNESCO 'Convention on the Means of Prohibiting and Precluding the Illicit Import, Export and Transfer of Ownership of Cultural Property' (Clement 1995) required the signatories to take steps to recover and return illicitly imported artefacts. There are eighty-one signatories to this convention include the USA, Canada, Australia. However, many European states, including the UK, Germany, France and the Netherlands did not sign because, it was claimed, of problems implementing this convention within the national legislation.

EU (European Union) countries, including the UK, are now bound to implement the European Council Directorate on 'Return of Cultural Objects Unlawfully Removed from the Territory of a Member State and Regulations on the Export of Cultural Goods'. This requires that all EU states will, when requested by another state, recover and return national treasures (artistic, historic and archaeological) removed from the host country at any time after 1 January 1993. The host country is required to reimburse the expenses of the country undertaking the recovery. This legislation is cumbersome and must be conducted on a state-to-state basis. More recently (1995) more practical legislation designed to be used by individuals seeking to recover property has been drafted – the UNIDROIT 'Convention on Stolen and Illegally Exported Cultural Objects' (Prott 1995). The UK has yet (1999) to ratify this convention.

The weak British legislation protecting items of cultural heritage and the strong laws on property ownership, which generally consider purchase 'in good faith' sufficient legal title to own almost any object, mean that a large market dealing in the purchase and sale of antiques, antiquities and works of art has become established in London. This market claims it deals principally in foreign antiquities, quoting that it required only ninety-eight licences to export under The Waverley Rules in 1992–3 (Morrison 1995). However, given the extensive limitations on excavation and export of objects from other countries, it has been suggested that 60 per cent or even 80 per cent of the antiquities in the antiquities trade come from illegal excavations or are illegally exported (Elia 1995).

Though objects in the ground and those of national value do enjoy some protection through existing legislation, it is clear that there are large numbers of illegal objects currently in circulation. This indicates that the problems lie principally in enforcing the existing legislation. In addition to the many illegally excavated and exported objects, there are also stolen goods. Despite museums and private collectors having substantial levels of security (Hoare 1990; Dovey 1992), objects are still stolen. Beyond physical security measures there are also agencies and publications to aid the recovery of stolen property. Publications such as the magazine *Trace* and *The Yearbook of Stolen Art*, databases such as the 'International Art and Antiquities Loss Register' and 'Thesaurus', and organizations such as the Council for the Prevention of Art Theft and the Art and Antiquities Unit at New Scotland Yard, all seek to aid in the recovery of stolen art and antiquities (Palmer 1995). Stolen or looted objects are often damaged and require conservation work (see Section 13.6).

In the United Kingdom, as in almost everywhere else in the world, even if an object is owned by, or in the care of, a national museum, local museum or an organization, such as The National Trust, there is no legal framework governing its care or treatment. Standards are slowly starting to be established in the UK through a national registration scheme for museums. This was first instituted in 1988 and is administered by the Museums and Galleries Commission. It requires museums to have strict guidelines regarding acquisition and disposal and is seeking to raise standards of object care and curation. Registered status is essential in order to receive government grants (Longman 1992).

11.6 Preservation *in situ*

Buildings and objects are unconsciously preserved where they were built or deposited *in situ*, if there is no subsequent development to sweep them away. Examples include the city of Charleston (South Carolina) which had a remarkable 3,600 intact historic buildings in the 1980s as a result of the poverty and consequent lack of development which gripped the southern states of the USA in the decades following the Civil War (Brand 1994).

The desire to leave or preserve monuments *in situ* has existed ever since antiquarians began to excavate and remove objects from the ground to museums. Austin Layard, the excavator of the Palace of Nimrud, was preparing in 1848 to move the huge winged-beast gate portals back to the British Museum. He was troubled by the decision to move them from their original position. It seemed almost sacrilege to 'tear them from their old haunts to make them a mere wonder stock to the busy crowd of a new world. They were better suited to the desolation around them for they had guarded the palace in its glory and it was for them to watch over its ruin' (Chamberlin 1979). Antiquities plucked from their original location for display back in the museums of the European capitals of the nineteenth century may have fuelled the interest in the past, but it was also clear that the objects lost much of their impact and meaning when removed from their original location.

Museums reacted by trying to recreate the impact which objects had *in situ* by constructing dioramas and naturalistic settings for their objects which made them appear in context. As early as 1938 this extended to the creation of a whole Victorian street scene 'Kirkgate' at the York Castle Museum. This tradition has been carried through to the present day with the creation of whole villages and landscapes such those at Beamish and the Welsh Folk Museum at St Fagans. This desire for a holistic view of the past has in recent years led organizations such as the National Trust to acquire not simply historic houses, but the landscape which surrounds them and of which they are an integral part.

The emergent interest in historic buildings and concern at the loss of the impact and information when objects were removed to the museum led to increasing attempts through the twentieth century to leave ancient buildings and artefacts *in situ*. This concept of the importance of the setting (see Sections 3.5, 9.1 and 10.1), is perhaps most apparent with mosaics, wall paintings and architectural and sculptured building details. Practice in the 1990s is, wherever possible, to preserve the building and the decorative details within it. Approaches to preserving buildings, their features and contents *in situ* include:

- Making the building sound, preserving all features and maintaining a modern use for the building which can help fund its upkeep; for example, Durham Castle is now part of the University of Durham or Peninsula Barracks, Winchester which have been converted to residential use (English Heritage 1998).

- Making the building sound, preserving all features and contents and attracting the general public to see the building and its contents. Through paying money the general public help fund the upkeep of the building and its contents (e.g. Chatsworth House).

- A government grant or agency funding the preservation of the building and its contents as a national treasure. This usually requires the building to permit public access (e.g. National Maritime Museum, Greenwich), though this can be on a limited basis.

- Reburying ruined or partially demolished buildings. This formed an effective solution in the case of the Roman villa at Woodchester in Gloucestershire (Wilson 1975), where the building was too costly to fully excavate and display. Consequently the mosaic floors and remnant walls were preserved through reburial under a generous layer of white sand, earth and turf.

- Ruined or partially demolished buildings can have a museum built over or around them (e.g. the Roman Palace of Fishbourne).

- Ruined or partially demolished buildings can form an open-air display. Whether in rainswept Britain or sundrenched Greece weather dictates that only robust stone structures such as ruined temples, abbeys or castles with minimal decorative features – such as The Parthenon (Athens), Fountains Abbey (Yorkshire) or Dryslwyn Castle (Dyfed) – are likely to survive such treatment.

- Many medieval and later buildings have been dismantled and re-erected in folk parks such as Avoncroft Museum of Historic Buildings, National Museum of Wales Folk Museum at St Fagans and the Ulster Folk Park Museum. Gathered together in such locations these buildings have an appropriate, if not original, context. Though this process has saved many buildings and objects, it falls short of the desirable aim of preserving the building or object in its original setting. There are several notable examples of this technique.

  By 1968 the London Bridge built by John Rennie in 1831 was insufficiently large or stable to carry the heavy flow of modern traffic and was to be replaced. It was purchased for just over £1 million by the McCulloch Oil Company and re-erected in Lake Havasu City. The bridge's fixtures and fittings and its granite cladding were stripped and sent to the USA, where it was attached to a concrete core, rather than the rubble core of the original. The moving and re-erection cost a further £2 million. During the 1970s the bridge attracted over 2 million tourists per year to Lake Havasu City, to which it was a source of much pride as well as tourism income (Chamberlin 1979). This piece of the past has been 'preserved', though in a new setting. These actions have been variously described as conservation, restoration and renovation, but are more accurately described as relocation and re-erection.

  In the 1960s, the massive temple of Rameses II, cut into the rock face at Abu Simbel in Upper Egypt, was threatened by the waters of Lake Nasser, which were rising fast behind the newly constructed Aswan High Dam (Chamberlin 1979). Numerous expensive and impractical schemes had been suggested to save the temple from inundation. Eventually a Swedish engineering firm Vattenbyggnodsbyron (VBB) developed and implemented a scheme where, behind a large coffer dam which was constructed to protect the temple from the rising water, the whole of the temple and associated rock face was cut into blocks of 20–30 tons, consolidated if necessary, had lifting bolts inserted which were adhered using epoxy resin and were hoisted 300 ft to a new site above the water. Here an artificial hill was created and the temple reassembled into it. The joints between each block were left visible so that evidence of the disassembly and re-erection of the monument is obvious to modern visitors (Chamberlin 1979).

- Some buildings only have their shell retained with much of the internal structure altered to accommodate new uses. This is usually the only means by which even the shell can be preserved; for example, the cluster of 1930s cylindrical concrete grain silos in Akron, Ohio, which were converted to form a hotel (Brand 1994).

- Ruined or partially demolished buildings – if too badly damaged, if insufficient funds are available for other forms of preservation or if demolition is planned ahead of development – can have their decorative features such as wall paintings removed to a museum, the building is recorded and then demolished.

The preservation of buildings or monuments *in situ* throws up a plethora of ethical (Matero 1993) and technical problems (Ashurst and Dimes 1990; Ashurst and Ashurst 1988). There remains a constant series of threats to the structure from the weather and from visitors. Whilst it is nessesary to attract visitors to the site in order to pay for the upkeep of the site, large numbers of visitors can generate considerable problems.

- Egyptian tombs. Attempts have been made to stabilize the structures of the tombs and their wall paintings. However, this has proved difficult to achieve as a result of the instability of the structure, soluble salts pushing off the surfaces of the wall paintings and the damaging effect of numerous visitors touching the walls and wearing away the floor (see Section 2.6). This has led to the closure of the most dangerous and easily damaged tombs and restricted visiting to many others.

- Lascaux. This French cave with its famous palaeolithic cave paintings was, by the 1970s, suffering from too many visitors, whose warm wet breath together with the lights installed in order to make the images visible, was encouraging the growth of moulds and algae over the paintings. To preserve the art the cave was closed to tourists and all but the most serious scholars. An exact replica of the cave with exact copies of the paintings was built nearby in order that the visitor can 'experience' the paintings within the cave environment.

- The National Trust experienced such large numbers of visitors at a number of its properties that it was degrading the experience for the individual visitor and placing the house and contents at increased risk of accidental damage and wear and tear (see Section 2.6). To reduce the visitor loads they stopped advertising some properties and reduced opening hours at others. At some properties which have limited visitor capacity (e.g. Mr Straw's House – a semi-detached house in Worksop preserved virtually intact with all fixtures and fittings from the 1930s), pre-booking and timed-entry tickets have been used to control visitor numbers (National Trust 1999). Other measures available, and utilized at some historic houses in private ownership, include convoying parties around the property and increasing admission charges. English Heritage has limited the use of some sites by not permitting the development of visitor facilities such as refreshments or car parking (Corfield, personal communication).

In recent years the concept of 'preservation *in situ*' has become more strictly applied amongst heritage organizations dealing with historic houses. Organizations such as English Heritage and The National Trust became conscious that their historic houses were being displayed in a repetitious style, with buildings or individual rooms restored to the fashion of a specific period. Consequently when the National Trust acquired Calke Abbey in 1985 (Colvin 1985) and when English Heritage acquired Brodsworth Hall in 1990 (English Heritage 1995), they sought to present these houses exactly 'as found'. Many private rooms which were filled with the junk of centuries were preserved in that state. These properties now demonstrate the country house in decline, suffering the problems of the rising cost of labour and falling income from estates experienced throughout the late nineteenth and twentieth centuries.

English Heritage have recently extended the concept of displaying 'as found' to their ancient monuments: Wigmore Castle in Herefordshire having been stabilized as a ruin on an overgrown hillside rather than being excavated and laid out with close cropped lawns between partially restored walls as had previously been the norm (Palmer 1999).

The increasing popularity for buildings and objects being seen *in situ* will result in an increasing requirement for conservators to safeguard buildings and objects in such environments. Consequently conservators need to develop the intellectual skills and technological expertise to advise on the sustainability of *in situ* preservation strategies. They must gain experience and develop their judgement in working with *in situ* sites, in order to advise and enhance the likely success of future *in situ* preservation projects.

11A   Case study: The Laetoli footprints (Demas *et al.* 1996; Agnew and Levin 1996; Agnew and Demas 1998)

In 1978–9 Dr Mary Leakey uncovered the footprints of a hominid, an early australopithecine, in the bedrock at Laetoli in Tanzania. They are 3.6–3.75 million years old and present the earliest and most important evidence of bipedalism in early hominids. The hominid tracks had been made, together with those of numerous animals, in wet volcanic ash which had then set hard so preserving the impressions. These impressions showed that the foot which made them had a raised arch, rounded heel, pronounced ball, forward pointing big toe and was thus very similar to a modern human foot. This demonstrates that bipedalism was almost fully evolved in early hominids of this date and was one of the earliest human traits to develop (Renfrew and Bahn 1991). Evidence of movement and soft-tissue form are both extremely rare in the study of early hominids, which is normally confined to the study of small scraps of fossilized bone. The footprints run in two tracks for over 27 m and contain over seventy individual prints. The principal track was made by a large individual with a stride length of 0.87 m, beside it walked a smaller individual. It is possible that a third individual followed the pair, walking in the footprints of the large individual.

After the footprints had been excavated and fully recorded, the tracks were covered over with loose soil capped with a layer of boulders in order to prevent damage to the site by the feet of cattle and elephants. In 1992 the condition of the trackway was re-assessed. The boulders had created shade and a condensation trap, which had led to the growth of acacia trees whose roots were now found to be damaging the trackway footprints (see Figure 11.3).

In 1992, the options for preserving the footprints were considered:

- It would be very costly to lift and transport the footprints to be stored, complete, in a museum. There is no museum big enough in Tanzania and thus a new one would need to be built.

- The rock which contains the footprints is friable, so lifting and transporting this rock would create a substantial risk to the well-being of these fossils.

- Creating open shelters to protect the footprints *in situ* has been shown, on other sites, not to work. Exposed or sheltered sites degrade very quickly.

Figure 11.3 The roots of acacia trees disturbing the trackway of 3.6-million-year-old human footprints, Laetoli, Tanzania (photograph courtesy of the Getty Conservation Institute, Los Angeles, California © *The J. Paul Getty Trust*).

- Laetoli is very remote and very few visitors are likely to come and see the foot-prints if they were on open display or in a museum at Laetoli.

- The footprints *in situ* have a context and a lot of associated information, such as associated animal hoof prints, the volcano which deposited the ash and the surrounding natural landscape. This would be lost should the trackway be moved.

- As part of the cultural heritage of the people of Tanzania, removal outside the country would neither be permitted nor was it desirable.

- The conservation of the trackway should be a solution which was viable and could be maintained by the existing authorities and people of Tanzania.

- Burial had proved effective preservation for the footprints for over 3 million years.

Consequently the best and most ethical solution was felt to be reburial since this preserves the footprints *in situ* ensuring that they retain their context and could be investigated in future if this was required.

In 1995, Site G, the southern end of the trackway which contained a 6.8-m-long stretch of the best (twenty-nine) footprints was re-excavated. Root damage from the acacia trees was fortunately limited to three of the footprints. The roots were carefully cut away and the friable tuff consolidated with an acrylic colloidal dispersion (Acrysol WS-24). The root voids were filled with Acrysol WS-24 and fumed silica. Any remaining root material was injected with a biocide and insecticide, both to kill off the root and remove any problem of potential infestation by termites. The footprints were recorded in great detail and fully resurveyed. They are not as clearly visible now as they were originally, because of the exposure upon excavation and the application of Bedacryl (polybutyral methacrylate) which was applied to consolidate the surface of the footprints prior to making casts of the footprints in 1979. This polymer could not be easily removed without potentially damaging the footprints so it was left in place.

To preserve the site it was provided with a covering which consisted of:

- Geotextile – a water-permeable long-lasting polypropylene textile, which will deflect any future root growth – marks the footprint horizon and protects the friable rock and sand beneath.

- Biobarrier – a polypropylene geotextile which has nodules that slowly release a long-acting root-growth inhibitor, 'Trifluralin', which will stop root growth but not kill off the plants and is largely insoluble and thus does not wash away.

- Sand from the Kakesio and Garusi rivers, in which the geotextile and biobarrier were seated. The sand was sieved so it contained no seeds or rocks, and has similar chemical and physical properties to the volcanic tuff rock so there should be no physical stress or chemical exchange between the rock and sand media.

- 'Enkamat' erosion-control matting to ensure that the sand was not lost, plus a second biobarrier layer.

- Local soil which was mounded up over the sand and geotextiles at an angle of 10–14° in order to deflect water away from the trackway.

- A substantial layer of lava boulders to provide physical protection from human and animal erosion.

These protection procedures were repeated in 1996 over the northern section of the hominid trackway. In addition:

- Laval-boulder banks were constructed to divert any rainwater run-off away from the site, so ensuring that there was no erosion of the site by running water.

- A committee of Tanzanian political representatives, national heritage officials and international experts was established to focus attention on the site and ensure that there is a mechanism for getting national and international assistance to the site if it is required.

- Employment of local people who have become involved with maintaining the site, both in terms of security and annually removing tree seedlings to limit any future damage to the site. Local-management agreements have become a feature of many of the successful arrangements for preserving sites throughout the world.

- The site was ceremonially adopted by the local Masai tribes as a sacred site. This raised its prominence and meaning to the people of the present day.

It is believed that a multiple strategy, involving both technical measures and monument management, will be the most likely chance of preserving the site intact for future generations. Conservation can be seen on this site to be working at numerous different levels.

12 Decisions

12.1 The nature of decision

When judgement uses specific options and outcomes, expresses the weighting factors as probabilities and leads to the selection of a specific course of action it is described as decision making. The development of the science or art of management in the 1970s led to the creation of theories and models concerning the making of decisions (Moore and Thomas 1976), many of them based on the mid-eighteenth century mathematical work on probability of Revd T. Baynes. Aspects of this work on formal decision making, such as decision trees, can be useful for considering conservation problems. Such consideration increases awareness of the range of possible options and helps estimate the probability of certain outcomes occurring more accurately. The responsibility for selecting and implementing the appropriate action rests, as it always has done, with the conservator.

Decision trees are perhaps the most useful decision/management tool for conservators. In any situation a number of actions are possible. These can be drawn as the first branches of the tree, not only the options of a number of actions (a), but also the options for not undertaking those actions ($1 - a$). Each action will have a number of outcomes, these are often expressed as probabilities. Where all probabilities are described they should sum to 1. At the end of this process, and there can be several steps of action and outcome, you arrive at a final outcome. The actions within this decision tree will cost money to enact and the costs for undertaking a particular course of action can be calculated. If all the aspects of the process are described in monetary terms, the outcome is a simple series of potential profits or losses. The route with the greatest profit can be selected, and is referred to as the highest EMV (expected monetary value). Alternatively the route with the least risk or the greatest return for the least investment can be selected (Moore and Thomas 1976). The objectives for conservation are invariably more complex.

12.2 Decision-tree example

In this example a simple mechanistic version of the decision tree process is used to explore the options which a conservator can face in deciding what course of action to recommend when cleaning archaeological ironwork. As with most models it is most easily understood when depicted in financial terms. Not all the options, especially not taking actions, are illustrated in the model.

A collection of 100 heavily corroded iron objects was retrieved from a medieval excavation (see Figure 12.1). They are brought into the laboratory by the archaeologist for assessment by the conservator. The archaeologist's objective is to identify the objects so

Figure 12.1 Cleaned archaeological ironwork from the medieval castle of Dryslwyn in West Wales (photograph courtesy of the author and Trevor Woods).

that they can help interpret the site. They are also interested in ensuring that they can be accurately drawn for the excavation report. A series of options for investigating and cleaning the objects are available at different costs. Using the estimates of likely success in identification these can be displayed as a decision tree (see Figure 12.2).

Costs: X-raying	£3.00 per object
Cleaning using an air-abrasive facility, total cleaning	£25.00 per object
Partial cleaning (tiger stripes) using an air-abrasive facility	£10.00 per object

The initial choice is between having all the objects X-rayed, at a cost of £300, or trying to visually identify them from the shape of the corroded lump (i.e. not X-rayed). This would not cost anything. At best 90 per cent or 0.9 of the objects will be identified using X-radiographs, at worst only 50 per cent or 0.5 of the objects will be identified. The visual-only analysis will yield approximately 20 per cent (0.2) identification at best and 2 per cent (0.02) at worst. The objects can then be cleaned in order to try and complete further identification. Since this is only for the purpose of identification, where 90 per cent of the objects are identified by X-ray only ten objects need to be cleaned. If totally cleaned then the costs would be $10 \times £25 = £250$ for cleaning, plus the £300 cost of X-raying, giving a total of £550. At best 80 per cent or 0.8 of the objects cleaned will be identified, at worst 40 per cent or 0.4. This option would thus yield a total of between 98 and 94 per cent of the objects identified, at a total cost for cleaning and X-raying of £550.

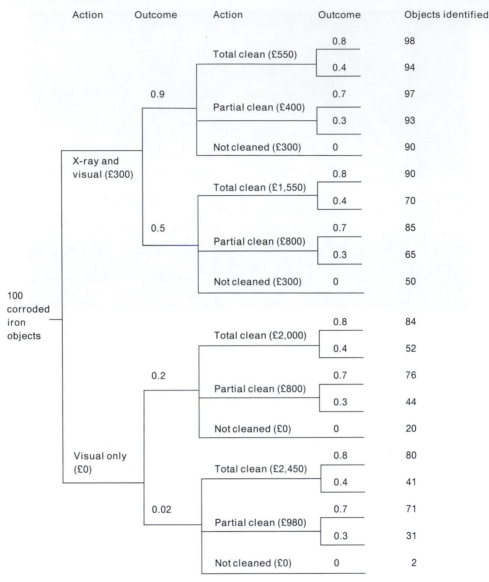

Figure 12.2 A decision tree for determining options for identifying 100 corroded iron objects. Since 100 objects were initially selected the final column can also be seen in percentage terms. In neither Figure 12.2 nor Figure 12.3 have all the outcomes been identified, and the costs are merely estimates for the purpose of calculation and are not real prices.

If partial cleaning rather than total cleaning were used it would yield 70 per cent identification at best, 30 per cent at worst. No cleaning will leave only the percentage identified by X-raying. If the X-raying had only limited success only 50 per cent would be identified and thus fifty objects would need to be cleaned at total cost of $50 \times £25.0 = £1,250$, plus £300 for X-raying, giving a total cost of £1,550. The percentage identification from cleaning will remain constant, thus 50 per cent (fifty objects) will be

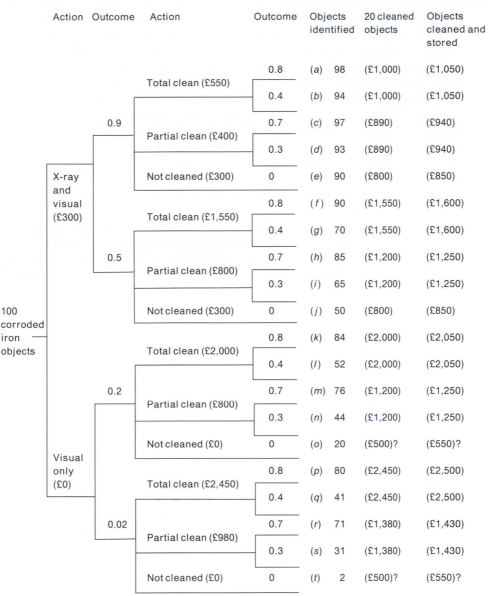

Figure 12.3 A decision tree for identifying, displaying and storing 100 corroded iron objects.

identified from X-radiographs plus fifty objects multiplied by 80 per cent (0.8) (totally cleaned) equals forty giving a total of ninety objects identified. Similar values of the number of identified objects can be established for every possible route in Figure 12.2. The poor levels of identification through not using X-raying and the necessity to clean large numbers of objects at high levels of expense are clarified using the decision tree. One uncertainty not resolved by the decision tree is the importance, or otherwise, of identifying an object. This will vary from site to site, and no single monetary value can easily be placed on it.

The model presented thus far is the simplest imaginable, where a single relationship of identification and its associated cost have been graphed. A more complete appreciation of the nature of the conservation process would include the costs of preparing objects for display or for preservation. If it was considered that twenty of the objects were required for display, this would involve totally cleaning twenty objects, ideally the 'most informative' from the assemblage. In Figure 12.3 the additional costs have been calculated and the option routes lettered. Where large numbers of objects have already been cleaned such as options (*k*) and (*l*) where eighty objects were totally cleaned, then you could select from these objects for display, thus there would be no additional cost. Options where there were only a few objects cleaned, such as options (*a*) and (*b*), additional objects would need cleaning. Since only ten objects were cleaned (the 10 per cent not identified by X-raying) only two of them are likely to form the 'most informative' 20 per cent of the collection. Thus a further eighteen objects should be cleaned with an additional $18 \times £25 = £450$ of additional expenditure. In the case of partially cleaned objects an additional £20 is likely to be charged for completing the cleaning. Thus for options (*c*) and (*d*) eighteen objects would need complete cleaning and two partially cleaned, an additional expenditure of £490. Whilst for options (*a*) to (*h*) a large percentage of the collection was identified and the most informative objects selected for cleaning, for options (*i*) and (*j*) only 65 and 50 per cent respectively of the collection have been identified. Though the cost has been calculated for twenty objects being cleaned, the low levels of identification mean that the 'most informative' objects will not have been selected. This problem becomes extreme for options (*o*) and (*t*) where very small numbers of objects have been identified and thus the twenty objects selected for cleaning will undoubtedly be far from the most informative. Consequently it is doubtful if cleaning objects with less than 70 per cent identified makes any sense for the museum or archaeologist paying for this work.

The processes involved in preservation comprise placing the objects in pierced polythene bags, and storing them with a desiccant, such as silica gel, in a sealed environment such as a polythene box, so maintaining a relative humidity (RH) less than 15 per cent which creates conditions that inhibit iron corrosion. Identification of the objects would allow a careful selection of which to retain, so time and effort is not expended storing hundreds of meaningless lumps of corroded iron, or relatively uninformative objects, such as nails. However, the costs involved in the storage process are low, both time and materials, circa £50 for 100 items, which would be only marginally reduced if only seventy or so were stored because thirty could be identified and discarded as uninformative. The greatest cost, over the period of the next 100 years, is the regular renewal of the silica-gel desiccant, which is necessary since water vapour slowly permeates through the walls of the polythene box (Horie and Francis 1984). The X-radiographs would also need to be stored properly (Walker 1990).

Whilst prices may vary, it can be seen from these estimates that certain processes appear much more cost effective in identifying objects. X-raying objects in order to identify them is clearly financially very effective and totally cleaning substantial numbers of objects is expensive. The nature of the objects, and the extent of their corrosion, will determine the ease with which they can be identified, and this has a considerable bearing on the costs. The differing emphasis between investigation, display and preservation will also have a bearing on the cost of the process. In the real world the conservator and archaeologist, who decide on the extent and nature of the cleaning process, will have their options limited by the budget available. The benefits of the different possible decisions will, however, have been clarified through the use of the decision tree. When the decision tree is used with financial information it can be regarded as performing a cost-benefit or cost-effectiveness analysis.

12.3 Estimating probability

The accuracy of the decision tree depends on how accurate the probability figures assigned to any given outcome of an action are. These are usually obtained in one of two ways:

- Where a large number of simple processes are carried out and provided accurate records are kept, then probability figures can readily be established from those records.

- Where conservation of unique objects occurs, or a rarely repeated action is proposed, the probability of success or failure is an estimate. If such estimates are inaccurate decision trees have little or no use.

A number of steps can be taken to improve the estimation of probability.

- Ensure that the person estimating the probability is the individual with the most experience, someone who actually does the job and who has a realistic approach to the problem.

- Break down the process into its component parts and assess each one carefully. Complex situations are often regarded as having low probabilities of success, but when treated as a sequence of simple processes, the probability of success increases.

- The estimator should discuss the reasoning behind the estimate and write down the outcomes and probabilities. These processes encourage careful consideration, and since failures loom larger in the mind than success discussing both generates a greater awareness and more accurate perception of the likelihood of success.

- Consider all the possible outcomes, assigning probability to them all. Even if they do not appear on the final decision tree they may aid the thought process.

- Assess the probability that an event will not occur. When this is combined with the probability of an event occurring the total must equal 1. Often both are underestimated!

- Ensure that there is no rush to complete the estimation. When short of time there is a tendency to revert to stereotype thinking and not to consider in a balanced fashion.

- The assessor should put aside any notions of what the final decision is likely to be since it could influence the probability values selected.

- Estimate in quantitative terms, phrases like 'quite likely' cannot be incorporated into a decision tree. Phrases such as a 1 in 5 chance or 'more probable than not' can be translated into percentages.

- Calibrate the assessor through asking them to estimate a situation with a known probability.

Though financial value (money) is usually used as the units in decision-tree calculations, the concept of utility, definable in terms of museum value or any term other than money, can be used.

12.4 Risk assessment for museums

Beyond looking at the most cost-effective way of cleaning and conserving objects decision trees are beginning to be used in conservation as part of risk assessment or risk analysis. This can be defined as predictions about the decay of objects and the consequent changes in the object's museum value (Ashley-Smith 1997, 1999). When carried out in a systematic manner it can quantify and evaluate risks and lead to preventive conservation strategies; for example, controlling the environment or disaster planning using 'Risk management procedures' as defined by Waller (1994).

The probability factors of success or failure of a process (e.g. storage at a given RH), may be defined as, the likelihood that the object will get mould at the given RH. Such factors are determined through the work of conservation scientists, such as Erhardt and Michalski (Erhardt and Mecklenburg 1994; Michalski 1993, see Section 11.3), or can be derived from conservation records. Some factors (e.g. light damage) are constant, others (e.g. the effects of theft, vandalism, insect infestation) are intermittent, but extensive when they do occur. The probability is effectively derived from the annual loss rate (see Section 11.3). Thus if fading-from-light figures are extrapolated until the image is obscured then if a collection has lost 100 images over the last 500 years the equivalent loss rate would be 0.2 objects per year. Since there are a large number of potentially damaging factors for any one object, these probabilities are invariably calculated on the speadsheet program of a computer. The effects of the different probabilities of success or failure on the values of the object can be calculated to yield a net value: Ashley-Smith's NEV (Ashley-Smith 1997). The current lack of data limits the present abilities to undertake such calculations.

If the loss rate for different agents of decay are calculated, the greatest threat to a collection can be identified and the limited resources available can be used to combat the greatest threat to the collection. Various improvements can also be assessed. By recalculating the change in loss rate from improved conditions, the improved net value can be set against the cost of achieving those conditions. These costs will be both capital costs and running costs to ensure the continued maintenance of the improved conditions. For example, the use of UV film and conservators to monitor and control light levels can be seen as improving the survivability of objects such as pictures expressed as a lower annual loss rate (Staniforth 1990). Costs for environmental protection will appear justifiable where marked improvements in the survivability of objects can be demonstrated (e.g. cold storage for photographic negatives). If and when condition surveys/collection audits become sufficiently accurate and precise they could provide data on rates of damage which could provide formulae or expressions for decay which could be fed into risk-analysis calculations and project accurate loss rates for whole collections.

Though the loss rate for sherds of archaeological ceramic and old-master paintings may be the same, those losses have very different values for the museum. The value of an object to the museum, or owner, through the factors of its exhibitability (aesthetic entity) and how informative it can be (historic document), needs to be included within the calculation of the impact of potential object loss. It can also be included in the calculation of the true cost effectiveness of a conservation treatment or storage provision. Such exhibitability and information values for objects have rarely been estimated by curators, and if done are achieved using a relative scale. The incorporation of object values from the display or information standpoint was seen to be incorporated with information on decay and interventive conservation in the work by Dollery and Henderson (1996) and in the Dutch Delta Plan assessments.

Expressing condition surveys and slow rates of decay in terms of number of objects lost per year, or additional hours of conservation (cost), brings home to curators, museum directors and auditors the loss as a result of the slow decay. Instead of recommended levels of light, RH, etc., which were seen by some curators as absolute limits, more sophisticated spreadsheets of risk analysis, programmed with details of objects in the collections will exist with rates of decay information such that if a curator opens the window the impact on the adjacent objects can be calculated.

12A Case study: The Bush Barrow Gold (Kinnes *et al*. 1988; Shell and Robinson 1988; Corfield 1988b; Chippindale 1988)

In 1985, the British Museum was asked to loan the Bronze Age gold objects recovered from Bush Barrow in Wessex to an exhibition 'Symbols of Power' at the National Museum of Scotland in Edinburgh. This they did after undertaking restoration, cleaning and remounting of the large sheet-gold lozenge from Bush Barrow. The subsequent exchange of views between Andrew Oddy and colleagues of the British Museum who undertook the restoration, Paul Robinson and colleagues of the Wiltshire Archaeological and Natural History Society who owned the object and Mike Corfield, chairman of UKIC, the representative body of conservators in the UK, demonstrated both the differences in approach and judgement which are seen within conservation on the subject of restoration and reshaping metal artefacts, and created a test case which has shaped subsequent discussions on conservation ethics.

Bush Barrow was excavated by William Cunnington in 1808. He uncovered a human skeleton surrounded with grave goods including several pieces of goldwork, amongst which was a large sheet-gold (85 per cent gold, 14 per cent silver, 0.5 per cent copper) lozenge (186 mm by 157 mm, 0.1–0.2 mm in thickness). It was bent over along each side forming a 3–4-mm ledge with the very edge of the foil being further bent over to grip the thin layer of wood which, according to Cunnington, had originally formed the backing to the object when discovered. The front surface was decorated in the form of a series of four concentric lozenges outlined with a group of three to four parallel incised grooves. The outermost of the four bands was decorated with an incised zig-zag pattern, the innermost with an incised criss-cross design, the second and third bands were undecorated (see Figure 12.4).

The Bush Barrow gold had become the property of Wiltshire Archaeological and Natural History Society in 1883 who displayed the material in the museum in Devizes until 1922 when it was deposited on 'indefinite' loan with the British Museum because of concerns over security at Devizes. Brief details about the lozenge and an idealized drawing were published along with full details of the excavation and contents of Bush Barrow in *Ancient History of South Wiltshire* written in 1812 by Sir Richard Colt Hoare who had financed Cunnington's excavation. Subsequently the lozenge was photographed in 1912 for Abercromby's book *Bronze Age Pottery*, where Corfield (1988b) suggests it is pictured 'considerably distorted and with a deep crease'. It was used as an illustration in Piggot's 1938 book *The Early Bronze Age in Wessex*, where Corfield (1988b) suggests the photographs indicate that it had been 'restored' to a form close to the original, including a slightly convex form at the edges. When photographed for Taylor's 1980 book *Bronze Age Goldwork of the British Isles*, Corfield

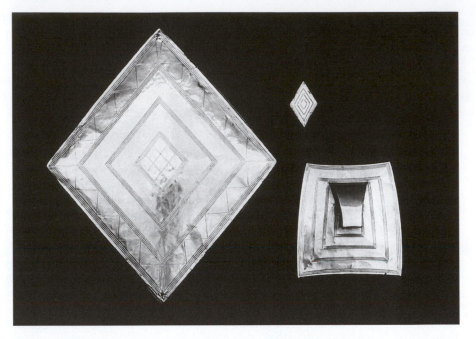

Figure 12.4 The gold objects from Bush Barrow, Wiltshire after conservation (photograph courtesy Wiltshire Archaeological and Natural History Society).

(1988b) observes that the lozenge had acquired a number of creases and dents and by the time it was photographed for the 'Symbols of Power' exhibition (Clarke *et al.* 1985) further dents had appeared in the surface. It has been suggested (Oddy, personal communication) that variations in lighting for the photographs have resulted in the variable published images of the object.

Noting the extremely fragile nature of the object, the continued demand for exhibitions and scholastic study and the ease with which thin gold foil is damaged the British Museum staff decided to 'remove the major undulations' (Kinnes *et al.* 1988), clean the lozenge and provide a firm new backing. The cleaning of the object and its fragile nature were discussed with Paul Robinson of Devizes Museum, though no permission to reshape the object was sought. The conservation staff of the British Museum have a long history and considerable expertise in restoring metal artefacts and believed they were carrying out minor conservation work which was appropriate for this object. They noted that the crumpled gold metal of the front surface of the lozenge was almost slack within the more rigid bent sides, they also noted that the outer incised lines were in the form of a slight curve. They concluded that the metal had originally had a shallow domed form, with a slight keel at the principal axes, and thus using fingers, wood, plastic hand tools and metal tools, applied through leather, the worst creases were eliminated from the lozenge which consequently had a form much closer to the envisaged original: a keeled domed form curving 8 mm above the horizontal. Measurements of the incised lines, taken using a series of 90° offsets, showed that in the reconstructed domed form, the lines form a very regular straight-lined lozenge design. This restoration has also helped to bring together the edges of the slight tears in the sides of the lozenge (Oddy 1994). Consequently the British Museum believe that the object now has the correct domed profile. An exact Perspex mount was created to fully support this restored form.

Corfield (1988b) quoting the UKIC 1983 'Guidance for Conservation Practice' described the aim of conservation as 'to reveal the true nature of the object', though since almost every object has a number of truths when restoring or reshaping metals, revealing one truth invariably destroys another. Therefore, a balanced judgement must be made as to what is the most important truth and the one which is revealed. It is not normally considered an ethical practice to remove any damage or distortion deliberately enacted upon an object during its life. A number of practices have evolved where reshaping metal may be considered ethical.

- Where it could be done so without damaging the object. Thus it should be done by an experienced and competent metalworker.

- Where the distortion of the metal resulted from the burial of the object or its excavation and it was clear that the distortion did not represent an important aspect of the past history of the object. Examples include removing the damage caused by the mechanical excavator to the Coppergate Helmet (Tweddle 1992), annealing and reshaping the Anastasius Dish crushed by the collapse of the Sutton Hoo burial chamber (Oddy 1994) and the restoration to its original form of a gold bracelet from Llanarmon yn Ial in Wales which had been unwound and flattened by the metal detectorist who found the object (Corfield 1988b).

- Where important information is uncovered; for example, the unrolling of Roman lead curses (thin sheets of lead on which worshippers scratched messages to the gods) to reveal the written information inside them (Dove 1989). Similarly the flattened and broken bronze bust of Lucius Aurelius Verus (Smith 1977) was reshaped in order to reveal this face from the past and identify who was depicted, whilst the Hockwold treasure was reshaped in order to determine how many objects were actually present (Oddy 1994). In these and other cases the reshaped object is seen to provide more information about the past than the flattened, rolled or distorted form.

The British Museum regarded the present distorted shape of the Bush Barrow lozenge as resulting from damage incurred during burial, excavation and subsequent handling. The post-excavation damage being suggested by the photographic history of the object. Consequently they restored it. It is clear that the object now more accurately reflects the original form and may be regarded as more aesthetically pleasing, though this remains a subjective judgement (Chippindale 1988).

Following reshaping, the lozenge was cleaned through the gentle application of Goddard's Long Term Silver Foam diluted with water and detergent. This cleaning agent in part cleans through the use of a very fine (1-micron-sized particle) abrasive. This cleaning, whilst preserving the tool marks and scratches from use or previous cleaning of the object, has given the surface a reflective shiny finish.

A number of concerns have been raised by Shell and Robinson (1988) and Chippindale (1988) regarding this reshaping and cleaning work.

- The need to undertake any work was questioned. Why allow the object to be studied, or go on exhibition if it is being damaged by this process? The same question can, however, also be asked about many archaeological excavations, which undoubtedly imperil and damage buried objects.

- The accuracy of the reshaping work and the necessity of cleaning. Measurements taken using an Omicron 3-D digitizer which determines surface contours to 0.001 mm on a cast of the electrotype of the Bush Barrow lozenge, taken in 1922, and housed in Devizes Museum, suggested that it had originally been a very shallow domed form with a maximum height of 3 mm above the horizontal.

- Shell and Robinson (1988) suggest that the domed form may have been due to distortion from post-excavation care between 1808 and 1922 and that the object may well have originally been flat. The evidence of the gently curved incised lines they dismiss as a deliberate decorative feature.

- All other gold from the Bush Barrow and surrounding barrows has a matt finish at present and there is no evidence to suggest that it was originally displayed in a highly reflective condition.

- Concerns that the British Museum reshaping plastically deformed the soft and easily deformed gold foil.

The British Museum suggest that the shape and measurement work of Shell and Robinson was based on a silicon rubber mould, which shrinks very slightly on casting, and since this was taken from an electrotype which would itself have been created using another mould, with associated shrinkage problems, the derived measurements may not accurately reflect the original dimensions of the lozenge. Since the work has already been carried out no further evidence can be obtained to resolve the issue as to whether the gold was plastically deformed. The question of the cleaning and degree of reflection from the surface is another area where it is difficult to be certain of the true nature of the object. The degree to which this was the original condition or something which has developed during burial (e.g. through etching of the silver from the surface of the metal during the decay of the body) is as yet unresolved. Consequently the present aesthetic experience, whether shiny or matt, is entirely subjective.

Having decided that the object was to be restored it is clear that although not regarded as major restoration work but 'standard practice' by the British Museum, others did not regard it in such a manner and greater consultation before the work was undertaken might have eliminated any later controversy. It remains a difficult judgement how far one should go in reshaping. Leaving our museums filled with broken crumpled objects gives a distorted view of the past, as does filling it with beautiful fully restored objects. Whilst all the items on loan from Wiltshire Archaeological and Natural History Society have now been returned to Devizes and the British Museum continue to robustly defend their actions (Oddy 1994), the most enduring legacy to conservation has been the exposure which this subject received. The level of research which was undertaken on this object occurred as a result of the controversy and was far greater than would have otherwise occurred.

The research emphasized the fragile and easily distorted nature of gold foil, it emphasized the threats posed to objects in museum care and questioned assumptions regarding the original form of objects. It moved the subject of conservation forward with wider awareness and debate on the issue of restoring and reshaping metal artefacts.

13 Responsibilities

13.1 Colleagues

As perception is based on pattern matching past images against the current image (see Chapter 1), each individual will view the same object in an entirely different way. Perception is as unique to an individual as fingerprints. When the cave paintings of Altimera were viewed by the influential archaeologist Abbe Breuil who had studied palaeolithic cave painting extensively, he described them as depicting 'active animals' such as the 'bellowing bison' and the 'trotting boar'. Consequently these animal images were interpreted as being drawn by hunters depicting animals they hoped to kill and capture in forthcoming hunts and the cave site was regarded as a ritual or religious place where hopes and aspirations were lodged (Abercromby 1960). When the images were re-examined by the artist, Learson, he noted that the animals had a slumped posture, the feet did not appear to either touch the ground or bear the weight of the animals and the tongues of the animals were often depicted hanging out. All these features, he argued, corresponded to the images of dead animals thrown on the floor of the cave. This would suggest that the cave would have been used as an area for storage or processing of animal carcasses (Abercromby 1960). Regardless of the rights and wrongs of either interpretation, the alternative interpretation caused existing evidence from the cave to be carefully studied for further facts to support either interpretation and for additional evidence to be sought. The sensitization to different interpretations and the acquisition of different forms of evidence informs and develops the debate, bringing truth closer – the aim of the conservation, as well as the archaeological, process.

Alternative interpretations about an object can be regarded as alternative patterns or schemata (see Chapter 1). Such alternatives reduce the temptation to:

- Push all the facts to a single interpretation.

- Overlook the absence of evidence which should be present.

- Overlook contradictory evidence which is present but which does not fit the existing pattern or schemata.

It is desirable that the conservator has as much information as possible so that proposed conservation work does not obscure or alter important aspects (the truth) of the work. It is, therefore, beneficial for a conservator to have colleagues who can suggest alternative interpretations about an object under examination and alternatives to the proposed conservation treatment. At the extreme alternative interpretations can be seen as leading to academic conflict (see Case study 12A: The Bush Barrow Gold). Though distracted by the rhetoric and heat of the debate, considerably more thought and effort has gone into the investigation and interpretation of the object than is normal. There is a responsibility on every conservator to seek a variety of ideas about an object before determining the final interpretation and the appropriate form of conservation. There is also a responsibility to be a good observer and interpreter of objects for others.

It is important that conservators are people who can change their minds. As shown in Chapter 1, having made a judgement it is a natural reaction to defend it, even when new information makes it appear a poor judgement. In modern Western societies changing one's mind appears to be associated with a loss of status (i.e. being wrong and someone else being right). This often leads to an unwillingness to communicate, in case information is proffered which makes earlier judgements appear inaccurate and require a change of mind. Such human frailties of ego must be overcome in order to achieve the best decisions about artefacts and provide the most appropriate conservation.

To achieve the care of historic and artistic artefacts most effectively within large organizations, it is necessary for conservators both to manage and to be managed. The purpose of management is to use finite resources most efficiently and effectively. Professional conservators are usually responsible for managing their own work and selecting the most efficient and effective methods for achieving the conservation aims. Where conservators have some element of responsibility for collections they routinely employ management techniques such as collection surveys, disaster planning and risk analysis to prioritize actions and expenditure (Keene 1996). Where a group of conservators work together, on a project or in a department, one individual is often responsible for leading or managing the group. Those individuals who have a capacity for 'seeing the big picture', being aware of conservation's role within the organization and have leadership and organizational skills, should be those in managerial positions. Often conservators work as part of a team managed by a curator or museum director who should have similar qualities. Where teams of different specialists working towards a goal can be developed, the input of the different experts can create a very powerful holistic effect as seen in the case of the research team investigating Lindow Man (see Case study 8A).

Numerous other individuals (e.g. museum directors, designers, councillors and trustees, scholars, teachers, archaeologists, researchers and curators) work alongside conservators. All have their own areas of responsibility and their own agendas which they seek to implement. Curators, art historians and archaeologists will frequently share the conservator's goal to investigate; teachers, curators and exhibition designers will share the conservator's goal to reveal objects to the public. Though all will wish to preserve the objects of the past, no group, other than conservators, has preservation as its primary responsibility.

Since other heritage professionals have different priorities to conservators, there is a risk of conflict. If conservators are to work effectively with these individuals, it is essential to understand fully other agendas and what they are trying to achieve. This will minimize conflict situations. Such conflict rarely results in either side achieving their aims. If conservators do not contribute to the overall process, they will become ignored and their advice is not sought (Barclay 1990). Conservation can end up as an expensive nuisance in the eyes of those trying to create exhibitions, run excavations, open museums, etc. The conservator can become typecast as 'an interfering nuisance with a negative attitude' (Ward 1986), or worse:

> The former, often curators, consider that the latter, often conservators, tend towards the same kind of inconvenient zealotry as Fire Prevention Officers, and lack understanding

of the underlying issues, while the latter accuse the former of recklessness and lack of professionalism.

(*Apollo* 1987: 390)

Stereotypes: Images of conservators are often stereotypes which, though they derive largely from hearsay, often contain a grain of truth. Such stereotypes can make it difficult for a conservator to function effectively and frequently the initial task facing a conservator when working in a museum or on excavation is to create a positive image. Examples of the stereotypes of the conservator, derived from a variety of professional colleagues, include:

- Technician: where others decide (curators, archaeologists, museum directors) and the conservator simply implements the decision. The view of the conservator as a technician was fostered by the authors of the period 1950–80 who frequently used the term. Coremans (1969) and Chamberlin (1979) refer to a conservator as 'a highly trained technician'. Though such a role may be appropriate for some who have only a basic-level training (Watkinson 1996b), for fully trained and qualified conservators this stereotype continues to deny the professional expertise, training and qualification level of the conservator.

- Scientist (mad). Speaking a language which others do not understand, doing things with chemicals (smells), living in a laboratory into which others do not go and doing things that nobody understands.

- Parent/mother/nurse. Anything which is broken, damaged, or just looks 'unhappy' is brought to the conservator for care. They will mend it. They will make it better. 'Whilst the curator adopts the role of pseudo ownership, the conservator adopts that of parent or carer' (Keene 1996).

- No, No, No! In attempts to safeguard the objects the conservator is seen as constantly turning down ideas for using or displaying objects. Appearing fussy, difficult, unrealistic, uncooperative, conservators are perceived as marching to the beat of their own (ethical) drum. Colleagues soon stop asking the conservator's opinion because they know what the answer will be. 'The conservator stereotype – being considered a pedantic nay-sayer by other museum professionals, especially exhibition designers, education officers, curators and management, – is a familiar one' (Frost 1994).

- Frustrated curator. An experienced conservator can often end up knowing more about the subject, particularly in specialist areas such as textiles, paper, paintings, archaeology, than the inexperienced curator or museum director. With such expertise in the material culture, the conservator ends up producing displays, planning research, answering enquiries and fulfilling a curatorial role.

- Artist/craftsman/restorer. Does lovely work but takes for ever. Lost in the 'art of conservation', all other things become secondary.

- Luxury. Too expensive, requiring costly equipment, a spacious laboratory and never appear to get anything done. An idle aristocrat who plays with their toys whilst the workers are short of the tools to get on with the job.

The general public often has an even less clear idea what a conservator does, invariably confusing the role with people who 'save trees and whales'.

Conservators need to be aware of these stereotype images that colleagues can hold and should seek to modify them. It is, therefore, essential to develop conservation as a positive experience for all curators, museum directors, archaeologists, painting historians, connoisseurs and owners of objects. This is most effectively achieved through creating an image of competence which derives from running successful conservation, storage, recording or exhibition projects. For inexperienced conservators running a series of smaller successful projects will give them experience and confidence and subsequently give them access to the resources necessary for larger projects. A positive attitude can be generated through:

- Successful completion of the project.

- The project estimates of time and funding being proved to be accurate (i.e. it is brought in on time and on budget), ensuring that the conservator is seen as someone who is responsible and can manage a budget.

- Awareness of colleagues' requirements, ensuring that their goals are achieved as well as the conservator's requirements. This creates the perception of the conservator as a broad-minded problem solver and dispels the myth of someone who always says 'no'.

- Colleagues seeing the conservator in a professional and managerial role, successfully organizing and running a project, dealing with fellow professionals on equal terms.

- Making difficult or awkward things happen. This creates the positive image of the conservator as an enabler. People who 'get things done' are always valued in any organization.

- Demonstrating skill at your craft, knowledge of your subject and mature well-considered judgement.

- Receiving a positive response from the public, or one's colleagues to the work which has been done. This may require publicising the successful project work.

13.2 Objects, conservators and owners

Conservators and owners: In the case of private ownership, the conservator is usually dealing with a single individual. In the case of public ownership, they are normally dealing with a representative of a public organization (e.g. the curator or archaeologist who, though a public servant, acts as the owner). Though responsible through a museum director and a board of trustees or councillors to the general public, in reality many curators adopt a highly proprietorial view of 'their' collections.

Drysdale (1988) has suggested that conservation can be seen by some owners as a 'distressed purchase', such as a TV licence or going to the dentist. We are fearful of the potential damage or loss if we do not get it 'fixed'. Large areas of personal and state spending are undertaken on this basis (e.g. pensions, mortgages, house repairs, etc.). Such purchases invariably focus on the trouble-free future and some aspects of preventive conservation, such as lining, backing, framing or storage, clearly fall into this category. However, other purchases like those to do with the car, garden and decorating the house focus on a dream, a beautiful vision of the future. Restoration work – readhering ceramics, repairing broken antique furniture, cleaning paintings, etc. – are undertaken in order to create such visions of beauty. When discussing conservation with the owner or curator of an object, the conservator is discussing their fears or their dreams. Such matters are frequently very personal and decisions are made, in part at least, on an emotional rather than a purely logical basis.

There are many potential areas of misunderstanding between the owner or curator of an object and the conservator, particularly when undertaking private contract work. It is important that owners or curators recognize that it is part of the conservator's duty to advise over the care and conservation of their object. Owners should be prepared to provide basic information about the object which may include some proof of ownership. It is often advisable that, prior to discussing conservation measures, conservators and owners/curators discuss the nature and importance of the object. This ensures that both parties have a common frame of reference. Following discussion of all the relevant conservation options and a decision over what work is to be done has been formulated, it is desirable that a formal written contract between the parties for the conservation work should be drawn up (UKIC 1998; MGC 1995b). This is particularly important when the work involves restoration up to a particular point. If a conservator is asked to undertake work which they consider inappropriate or unethical they can always decline to undertake such work and should do so before any contract is signed. They should always advise the owner/curator of why such actions are unethical and seek to persuade them to a more appropriate and ethical course of action.

Conservators, as a result of their training and natural inclination, hold objects in high regard. Consequently they see part of the role of the conservator as protecting objects. Where an owner or curator damages or neglects an object, a conservator will frequently feel it their duty to protect the object against the owner (see Figure 13.1), developing

Figure 13.1 Preventive conservation: The conservator's responsibility to the object? (Cartoon drawn by Richard Stansfield.)

emotional involvement with the object, and experiencing moral indignation, even direct conflict, with the owner (private or state). This often results in censuring owners for not taking good and proper care of their objects. Aggressive, angry, censorious reactions are usually unhelpful, as they simply dissuade the owner/curator from taking conservation advice in future. The conservator needs to develop the emotional detachment of medical staff, to keep working to improve the condition of objects and see the 'big' picture of collections and future objects rather than focusing on any one individual object. This means seeking to slowly improve the standing of the object in the owner's eyes, usually through developing understanding of what is important to the owner (their agenda) and showing how the object has facets which make it valuable in such terms (i.e. advocacy, see Section 13.8). Making the owner treasure the object is the only long-term solution. The reaction to mend or do immediate conservation action is only a short-term solution which merely delays the inevitable decay of the object.

Conservators and objects: Conservators spend almost all their time working with objects. Drysdale (1988) noted, in psychoanalytical terms, that conservators can develop an object cathexis (an idea or fixation). This is a prop compensating for the failure to establish the proper balance between internal psychic reality and the real world. This is, perhaps, a relatively frequent occurrence. From the much cherished and highly polished car to a tightly gripped childhood teddy bear, all of us have sought certainty in the form of an object, an anchor of certainty that acts as comforter in a world of uncertainty to which we will, literally, cling. Few conservators will go as far as to identify with Ruskin who in a letter to his father wrote 'whatever feelings of attachment I have, are to material things' (Drysdale 1987). The vast majority of conservators recognize that excessive attachment to an object is not healthy since it distorts an accurate appreciation of reality. It is where objects have become symbols, particularly religious icons such as the relics of saints which exemplify the extent of the distortion of reality. Rycroft offers a slightly less perturbing definition of an object in psychoanalytical terms as 'that towards which an action or desire is directed: that which the subject requires in order to achieve instinctual satisfaction' (Drysdale 1988). This can be seen in any form of artefact, tool or machine with which the individual has frequent contact. Musicians certainly achieve instinctual satisfaction playing an instrument and many who use a machine or drive a car regularly enjoy the operation or action involved. A degree of attachment frequently forms with an instrument or machine which is regularly used, they often acquire a 'personality' and even a name in the user's mind.

Conservators often examine objects in greater detail than anyone else, other than their creator. For many objects, especially works of art, this gives rise to a deep insight into, and attachment to, the object. Many conservators talk to their objects and even dream about them. Conservators frequently spend hundreds even thousands of hours with an object, and since they value themselves and their time, this value must also apply to the object. This gives the object a value to the conservator far beyond its monetary value, its museum value and its value to others. This can lead to problems of perspective since the conservator sees the object as far more valuable than the curator or museum director, who has many other objects and concerns, and this can lead to conflict. Clearly it is beneficial, if investing a lot of time with a single object, to ensure that curators, directors and others also spend time dealing with this object so that they will also consider it valuable.

If the conservator's desire to be with objects can be seen as a normal, understandable (if slightly insecure) part of the human condition, what of the desire to conserve? Most potential conservators first approach the subject without the rational 'academic' approach which has been detailed in this book up to the present. In truth, more basic instincts probably apply: the desire to clean, make perfect, correct, make whole, make work again, make beautiful, investigate. These may stem from childhood notions of right and wrong and Victorian attitudes of cleanliness (next to godliness, see Section 7.2). Over the last few years it has become increasingly important for the conservator to temper their basic instinct to mend and clean, with a high level of intellectual control.

- The importance of objects as historic documents has grown and there is a need to preserve the traces of use: the dust, dirt and scratches that accompany every object.

- The importance of collections as a whole has become appreciated and thus the need for collection surveys and prioritizing and managing scarce time.

- The importance of building surveys, materials testing, storage and packaging and environmental monitoring and control, in order to ensure that the object's long-term condition is not jeopardized, has been understood.

- The importance of training staff in handling objects and all advocacy activities (see Section 13.8) has become better appreciated.

- The importance of recording and research has been realized.

Such activities, though often less personally satisfying, also place preservation and investigation of objects at the centre of the conservator's role, rather than the personal gratification of cleaning and restoration craft skills (revelation). The balanced approach which a present-day conservator needs to have towards any object being described through the RIP triangle (see Section 3.4).

13.3 World heritage

Some monuments and objects are important to several nations with complex aspects of legal and moral ownership. Thus the Elgin Marbles are claimed as part of the heritage of the peoples of both Greece and Britain and the slave forts of West Coast Africa are important to the history of the people of Ghana and the other countries of West Africa and the black community of the USA. Images and ideas from ancient cultures from all over the world have directly affected all modern-day societies. Consequently those societies have an interest, and arguably some right, to preserve that which has shaped their culture.

The 1954 Hague Convention asserts 'cultural property belonging to any people' is also 'the cultural heritage of all mankind'. This suggests that although cultural-heritage resources are located in individual countries and belong to the people of that country, the cultural heritage is the inheritance of all the peoples of the world and each country is responsible to the global community for the cultural property in its care.

Such concepts were undreamed of in the nineteenth century when national power was dominant. However, the interlinking of the global economy in the late twentieth century, emphasized by two world wars, as well as transnational pollution, transport, media and the development of international events and organizations, has resulted in concepts such as world heritage. Most countries in the world have joined the World Heritage Convention, created in 1973, which requires national governments to 'ensure the identification, protection, presentation and transmission to the future generations of its natural and cultural heritage' (Young 1998). World heritage has been manifest in physical form through:

- The creation of international agencies such as ICOM and ICCROM which have an international role in preserving both movable cultural treasures and ancient monuments and buildings of cultural and historic importance. These agencies have an important role to play in the case of threats to heritage sites and objects of world importance when large sums of money are required to achieve the necessary conservation, such as the saving of the temple at Abu Simbel (see Section 11.6).

- The creation by UNESCO and its World Heritage Committee of 506 'World Heritage Sites' in 107 countries (1998) (Young 1998). This is designed to highlight the importance to world culture of these sites and to aid their preservation.

A significant factor in developing the concept of world heritage is heritage tourism and the economic power it represents. For many countries, such as Egypt and Great Britain, heritage is a significant factor in tourism which is one of a country's largest industries and which brings significant economic benefits to it. The economic power provided by these tourists affects the nature and extent of the heritage on display (see Section 2.6).

The involvement of one country with another's national past has always been a delicate area. Nineteenth-century ethnographic collecting and archaeological expeditions and the purchase of one country's art by another, invariably favoured the economically powerful European countries. During the later half of the twentieth century America and Japan have become powerful importers of the material culture of South America, Africa and Asia. Resentment at the loss of their material culture has led to the banning of exports of ancient cultural heritage by countries such as Greece, Italy, Turkey, Egypt, Iran, Iraq, Syria and other countries of North Africa, the Middle, Near and Far East as well as South America.

Modern expeditions from the developed world to the developing world are now increasingly collaborative affairs often focusing on efforts to research and preserve the heritage of the host country. Organizations, such as the Getty Conservation Institute, have worked with host countries, such as China at the Yungang and Mogao Grottoes (Agnew 1995), Egypt at the tomb of Nefertari (Corzo and Afshar 1993) and Tanzania at the site of the Laetoli footprints (see Case study 11A), to preserve the sites and their content, establish long-term management solutions for the sites and train local personnel in the relevant conservation skills.

The concept of world heritage aims to ensure that objects and monuments are preserved for the peoples of the world and not merely for the interests of the host nation of the antiquity. Through grants, training and public support the world community encourages a long-term approach preserving the material culture of the past for posterity. They encourage both techniques and materials which have been internationally proven and solutions which are locally based and can be effectively run with the resources and personnel available. Management plans are encouraged for all important ancient sites and are required for World Heritage Site designation. The world community discourages short-term 'cosmetic' conservation using techniques where there is limited local knowledge and unproven materials.

13.4 Objects of belief

Native peoples: As discussed in Section 10.1, the concept that the importance of an object derives principally from the physical form of the object comes largely, though not exclusively, from modern Western civilization. In societies which have different cultural roots, such as the native people of the Americas or Asia, the Maori of New Zealand or the Aborigines of Australia, objects are often considered to possess the spirit of their creator or owner. This makes them essentially living things and endows the object with feelings, life processes and rights. In collections such as those of the Museum of the American Indian, the objects are considered as they would be by the native peoples who originally created and owned them and the feelings, life processes and rights of the object are respected. In such a museum environment it is not regarded as appropriate to treat an insect-infested object by fumigation or freezing since this would 'kill' the object (Drumheller and Kaminitz 1994). Therefore, approaches such as isolating the object and using natural insect-repellent plant secretions which would not harm a human being are used. There are also considerable limitations on who can touch the objects (with restriction on groups such as menstruating women), what objects may be stored together and which way they face (Drumheller and Kaminitz 1994; Clavir 1994). These 'human' attributes have been vested in objects to support social beliefs and customs (see Section 6.3). As such they formed an important element in the belief system and social structure of the culture which created them and a device to remind and reinforce that belief system (Peters 1981; Barton and Weik 1984; Labi 1993; Mellar 1992). The continued supporting of these attributes and traditions within the museum can be seen as 'preserving the true nature of the object'.

Whilst a conservator is encouraged to respect the beliefs associated with any object, in the AIC and other conservation ethical codes, how far the conservator should go in enacting these beliefs is a matter of careful judgement (Clavir 1996). Museum policies on such matters are highly variable depending on the nature of the institution and the local community they serve.

- The adoption of special practices is perhaps not done for the physical benefit of the object, but for the benefit of modern-day adherents of the belief system from which the object is believed to derive.

- How effective are the procedures if there is no personal belief on the part of the conservator? Can only conservators who are adherents of the belief system treat the object?

- The folkways and belief systems, the non-material traditions, are an essential element of the past and it can be argued are every bit as important as the physical form of material possessions (see Section 10.1). They have fundamentally shaped the world in which we live. Consequently every effort should be made to preserve these folkways and belief systems as much as the physical world.

- The concept of the native peoples of the world as 'First Nations' is often inaccurate, many are invaders who drove out earlier native predecessors. Most of these tribes of native peoples, whilst respecting their own traditions and those of their allies, did not respect those of other tribes especially those whom they had conquered or with whom they were at war. In some cases they deliberately denied the existence of the other tribes and sought to remove or eliminate the material culture of other tribes (Drumheller and Kaminitz 1994).

- Modern Western society has been formed from many groups, each of which had traditions and ideas about their objects which do not correspond with present museum practice. Nineteenth-century housekeepers would be horrified at the ideas of preserving evidence such as stains on textiles, and regimental standing orders would require that metalwork was regularly polished regardless of need. Are such belief systems 'cleanliness next to godliness' and 'the beneficial nature of hard work' any more or less important than those of nineteenth-century native peoples?

- How does one reconcile two different belief systems which venerate the same object in different ways? Should a conservator treat the venerated 'lucky rabbit's foot' in a different way to all other rabbits' feet?

- It is important to understand the tradition fully in order to avoid removing its significance such as the 'lucky' attribute of the rabbit's foot. Conservators will deal with such a large number of objects from many different cultures. Even with the guidance of experts, there is often too much information for an individual conservator to learn (Odegaard 1995). Consequently there remains a considerable risk of unintentionally damaging the non-visible belief or 'living' aspect of an object.

- The limits of time and money.

- There may be much inherent wisdom contained within the belief systems of those who created the artefacts. Though undoubtedly geared to the native use of the objects rather than the object use in a modern museum, there may yet be much to be learnt about object care from other societies who have successfully cared for their objects for many decades.

Religious objects: The question of religious and sacred objects is the extreme example of objects having meaning and symbolism well beyond their physical form. Objects such as a cross were intended to be primarily representational, though they have frequently been manifest as physical forms which have become venerated in their own right. Sacred objects are often over-represented in collections since they tend to be venerated, cared for and have consequently been preserved.

The world's religions have taken different attitudes to conservation and in particular to investigation of religious objects. Christianity has experienced the questioning and doubting of science for many centuries. This has led to some perception of the separate nature of religious belief from the physical form of the object. This was demonstrated by the Catholic Church granting permission to radiocarbon date a thread from the Turin shroud. Christian relics can consequently be cleaned and preserved through the ministrations of conservators. In the 1980s the cowl and chasuble of St Anthony housed in the Basilica del Santo at Padua were cleaned and supported by a textile conservator (Brooks *et al.* 1996). Other religions maintain an investment of religious meaning in physical objects. Thus Tibetan religious leaders condemn as desecration the opening of Tibetan bronze statues to remove and examine the textile or birch-bark scrolls of religious writings which they frequently contain (Brooks *et al.* 1996; Reedy 1992).

Many religious objects remain primarily symbols of belief, objects in active use to the present day (see Figure 5.1). Regardless of age those objects still need to meet the needs of present-day believers (Weersma 1987; Greene 1992). The conservators treating a series of medieval polychrome crucifixes and religious statues in northern France adopted a minimal conservation approach removing surface dirt and consolidating the fragile painted surface. This was seen as inappropriate by some of the priests and congregations who owned the objects and who wanted clear symbols for veneration. They expected restoration to mean a new coat of brightly coloured paint and in a number of instances following minimal conservation the objects were overpainted by the local community (Molina and Pincemin 1994).

Objects of veneration can be very modern symbols such as regimental regalia, miners' trade-union banners, even mementoes of sporting or other events. The colour, orientation and numerous other small features of presentation of these objects are regarded as extremely important by the believers, and consequently need to be respected and preserved. All these cases highlight the need for consultation when dealing with religious or devotional objects. It is desirable for views of those who venerate the object as well as those who own the object, often separate entities for religious objects in museums, to be known and consulted prior to commencing conservation treatment.

Human remains: There is a fascination with human bodies. Staring at mummified or preserved bodies one comes literally face to face with the past, and Egyptian mummies or bog bodies have always been popular exhibits in museums (Berger 1992). Human remains are always a sensitive subject and remains, such as the shrunken heads of Indonesian and Amazonian tribes, have often been removed from display in deference to the sensitivity which such objects have acquired in the late twentieth century. Modern sensitivities, particularly those of native peoples such as native American Indians, Maori, Aborigine and Inuit, to the treatment of the bones and bodies of their ancestors have led to repatriation and reburial of much skeletal material (MacGowan and LaRoche 1996).

Human remains were principally collected by museums in the nineteenth century and early twentieth centuries when all museums considered themselves centres for serious research and learning. As many museums have evolved in the late twentieth century from centres of learning and scholarship to foci for entertainment and leisure time as well as education, sensitivity to late twentieth-century public opinion and visitor numbers have led to the removal from display of all but the most ancient human remains. A similar sensitivity was also observed in the display of 'stuffed animals'. The animal and human remains in museums' collections are, with the loss of animals in the wild and the advent of DNA studies, being recognized as a valuable scientific resource, which should be respected and preserved.

The human body has been an important form of expression of human beliefs from present-day body piercing, through tattooing, scarring, castration and mutilation to ritual sacrifice and mummification. Human remains from the past also contain indirect information on diet, disease, poisoning, ancient medical practices, execution, race, genetics and human parasites. In all these cases the bodies are the only form of information and it is only through examination of bodies and body tissues that these aspects of the human past can be understood (see Case study 8A: Lindow Man). Consequently it is essential both to preserve and investigate human remains. There is a fine balancing act to be achieved between reconciling the requirements of those who claim ancestry from those whose bones or bodies are retained in the museum collections and the rights of the wider public and scientific community who through the law, conquest or purchase have acquired these objects. The conservator has the same responsibility of care to human remains in museum collections as any other object. Many countries now have clear guidelines related to the collection, storage and display of human remains, which should always be treated with respect (Museum Ethnographers Group 1991).

13.5 Artist/creator of the object

Both the American (AIC) and Australian (AICCM) conservation codes make special reference to the 'need to respect cultural property and the people who created it'. This refers both to living artists and those who created culture in the past, such as the native peoples (Brooks *et al.* 1996). The rights of living artists have been enshrined in the Berne Convention for the Protection of Literary and Artistic Works (1971) (Fry 1997). This asserts:

- Copyright exists for every artistic work without the need for registration or formality.

- The rights are first given to the author or artist.

- The protection period continues to be active until at least 50 years after the death of the artist.

The convention has now been signed by ninety countries including the USA, UK and all major European states. It is being slowly incorporated into national legislation, in the case of the UK into the Copyright Designs and Patents Act of 1988, in Canada in the Copyright Act of 1988 (Curnoe 1990) and in the USA in the Visual Artists Rights Act (VARA) (Garfinkle *et al.* 1997). Of particular relevance to conservators is the statement in the Berne Convention that 'the author shall have the right to claim authorship of the work and to object to, any distortion, mutilation or other modification of, or derogatory action in relation to, the said work, which would be prejudicial to his honour or reputation'. In practice this has meant that any work by a conservator on a work of art by a living artist is normally only done with the artist's permission. Some artists, particularly those working in unstable materials, have requested that the objects are not conserved and are allowed to degrade naturally, such as Joseph Beuys *Fat Battery* and Dieter Roth's *Chocolate Bust*. Other artists feel the form of their work is important and will allow varying degrees of action to preserve them, such as Claes Oldenburg's *Earthquake* a chocolate, enamel paint and polyurethane resin sculpture which was frozen and then sprayed with methyl bromide to stop insect activity (Heuman 1995). Some artists are involved actively in the conservation process; for example, the architect Lubetkin who worked with John Allan of Avanti Architects in the 1987 restoration of his 1934 masterpiece of Early Modern architecture, the Penguin Pool at London Zoo (Pearce 1989). There is, however, a demonstrable risk that artists will not have the restraint merely to restore and will seek to recreate the work (Barclay 1990; Smith 1990). Conservators are invariably the most appropriately skilled people to intervene with objects provided the intervention would not be considered prejudicial to the honour and reputation of the artist. However, with works of conceptual art or works of unstable materials it may be argued that conservation was directly altering the artist's intent and fundamentally changing the nature of the work of art. Thus it is a difficult area and consultation with the artist is always to be encouraged.

13.6 Stolen or looted objects

Despite attempts to limit the rise in the trade in stolen or looted objects through the 1970 UNESCO Convention on the Means of Prohibiting and Preventing the Illicit Export and Transfer of Ownership of Cultural Property and the 1995 UNIDROIT Convention on the International Return of Stolen or Illegally Exported Cultural Objects (see Section 11.5), the rising price of antiquities has led to large numbers of illegally exported (looted) or stolen items on the antiquities market. This has led to many conservators being faced with the prospect of being asked to treat objects which they suspect are stolen or looted (Tubb 1995; Tubb and Sease 1996). There are two responses:

- Conservators may choose to work on 'objects of dubious provenance' since this ensures that the object is at least fully and properly recorded (see Section 6.2). This may be the only opportunity to ensure that information about this object enters the public domain. The aim of such actions by the conservator is to preserve the object for future generations. Even if the conservation work benefits the private owner now, it will also ensure that the object can survive and could eventually become public property.

- Conservators may choose not to work on 'objects of dubious provenance' since this denies the object any respectability and denies the perpetrators or collaborators in the crime the financial gain which a well conserved and thus seemingly respectable object would attract. Reducing the financial gain means that there is little benefit to be gained from looting sites or stealing objects and this would eventually suppress the trade in illegal objects and the damage to sites.

Both arguments can be seen as naive and idealistic. It is difficult to turn away a beautiful damaged object in need of care, particularly as it provides the conservator with much needed employment. However, such actions will help support and maintain the stealing of objects and the looting of sites. Equally refusal to treat one object will do little to suppress the trade in stolen or looted art and antiquities which, it is claimed, is the second most profitable criminal activity after drug trafficking (Palmer 1995).

Though the AIC (1994) and UKIC (1996) ethical codes do not forbid working on stolen or looted objects, they do emphasize the importance of working within the law. The public statements of conservators (Tubb 1995; Tubb and Sease 1996), however, clearly urge conservators to refuse to work on such objects. Such a stance indicates that the conservator's responsibilities lie primarily with the majority of objects even the, as yet, unexcavated ones rather than to the immediate well-being of any one looted or stolen, damaged object. Other bodies such as ICOM and the UK Museums Association prohibit their members from purchasing stolen or looted objects, thus clarifying their priorities (Boylan 1995). Refusing to treat objects which are stolen, looted and are thus devoid of their archaeological or artistic context, emphasizes the importance of objects as historical documents.

It is, frequently, not a simple matter to know that an object is stolen or looted, and often the conservator's suspicions may only be aroused during the conservation process. It is always legitimate to raise concerns and enquire about the ownership of an object with the relevant authorities.

13.7 Competence

The most strongly imprinted images or memories are those events and activities which are personally experienced (see Sections 1.3 and 1.5). Consequently, personal experience is one of the strongest factors in making a judgement. The wider the conservator's experience, the potentially better their judgement. The most powerful experiences are those involving all the senses, thus practical work is a far more powerful learning tool than anything read or heard. This makes practical work essential in training conservators, hence the emphasis on practical work, placements and internships on conservation courses. It is essential that inexperienced conservators are conscious of the need to continue learning and developing their conservation skills throughout the rest of their working life. This consciousness is aided by the encouragement for practising conservators to become involved in 'continuing professional development' (CPD) (e.g. through attending seminars, conferences, visits and workshops). The benefit derived from a practical experience can be enhanced by debriefing whether through discussion or writing a report since it draws out the key points and makes the individual aware of what has been learnt from the experience.

Child (1994) has noted the present emphasis on preventive conservation encourages a 'hands off' attitude to conservation. This unfortunately reinforces an inexperienced conservator's natural lack of confidence in using vigorous interventive methods with important historic and archaeological objects. It is, therefore, important for conservation students to take opportunities, especially during their student years or early professional experience, to become familiar with undertaking substantive intervention conservation work, such as extensive cleaning or restoration. This reduces the risk that their future judgements will be clouded by caution because of their own lack of confidence or experience and decisions to pursue preventive conservation methods are made purely on the grounds of appropriateness.

Though the AIC and UKIC codes both refer to conservators not working in areas beyond their competence, it is difficult for the conservator to judge when they have reached the edge of their competence and an object is imperilled. All conservation processes carry risks, and although the conservator always tries to minimize that risk, since no two objects ever react exactly the same, there is always some element of risk. Practitioners in all professions only learn through working at the edge of their competence. This is made safer by:

- The presence and advice of a senior colleague who can act as a guide and safety net in such situations.

- Qualified conservators should, through their training courses, further reading and experience, be well aware of the many other areas of specialist conservation expertise which exist. In such areas consultation with a fellow conservator in the field is essential. As a result of such discussions it will become clear who has the appropriate level of competence to undertake the conservation work required.

- Trying procedures, where possible, on fragments, samples or 'less valuable' objects is a process often used by conservators of all levels of experience to build up their confidence and expertise to a level where they can successfully tackle new or difficult treatments on 'valuable' or difficult objects.

13.8 Advocacy

A conservator's work is limited by the fact that 'they only have one pair of hands'. Greater volumes of conservation work will be achieved if others are persuaded to do conservation work as well. This persuasion or advocacy can take many forms: publication in conservation journals and conferences, publication in the journals of the numerous related fields, public speaking (whether to the local Women's Institute or international conferences), exhibitions and appearances in the media. All such communication emphasizing the values and basic principles of conservation will encourage people to take good care of their own objects and it will inform a wide range of people about conservation (MGC 1993c, 1997). It may also encourage financial and political support for larger conservation projects. The people who receive this communication represent an enormous group of potential preservers of, and carers for, objects. They can do infinitely more good for more objects than any single conservator could achieve.

Advocacy can be a powerful tool; however, there are risks in describing conservation work, as unqualified individuals may attempt to copy some of the things mentioned and through lack of skill and understanding damage objects. Consequently conservators should provide minimal details of materials and practices for widespread public consumption. Conservators should also be aware that radio, television, magazines and particularly newspapers are in the business of making a profit, thus they will amend (edit) the information provided by the conservator in order to make a more dramatic or controversial story (see Case study 7A). Where conservators control the delivery of the message – as in the case of exhibitions such as 'Stop the Rot' at York Castle Museum and 'Preserving the Past' by the Getty Conservation Institute (Podany and Lansing Maish 1993) – it can be delivered with clarity and subtlety.

13A Case study: Cartoon – Leonardo da Vinci – *The Virgin and Child with St Anne and St John the Baptist* (Harding and Oddy 1992)

The cartoon *The Virgin and Child with St Anne and St John the Baptist* was drawn by Leonardo da Vinci in 1507–8 using chalk and charcoal on paper. It was purchased by The National Gallery in 1962–3 from the Royal Academy. On 17 July 1987 a man entered the National Gallery and fired a shotgun at the picture. He was subsequently detained in Broadmoor high-security hospital. The picture, which had been protected behind laminated glass, sustained an approximate 100-mm circle of extensive damage. The National Gallery employs some of the world's finest conservators of oil paintings amongst their conservation staff. However, they have less expertise in dealing with works of art on paper and, after seeking advice from a number of experts, seconded Eric Harding, Chief Conservator of Western Pictorial Art at the British Museum (and previously a member of staff at the National Gallery) to conserve the damaged picture.

Detailed observation established that none of the shotgun pellets had penetrated the plastic laminate layer in the glass, although the force of the blast had pushed fragments of glass into the paper, fragmented the paper and caused pigment loss in the damaged area. Small fragments of the detached paper and pigment were analysed, as was the construction of the picture itself. The cartoon is drawn in white chalk and black charcoal, without any binder, on to a piece of paper composed of six smaller sheets stuck together. The surface of the paper had been coloured with a mixture of chalk, soot and iron oxide which had been rubbed into the surface to give a mid-red-tone background on to which the image of the picture was drawn. At a later date, possibly in the eighteenth century, the cartoon had been stuck on to canvas secured over a wooden stretcher. The paper had been poorly attached to the canvas with a number of tears and wrinkles clearly visible. Prior to the attachment to the canvas there had been a number of repairs and patches applied to support tears and cover missing areas of the cartoon; the picture had clearly received poor treatment earlier in life. Several of these repairs were of poor quality. It was desirable to remove the cartoon from its now distorted canvas backing, relax the paper so removing the creases and wrinkles, reback it on to a stable support, redo the earlier repairs and de-acidify the paper which had become brittle because of acidity, a condition which is considerably increased by the adhesive and canvas backing. However, it was felt that such remedial conservation action could not be undertaken since it would risk greater damage to the object:

- Any attempt to remove the paper from the canvas would risk weakening the adhesive holding the six sheets of paper together and thus offsetting part of the original image.

- Unbacked the paper would be difficult to handle and very weak thus there would be a considerable risk of exacerbating some of the existing tears.

- The moisture would differentially affect the pigments dislodging some, whilst binding others closer to the paper. There could consequently be considerable alteration to the visual effect of the image.

- Any dry backing would require working on the picture, face down, with consequent loss of surface pigments.

- Any non-aqueous de-acidification would again require the use of a solvent which would have some effect on the pigment particles and thus alter the visual effect of the image. The chalk highlights appeared particularly vulnerable to alteration through aqueous or solvent treatment.

In view of these factors it was decided that only very localized and limited conservation would be undertaken. After collecting all the shattered pieces of paper and removing all pieces of glass embedded in the paper, the distorted canvas was flattened through localized humidification, using an ultrasonic humidifier and modified suction tables. When flattened the canvas was removed from the wooden stretcher and backed on to another piece of paper and canvas using wheat-starch paste. All the pieces of shattered paper from the damaged area were readhered in place, eventually only leaving approximately $1\,cm^2$ empty. This was filled with a piece of new paper visually similar to the original which was cut to shape and inserted. There were many thin lines of pigment loss as well as the new piece of paper. Powdered chalk, charcoal and other pigments were used to tone down these areas to harmonize with the rest of the image. Applied dry to the surface this pigment

Figure 13.2 Leonardo da Vinci cartoon, *The Virgin and Child with St Anne and St John the Baptist*, after restoration (photograph courtesy of The National Gallery).

could readily be removed by future conservators if required. The cartoon, mounted in a new frame, again protected with laminated glass, was returned to display in May 1989. The damage is not visible to the casual observer, only detectable upon detailed inspection (see Figure 13.2).

This conservation work, whilst restoring the image, demonstrated the careful consideration which is needed by a conservator. There was clear recognition of the limitations of their own skills by the conservators of the National Gallery and the benefits of involving more specialized and experienced colleagues clearly paid dividends.

Examination gave clear information about the materials and techniques used to create this work of art, providing a clear indication of the sensitivity of the materials used. There was very careful judgement made in the extent of conservation, with the potential improvement to the stability and longevity of the cartoon balanced against the risk of further damage.

14 Conclusion

14.1 The evolution of conservation

Conservation is no longer the scraping clean, recarving and affixing of missing limbs to the damaged Roman statues of a minor Renaissance prince. It has become a widespread public concern for preserving, revealing and studying the past. This evolution of conservation has been based on a number of separate phenomena, many of which have been exemplified by the case studies used in this book.

The rise of the concept of accuracy and provable (absolute) truth

In the sixteenth century, 'conservation' was an inherently subjective discipline, cleaning and restoring the great and beautiful works of art of the past. Conservators responded to objects purely as aesthetic entities. Through the growth of scholarship in the seventeenth, eighteenth and nineteenth centuries, restoration work became more sophisticated leading to the 'in the style of' restoration of the nineteenth century. The development of the concept of certainty and physical proof, aided by the developments in technology, social justice and education, had by the late twentieth century created a public expectation for truth and accuracy in all things. The expectation of increasingly truthful restoration work is shown by the re-restoration of the Sutton Hoo Helmet and Holbein's *The Ambassadors*.

The modern desire for truth will no longer merely accept scholarly opinion, it demands a provable truth supported with evidence from a battery of scientific techniques. These are now capable of dating and revealing the details of the last meal, and manner of execution, of Lindow Man, killed nearly 2,000 years ago. However, the search for greater truth, and in particular the revealing of that truth, can lead to the problems as seen with the garden of the Elkanah Deane House in Colonial Williamsburg and the cleaning of the Sistine Chapel ceiling.

The evolution of the subject of conservation, and the rising quest for the truth, has seen the recognition of objects as historic documents. The presence of this valuable evidence of the past, in every object, was articulated in the late nineteenth century by William Morris and the members of the Society for the Protection of Ancient Buildings. One result of this has been much greater appreciation of the value which objects, often of limited aesthetic impact, contain in terms of historic information (e.g. the Laetoli footprints and the body of Lindow Man). The presence of soiling and information related to the use of the object is increasingly seen as crucial to the truth of the object and greater efforts are being made to record, investigate and retain this information.

Wider social development

The growth of democracy and the power of the people through the twentieth century has meant that it is no longer the art of an elite which is conserved, but objects and symbols which are important to a wide range of people such as the Forth Railway Bridge and the Statue of Liberty which are conserved. The popular enthusiasm for objects of the recent past has resulted in the establishment of many industrial and folk museums containing working objects. Though they provide informative activity many working objects have been excessively restored and have thus lost some of their value as historic objects.

The decline in the eighteenth- and nineteenth-century European empires and the rise by the late twentieth century of national independence for most countries of the world has led to increased emphasis on the preservation by each country of its own historic national culture. Thus an increasingly diverse range of objects is being preserved and displayed.

The public enthusiasm for scientific and technical advances developed during the nineteenth century and continued into the 1960s producing products such as man-made fibres and putting a man on the Moon. However, the social cost of developments such as atomic power (CND formed in 1958) and drugs like thalidomide (withdrawn in 1961) led to a perceptible public caution, from the 1960s onwards, regarding some of the uses of chemicals, radioactivity and biotechnology. This appears to have influenced conservation to reduce its use of chemicals with far greater awareness of health-and-safety issues when handling and using chemicals (see Section 8.6). There has been a reduction in the use of fumigants and biocides with research and development having focused on anoxia and freezing treatments for insect eradication. There is also greater caution in the use of polymers since many used in the past have proved unstable.

The recognition of the importance of context

The loss of associated information, caused by removing objects from their original settings and mounting them like trophies in nineteenth-century museums, led to the increasing preference for preserving objects such as the Laetoli footprints *in situ*. Expressed in many different forms this approach has led to historic houses being preserved 'as found' and where possible preserved within their landscape.

The increasing ability to travel means that it is possible to visit many of the countries of the world and see their culture *in situ*. Tourism and the media have encouraged a globalization of culture which is leading to the development of concepts such as world heritage, an increased sensitivity to the culture of native peoples and recognition of the non-physical attributes of objects.

The desire for a more holistic experience of the past has led to the creation of museums, such as Colonial Williamsburg and the National Museum of Wales Folk Museum at St Fagans. This has resulted in the preservation of a large cross-section of historic objects.

Increased efforts to preserve the past *in situ*, often spurred on by ideas of a loss of national (heritage) identity, has resulted in legislation which protects historic buildings and ancient monuments, including unexcavated archaeological sites.

The development of science and technology of the nineteenth and twentieth centuries

The creation of instruments for elemental analysis (AAS, EDXRF, ICPMS, etc.) and investigation (X-radiography, IR imaging, SEM) has permitted the accurate analysis of

Figure 14.1 Conservators Phil Clogg and Jennifer Jones 'freeze lifting' a neolithic hurdle on the beach at Seaton Carew (photograph courtesy of the author and Jennifer Jones). An early neolithic hurdle, composed of a waterlogged mat of interwoven degraded hazel withes which was exposed by the tide on the beach at Seaton Carew, County Durham. Following excavation and recording of the hurdle by the Cleveland Archaeological Unit the hurdle was frozen solid using solid CO_2 pellets and lifted just ahead of the incoming tide.

ancient materials such as the De Walden Helmets, the Bush Barrow Gold and the Benwell Box. An increasingly reliable body of knowledge is consequently being assembled about ancient materials permitting some objects to be identified as fakes and others to be reconstructed from scant remains.

Improvements in technology and materials have enabled many objects which would previously have perished to be conserved. The invention of freeze-drying and the creation and use of water-soluble waxes, such as polyethylene glycol, have enabled bog bodies such as Lindow Man to be preserved. The range of modern polymers available as solvents, adhesives and consolidants permitted a reversible treatment to be applied to the fragmentary remains of St Cuthbert's Coffin (Cronyn and Horie 1985) whilst root-growth-retarding geotextiles could be utilized for preserving the Laetoli footprints. The development of techniques such as laser cleaning (Cooper 1998) and freeze lifting (Jones 1997, see Figure 14.1), and products for adsorbing gaseous pollutants such as 'Microchamber' products (Hollinger 1994) are continually improving the conservator's ability to reveal, investigate and preserve objects.

Conservation evolving from its own mistakes

Failure of materials and treatments of the past have influenced conservation ethics leading to concepts such as reversibility and minimum intervention. This has led to careful selection of materials and techniques as reflected in the materials used in the conservation of the Laetoli footprints or the Portland Vase. Many of these materials are selected because of their long-term stability

The absence of information regarding earlier conservation work (e.g. experienced in the reconservation of The Portland Vase and Holbein's painting *The Ambassadors*), has emphasized the need for the creation of accurate conservation records. The creation of such records marked the change from the ideals of a craft, where the immediate quality of the visual image of the object was important, to a profession which recognized the need for long-term care including retreatment of objects. The large volume of information now generated through analysis and study of objects as historic documents has created the need for long-term storage of these 'permanent' conservation records.

Taking a step back from the immediacy of interventive conservation to look at the generic causes of damage and decay of objects in museum storage led to the development of preventive conservation. The benefits for objects of establishing proactive regimes of stable storage environments, testing display and storage materials and disaster planning led to their widespread adoption. This change saw conservators moving their thinking from the level of the individual object to that of the whole collection.

Much of the present emphasis in conservation is on preservation for posterity, ensuring that the remains of the past will be available for future generations to study. This stems from a recognition of the continually advancing nature of technology and knowledge and the concern that, as has occurred in the past, the conservation techniques of the present day could be stripping away useful information obtainable in the future. The concept of stewardship encapsulates the concept of care for the future, responsibility without absolute ownership. Efforts are, therefore, made to ensure that evidence, such as the conserved remains of Lindow Man, are preserved for future research through storage in stable environmental conditions.

The continued desire to restore the aesthetic entity of objects

There remains a very human desire in conservators to clean, mend and restore. This is harnessed to the essential need to have objects available to educate, amaze and attract the visiting public. The increasing development of the skills of conservation practitioners allows the treatment of objects which previous generations have struggled to achieve, such as the reconservation of the Portland Vase, the Sutton Hoo Helmet and the da Vinci *The Virgin and Child with St Anne and St John the Baptist*. The natural desire to clean, uncover and make whole is, however, balanced by the intellectual requirements to preserve, investigate and record.

Organization and resources

The continued growth in collection of historic and artistic artefacts has to be reconciled with the limited resources available for storage and conservation of these collections. Efforts to maximize the benefit of limited resources (i.e. management) have resulted in prioritization achieved primarily through collection surveys, disaster planning, differing levels of conservation, estimation and contract conservation, work scheduling, cost–benefit analysis, team and project working and the use of conservation managers.

Debate and conflict

Undoubtedly the most difficult way in which conservation evolves is through conflict. The controversies within the profession are usually those associated with developing technology and science of materials, demonstrating the problems caused by earlier treatments; for example, the use of soluble nylon (Bockhoff *et al.* 1984) and Chloramine T (Bomford 1994). A healthy debate within the profession, such as that surrounding the Bush Barrow Gold, is desirable in order to move the subject forward. Public debate, such as that surrounding the cleaning of the Sistine Chapel, is also important since it reminds conservators of the importance which objects can still have for the public. Unfortunately the level of the public debate is often uninformed and retreats to stereotypes. Such incidents remind conservators that conservation is an area which is largely publicly funded and that conservators must be prepared to defend their actions in the public arena.

Conservation is essential to ensure that historic and artistic artefacts are preserved and continue to fascinate and inform people about their past. The subject must evolve if conservators are to remain effective in a world with continually changing social and financial priorities. An awareness of the way in which the past is important to the present, and the way in which the human brain reaches judgements, should enable conservators to make the best possible judgements regarding the conservation of historic and artistic artefacts within the context of the society in which they operate.

14.2 Good judgement

Whilst good judgement frequently develops through experience, it also develops through a constant willingness to question what one is doing and why one is doing it. Two of the strongest questioning approaches have been those of Child, and Ashley-Smith and the staff of the V&A Museum.

Ethical questions based on those of Child (1994):

- What is the value of this object for the museum/owner?

- What is the value of this object to the future?

- How will this value change over time?

- What effect will the various forms of conservation (preservation, investigation, cleaning, restoration) have on this value?

- What benefit does the museum/owner derive from this conservation?

- Does the museum have the money, time, facilities and expertise to undertake the conservation?

- Does the conservation laboratory have the time, facilities and expertise to undertake the conservation?

- Can the museum maintain the object in the relevant stored, displayed or restored state?

Ethical questions based on those of Ashley-Smith and the V&A Conservation Department (1994):

- Why is conservation needed?

- Have I consulted existing records?

- Do I need to consult the clients, my peers, other specialists?

- Have I considered all the factors contributing to the identity and significance of the object: historical, technical, associations, sanctity, creator's intention?

- What effects will the conservation have on the evidence of these factors?

- Do I have sufficient skill and information to assess and implement the conservation?

- What are my options for conservation which will produce an acceptable result with minimum intervention?

- What are the advantages of each course of conservation?

- Can the use of environment be adapted instead of intervening on the object?

- What are the resource implications of my actions, and does my intended conservation make best use of resources?

- Do established courses of action need to be adapted or new ones developed?

- Are all my actions fully documented to a known and accepted standard?

- Are my records accessible to appropriate users?

- How will my conservation affect subsequent conservation work?

- Have I taken account of the future use and location of the object?

- How will I assess the success of the conservation and how will I get feedback from owners/curators and peers?

All these questions should be answered before proceeding with any conservation work. They raise crucial questions, but the focus of any envisaged conservation work is determined by knowing:

- What are the truths contained within the object?

and then judging:

- Where does the best balance lie between seeing this object as an aesthetic entity and a historic document?

or for working objects:

- Where does the best balance lie between seeing this object as an aesthetic entity, a historic document and an informative activity?

and crucially:

- Where does the best balance lie between revelation, investigation and preservation for this object?

Bibliography

Abercromby, M. L. J. (1960) *The Anatomy of Judgement*, Harmondsworth: Penguin.

Adkins, L. and Adkins, R. A. (1989) *Archaeological Illustration*, Cambridge: Cambridge University Press.

Agnew, N. (1995) 'The China projects', *Conservation, The GCI Newsletter* X(III): 6.

Agnew, N. and Demas, M. (1998) 'Preserving the Laetoli footprints', *Scientific American* September 1988: 26–37.

Agnew, N. and Levin, J. (1996) 'Adapting technology for conservation', *Conservation, The GCI Newsletter* 11(3): 16–18.

AIC (American Institute of Conservation) (1985) *Code of Ethics and Standards of Practice*, New York: AIC.

—— (1994) 'Code of Ethics and Guidelines for Practice', *AIC News* May 1994: 17–20.

AICCM (Australian Institute for the Conservation of Cultural Material) (1986) *Code of Ethics and Guidance for Conservation Practice*, Canberra, Australia: AICCM.

Aitken, M. J. (1990) *Science Based Dating in Archaeology*, London: Longman.

Ames, M. (1994) 'Cannibal tours, glass boxes and the politics of interpretation' in S. M. Pearce (ed.) *Interpreting Objects and Collections*, London: Routledge.

Andrews, T. M., Andrews, W. M. and Baker, C. (1992) 'An investigation into the removal of enzymes from paper following conservation treatment', *Journal of the American Institute of Conservation* 31(3): 313–23.

Apollo (1987) 'Editorial: Mass tourism and the conservators', *Apollo* 126: 390–1.

Appelbaum, B. (1987) 'Criteria for treatment: Reversibility', *Journal of the American Institute for Conservation* 26: 65–73.

Appleyard, H. M. (1978) *Guide to the Identification of Animal Fibres*, Leeds: British Textile Technology Group.

Ashley-Smith, J. (1982) 'The ethics of conservation', *The Conservator* 6: 1–5.

—— (1994) 'A constant approach to a mixed collection', in A. Oddy (ed.) *Restoration: Is It Acceptable?*, British Museum Occasional Paper No. 99, London: British Museum Press.

—— (1997) 'Risk analysis', in S. Bradley (ed.) *The Interface Between Science and Conservation*, British Museum Occasional Paper No. 116, London: British Museum Press.

—— (1999) *Risk Assessment for Object Conservation*, Oxford: Butterworth-Heinemann.

Ashley-Smith, J., Umney, N. and Ford, D. (1994) 'Let's be honest – realistic environmental parameters for loaned objects', in A. Roy and P. Smith (eds) *Preventive Conservation Practice, Theory and Research*: 1994 IIC Ottawa Congress, London: IIC.

Ashurst, J. and Ashurst, N. (1988) *Practical Building Conservation*, English Heritage Technical Handbooks Vols 1–5, Aldershot: Gower.

Ashurst, J. and Dimes F. G. (1990) *Conservation of Building and Decorative Stone*, Vols 1 and 2, Oxford: Butterworth-Heinemann.

Baboian, R., Cliver, E. B. and Bellante, E. L. (eds) (1990) *The Statue of Liberty Restoration*, Houston, Texas: National Association of Corrosion Engineers.

Baillie, M. G. L. (1995) *A Slice Through Time*, London: Routledge.

Ball, S. and Winsor, P. (1997) *Larger and Working Objects: A Guide to Their Preservation and Care*, London: Museums and Galleries Commission.

Barclay, M. H. (1990) 'An art gallery conservator: Roles and responsibilities', in B. Ramsay-Jolicoeur and I. N. M. Wainwright (eds) *Shared Responsibility*, Ottawa: National Gallery of Canada.

Barclay, R. L. (1997) *The Care of Historical Musical Instruments*, Edinburgh: MGC, CCI, CIMCIM.

Barton, G. and Weik, S. (1984) 'Maori carvings: Ethical considerations in their conservation', in *ICOM-CC 7th Triennial Meeting, Copenhagen 1984*, Copenhagen: ICOM-CC.

Batchelor, R. (1994) 'Not looking at kettles', in S. M. Pearce (ed.) *Interpreting Objects and Collections*, London: Routledge.

Beck, J. and Daley, M. (1993) *Art Restoration: The Culture, the Business and the Scandal*, London: Murray.

Beeton, I. (1859) *Mrs Beetons's Household Management*, London: Ward Lock.

Belk, R. W. (1994) 'Collectors and collecting', in S. M. Pearce (ed.) *Interpreting Objects and Collections*, London: Routledge.

Berducou, M. (1996) 'Introduction to archaeological conservation', in N. Stanley Price, M. Kirby Talley, Jr and A. M. Vaccaro (eds) *Historical and Philosophical Issues in the Conservation of Cultural Heritage*, Los Angeles: The Getty Conservation Institute.

Berger, C. (1992) 'The Queen and Madame X', *The Independent on Sunday*, 19 January 1992: 10–11.

Bilz, M. and Grattan, D. W. (1996) 'The ageing of Parylene: Difficulties with the Arrhenius approach', in *ICOM–CC 11th Triennial Meeting, Edinburgh 1996*, Edinburgh: ICOM-CC.

Bilz, M., Dean, L., Grattan, D. W., McCawley, J. C. and McMillen, L. (1993) 'A study of the thermal breakdown of polyethylene glycol', in P. Hoffmann (ed.) *Proceedings of the 5th ICOM Group on Wet Organic Archaeological Materials Conference, Portland, Maine 1993*, Bremerhaven: ICOM-CC.

Bintliff, J. (1988) 'A review of contemporary perspectives on the 'meaning' of the past', in J. Bintliff (ed.) *Extracting Meaning from the Past*, Oxford: Oxbow.

Black, J. (1997) 'Letter: The Forth Bridge as a work of art', *The Times*, 26 June 1997: 23.

Blackshaw, S. M. and Daniels, V. D. (1979) 'The testing of materials for use in storage and display in museums', *The Conservator* 3: 16–19.

Blyth, V. and Hillyer, L. (1993) 'Carpet beetle – A pilot study in detection and control', *The Conservator* 16: 65–77.

Bockhoff, F., Guo, K-M., Richards, G. E. and Bockhoff, E. (1984) 'Infrared studies of the kinetics of stabilisation of soluble nylon' in N. Bromelle, E. Pye, P. Smith and G. Thomson (eds) *Adhesives and Consolidants: 1984 IIC Paris Congress*, London: IIC.

Bomford, D. (1994) 'Changing taste in the restoration of paintings', in A. Oddy (ed.) *Restoration: Is It Acceptable?* British Museum Occasional Paper No. 99, London: British Museum Press.

Bowditch, G. (1993) 'Painting the Forth Bridge halts at last', *The Times*, 2 February 1993: 3.

Boylan, P. J. (1995) 'Illicit trafficking in antiquities and museum ethics', in K. W. Tubb (ed.) *Antiquities: Trade or Betrayed*, London: Archetype.

Bradley, S. (1983) 'Conservation recording in the British Museum', *The Conservator* 7: 9–12.

Brand, S. (1994) *How Buildings Learn*, London: Orion.

Brandi, C. (1996) 'Theory of restoration I', in N. S. Price, M. Kirby Talley and A. M. Vaccaro (eds.) *Historical and Philosophical Issues in the Conservation of Cultural Heritage*, Los Angeles: Getty Conservation Institute.

Brandt, K. W–G. (1987) 'Twenty-five questions about Michelangelo's Sistine Ceiling', *Apollo* 126: 392–400.

Brewster, D. (1861) 'Optical phenomena of ancient decomposed glass', *Transactions of The Royal Society of Edinburgh* 23: 193–204.

Brinch Madsen, H. (1987) 'Artefact conservation in Denmark at the beginning of the last century', in J. Black (ed.) *Recent Advances in the Conservation and Analysis of Artefacts*, London: Summer Schools Press.

British Leather Manufacturers Association (1957) *Hides, Skins and Leather under the Microscope*, Egham, Surrey: British Leather Manufacturers Association.

Brodie, F. (1994) 'Clocks and watches, a re-appraisal?', in A. Oddy (ed.) *Restoration: Is It Acceptable?* British Museum Occasional Paper 99, London: British Museum Press, 27–32.

Bromelle, N. S. and Thomson, G. (eds) (1982) *Science and Technology in the Service of Conservation: 1982 IIC Washington Congress*, London: IIC.

Brooks, M. M. (1998) 'International conservation codes of ethics and practice and their implications for teaching and learning ethics in textile conservation education with special reference to the Diploma in Textile Conservation taught at the Textile Conservation Centre', in D. Eastop and A. Timar–Balazsy (eds) *International Perspectives in Textile Conservation*, London: Archetype.

Brooks, M. M., Clark, C., Eastop, D. and Petschek, C. (1994) 'Restoration or conservation – issues for textile conservators, a textile conservation perspective', in A. Oddy (ed.) *Restoration: Is It Acceptable?*, British Museum Occasional Paper No. 99, London: British Museum Press.

Brooks, M., Lister, A., Eastop, D. and Bennett, T. (1996) 'Artefact or information? Articulating the conflicts in conserving archaeological textiles', in A. Roy and P. Smith (eds) *Archaeological Conservation and Its Consequences: IIC 1996 Copenhagen Congress*, London: IIC.

Brostoff, L. B. (1995) 'Investigation into the interaction of benzotriazole with copper corrosion minerals and surfaces', in I. D. MacLeod, S. L. Pennec and L. Robbiola (eds) *Metals 95, Proceedings of the International Conference on Metals Conservation*, London: James & James.

Bruce-Mitford, R. (1978) *The Sutton Hoo Ship Burial: Vol. 2, Arms, Armour and Regalia*, London: British Museum Publications.

Buys, S. and Oakley V. (1993) *The Conservation and Restoration of Ceramics*, Oxford: Butterworth-Heinemann.

Byrne, A. F. and Cook, I. L. (1976) 'The preparation and examination of cross sections', in C. Pearson and G. L. Pretty (eds) *Proceedings of the National Seminar on the Conservation of Cultural Material, Perth, 1973*, Perth: ICCM (Institute for the Conservation of Cultural Material).

Caldararo, N. L. (1987) 'An outline history of conservation in archaeology and anthropology as presented through its publications', *Journal of the American Institute for Conservation* 26(2): 85–104.

Campbell, L. (1998) 'The conservation of Netherlandish paintings in the fifteenth and sixteenth centuries', in C. Sitwell and S. Staniforth (eds) *Studies in the History of Painting Restoration*, London: Archetype.

Caple, C. (1996) 'The creation of self-development learning packages (SDLP) and formalised object construction and use sequences (FOCUS)', *ICOM-CC 11th Triennial Meeting, Edinburgh 1996*, Edinburgh: ICOM-CC.

Caple C. and Murray, W. (1994) 'Characterisation of a waterlogged charred wood and development of a conservation treatment', *Studies in Conservation* 39(1): 28–38.

Caple C., Dungworth D. and Clogg, P. (1997) 'The assessment and protection of archaeo-logical organic materials in waterlogged burial environments', in P. Hoffmann, T. Grant, J. A. Spriggs and T. Daley (eds) *Proceedings of the 6th Waterlogged Organic Archaeological Materials Conference, York 1996*, Bremerhaven: ICOM-CC Working Group on Wet Organic Materials.

Cassar, M. (1995) *Environmental Management Guidelines for Museums and Galleries*, London: Butterworth-Heinemann.

Catling, D. and Grayson, J. (1982) *Identification of Vegetable Fibres*, London: Chapman & Hall.

Cellini, B. (1878) *Memoirs of Benvenuto Cellini, A Florentine Artist*, trans. T. Roscoe, London: G. Bell.

Chamberlin, E. R. (1979) *Preserving the Past*, London: Dent.

Champion, T. (1996) 'Protecting the monuments: Archaeological legislation from the 1882 Act to PPG 16', in M. Hunter (ed.) *Preserving the Past*, Stroud: Alan Sutton Publishing.

Child, R. E. (1988) 'Ethics in conservation of social history material', in V. Todd (ed.) *Preprints for the UKIC 30th Anniversary Conference*, London: UKIC.

—— (1994) 'Putting things in context – The ethics of working collections', in A. Oddy (ed.) *Restoration: Is it Acceptable?*, British Museum Occasional Paper No. 99, London: British Museum Press.

—— (1997) 'Ethics and museum conservation', in G. Edson (ed.) *Museum Ethics*, London: Routledge.

Child, R. E. and Pinniger, D. B. (1987) 'Insect pest control in UK museums', in J. Black (ed.) *Recent Advances in Conservation and Analysis of Artefacts*, London: Summer Schools Press.

—— (1994) 'Insect trapping in museums and historic houses', in A. Roy and P. Smith (eds) *Preventive Conservation Practice, Theory and Research: 1994 IIC Ottawa Congress*, London: IIC.

Chippindale, C. (1983) *Stonehenge Complete*, London: Thames & Hudson.

—— (1988) 'Editorial', *Antiquity* 62: 207–8.

Clarke, D. V., Cowie, T. G. and Foxon, A. (1985) *Symbols of Power, at the Time of Stonehenge*, Edinburgh: HMSO.

Clavir, M. (1994) 'Preserving conceptual integrity: Ethics and theory in preventive conservation', in A. Roy and P. Smith (eds) *Preventive Conservation Practice, Theory and Research: 1994 IIC Ottawa Congress*, London: IIC.

—— (1996) 'Reflections on changes in museums and the conservation of collections from indigenous peoples', *Journal of the American Institute for Conservation* 35(2): 99–107.

Cleere, H. (1984) 'Great Britain', in H. Cleere (ed.) *Approaches to the Archaeological Heritage*, Cambridge: Cambridge University Press.

Clement, E. (1995) 'The aims of the 1970 UNESCO Convention on the Means of Prohibiting and Preventing the Illicit Import, Export and Transfer of Ownership of Cultural Property and action being taken by UNESCO to assist in its implementation', in K. W. Tubb (ed.) *Antiquities: Trade or Betrayed*, London: Archetype.

Colalucci, G. (1991) 'The frescoes of Michelangelo on the vault of the Sistine Chapel: Original technique and conservation', in S. Cather (ed.) *The Conservation of Wall Paintings*, Los Angeles: Getty Conservation Institute.

Colvin, H. (1985) *The National Trust, Calke Abbey, Derbyshire: A Hidden House Revealed*, London: Antler Books.

Cooper, M. (1998) *Laser Cleaning in Conservation*, Oxford: Butterworth-Heinemann.

Coremans, P. (1969) 'The training of restorers' in ICOM (ed.) *Problems of Conservation in Museums*, London: Allen & Unwin.

Corfield, M. (1983) 'Conservation records in the Wiltshire Library and Museums Services', *The Conservator* 7: 5–8.

—— (1988a) 'Towards a conservation profession', in V. Todd (ed.) *Conservation Today, Papers Presented at the UKIC 30th Anniversary Conference 1988*, London: UKIC.

—— (1988b) 'The reshaping of archaeological metal objects: Some ethical considerations', *Antiquity* 62: 261–5.

—— (1992) 'Conservation documentation', in J. Thompson (ed.) *The Manual of Curatorship*, Oxford: Butterworth-Heinemann.

—— (1993) 'Monitoring the condition of waterlogged archaeological sites', in P. Hoffmann (ed.) *Proceedings of the 5th ICOM Working Group on Wet Organic Archaeological Materials Conference, Portland, Maine*, Bremerhaven: ICOM-CC.

Corzo, M. A. and Afshar, M. (eds) (1993) *Art and Eternity, the Nefertari Wall Paintings Conservation Project 1986–1992*, Marina del Rey: GCI & J. Paul Getty Trust.

Craddock, P. T. (1978) 'The composition of the copper alloys used by the Greeks, Etruscan and Roman civilisations: 3, The origins and early use of brass', *Journal of Archaeological Science* 5: 1–16.

Cronyn, J. (1990) *The Elements of Archaeological Conservation*, London: Routledge.

Cronyn, J. M. and Horie, C. V. (1985) *St. Cuthbert's Coffin*, Durham: The Dean and Chapter of Durham Cathedral.

Curnoe, G. (1990) 'Owning ideas, appropriation and protective collectives', in B. Ramsay-Jolicoeur and I. N. M. Wainwright (eds) *Shared Responsibility*, Ottawa: National Gallery of Canada.

Dauma, M. and Henchman, M. (1997) 'The scientific evaluation of images', in S. Bradley (ed.) *The Interface Between Science and Conservation*, British Museum Occasional Paper No. 116, London: British Museum Press.

Davy, H. (1821) 'Some observations and experiments on the papyri found in the ruins of Herculaneum', *Philosophical Transactions of the Royal Society of London* 111: 191–208.

Davy, V. (1826) 'Observations on the changes that have taken place in some ancient alloys of copper', *Philosophical Transactions of the Royal Society of London* 116: 55–9.

Deetz, J. and Dethlefsen, E. S. (1994) 'Death's head, cherub, urn and willow', in S. M. Pearce (ed.) *Interpreting Objects and Collections*, London: Routledge.

Demas, M., Agnew, N., Waane, S., Podany, J., Bass, A. and Kamamba, D. (1996) 'Preservation of the Laetoli hominid trackway in Tanzania', in A. Roy and P. Smith (eds) *Archaeological Conservation and Its Consequences: 1996 IIC Copenhagen Congress*, London: IIC.

Dollery, D. (1994) 'A methodology of preventive conservation for a large, expanding and mixed archaeological collection', in A. Roy and P. Smith (eds) *Preventive Conservation Practice, Theory and Research: 1994 IIC Ottawa Congress*, London: IIC.

Dollery, D. and Henderson, J. (1996) 'Conservation records for the archaeologist?', in A. Roy and P. Smith (eds) *Archaeological Conservation and Its Consequences, 1996 IIC Copenhagen Congress*, London: IIC.

Dorrell, P. (1989) *Photography in Archaeology and Conservation*, Cambridge: Cambridge University Press.

Dove, S. (1989) 'Conservation of glass-inlaid bronzes and lead curses from Uley, Gloucestershire', *The Conservator* 5: 31–5.

Dovey, B. (1992) 'Security', in M. A. Thompson (ed.) *Manual of Curatorship* (2nd edn), Oxford: Butterworth-Heinemann.

Dowman, A. (1970) *Conservation in Field Archaeology*, London: Methuen & Co. Ltd.

Down, D. (1983) 'Record keeping – Notes from a private restorer', *The Conservator* 7: 17.

Down, J. L. (1995) 'Adhesion projects at the Canadian Conservation Institute', in M. Wright and J. H. Townsend (eds) *Resins: Ancient and Modern*. Edinburgh: SSCR.

Drumheller, A. and Kaminitz, M. (1994) 'Traditional care and conservation, the merging of two disciplines at the National Museum of the American Indian', in A. Roy and P. Smith (eds) *Preventive Conservation Practice, Theory and Research: 1994 IIC Ottawa Congress*, London: IIC.

Drysdale, L. (1987) 'Me and my object – A very special relationship', *Conservation News* 33: 9.

—— (1988) 'The eternal triangle: Relationships between conservators, their clients and objects', in V. Todd (ed.) *Conservation Today, Papers Presented at the UKIC 30th Anniversary Conference 1988*, London: UKIC.

Duncan, C. (1994) 'Art museums and the ritual of citizenship', in S. M. Pearce (ed.) *Interpreting Objects and Collections*, London: Routledge.

Dungworth, D. (1995) 'Iron Age and Roman copper alloys from Northern Britain', unpublished PhD thesis, Department of Archaeology, University of Durham.

Eastop, D. (1998) 'Decision making in conservation: Determining the role of artefacts' in A. Timar Balazsy and D. Eastop (eds) *International Perspectives on Textile Conservation*, London: Archetype.

Eastop. D. and Brooks, M. (1996) 'To clean or not to clean: The value of soils and creases', *ICOM-CC 11th Triennial Meeting, Edinburgh 1996*, Edinburgh: ICOM-CC.

Edge, D. (1994) 'The armourer's craft: Restoration or conservation?', in A. Oddy (ed.) *Restoration: Is It Acceptable?*, British Museum Occasional Paper No. 99, London: British Museum Press.

Edson, G. (1997) *Museum Ethics*, London: Routledge.

Ekserdjian, D. (1987) 'The Sistine Ceiling and the critics', *Apollo* 126: 401–4.

Elia, R. (1995) 'Conservators and unprovenanced objects: Preserving the cultural heritage or servicing the antiquities trade?', in K. W. Tubb (ed.) *Antiquities: Trade or Betrayed*, London: Archetype.

Elliot, R. *et al.* (1994) 'Towards a material history methodology', in S. M. Pearce (ed.) *Interpreting Objects and Collections*, London: Routledge.

English Heritage (1991) *Exploring Our Past. Strategies for the Archaeology of England.* London: English Heritage.

—— (1995) *Brodsworth Hall*, London: English Heritage.

—— (1998) *Conservation led Regeneration*, London: English Heritage.

Erhardt, D. and Mecklenburg, M. (1994) 'Relative humidity re-examined', in A. Roy and P. Smith (eds) *Preventive Conservation Practice, Theory and Research: 1994 IIC Ottawa Congress*, London: IIC.

Evans, A. C. (1986) *The Sutton Hoo Ship Burial*, London: British Museum Publications.

Faraday, M. (1843) *On the Ventilation of Lamp Burners*, Royal Institution Lecture, 7 April 1843, London.

Fell, V. (1996) 'Washing away the evidence', in A. Roy and P. Smith (eds) *Archaeological Conservation and Its Consequences, 1996 IIC Copenhagen Congress*, London: IIC.

Feller, R. L. (1978) 'Standards in the evaluation of thermoplastic resins', ICOM-CC Fourth Triennial Conference, Zagreb 1978, Zagreb: ICOM-CC.

—— (1997) *Artists Pigments: A Handbook of Their Histories and Characteristics*, Vol. 1, Washington: National Gallery of Art.

Fowler, J. (1880) 'On the processes of decay and, incidentally, on the composition and texture of glass at different periods, and the history of its manufacture', *Archaeologia* 46: 65–162.

Fowler, P. (1992) *The Past in Contemporary Society: Then, Now*, London: Routledge.

France-Lanord, A. (1996) 'Knowing how to question the object before restoring it', in N. Stanley Price, M. Kirby Talley Jr and A. M. Vaccaro (eds) *Historical and Philosophical Issues in the Conservation of Cultural Heritage*, Los Angeles: The Getty Conservation Institute.

Frost, M. (1994) 'Working with design professionals: Preventive conservators as problem solvers, not problem creators', in A. Roy and P. Smith (eds) *Preventive Conservation Practice, Theory and Research: 1994 IIC Ottawa Congress*, London: IIC.

Fry, M. (1996) 'Buried but not forgotten: Sensitivity in disposing of major archaeological timbers', in A. Roy and P. Smith (eds) *Archaeological Conservation and Its Consequences: 1996 IIC Copenhagen Congress*, London: IIC.

Fry, R. (1997) 'Preservation or desecration? The legal position of the restorer', in P. Lindley (ed.) *Sculpture Conservation: Preservation or Interference*, Aldershot: Scolar Press.

Ganiaris, H. and Sully, D. (1998) 'Showcase construction: Materials and methods used in the Museum of London, *The Conservator* 22: 57–67.

Garfinkle, A. M., Fries, J., Lopez, D. and Possessky, L. (1997) 'Art conservation and the legal obligation to preserve artistic intent', *Journal of the American Institute for Conservation* 36(2): 151–63.

Geddes, J. (1982) 'The Sanctuary Ring of Durham Cathedral', *Antiquity* CVII: 125–9.

Gilardoni, A., Orsini, R. and Taccani, S. (1994) *X-Rays in Art* (2nd edn), Mandello Lario, Lecco, Italy: Gilardoni SpA.

Gilberg, M. (1987) 'Friedrich Rathgen: The father of modern archaeological conservation', *Journal of the American Institute for Conservation* 26(2): 105–20.

—— (1991) 'The effects of low oxygen atmospheres on museum pests', *Studies in Conservation* 36(2): 93–8.

—— (1997) 'Alfred Lucas: Egypt's Sherlock Holmes', *Journal of the American Institute for Conservation* 36(1): 31–48.

Gilberg, M. and Grattan, D. (1994) 'Oxygen free storage using "Ageless" oxygen adsorber', in A. Roy and P. Smith (eds) *Preventive Conservation Practice, Theory and Research: 1994 IIC Ottawa Congress*, London: IIC.

Giusti, A. (1994) 'Filling lacunae in Florentine mosaic and tessera mosaic: Reflections and proposals,' in A. Oddy (ed.) *Restoration: Is It Acceptable?*, British Museum Occasional Paper No. 99, London: British Museum Press.

Glob, P. V. (1969) *The Bog People: Iron-Age Man Preserved*, London: Faber.

Graham, R. and Eddie, T. (1985) *X-Ray Techniques in Art Galleries and Museums*. Bristol: Adam Hilger Ltd.

Green, L. (1991) 'Microchemical test', *Conservation News* 45: 35.

Green, L. and Thickett, D. (1993) 'Interlaboratory comparison of the Oddy Test', in N. Tennant (ed.) *Conservation Science in the UK*, London: James & James.

Greene, V. (1992) 'Accessories of holiness, defining Jewish sacred objects', *Journal of the American Institute for Conservation* 31(1): 31–9.

Griffiths, N., Jenner, A. and Wilson, C. (1990) *Drawing Archaeological Finds: A Handbook*, London: Archetype.

Hanssen-Bauer, F. (1996) 'Stability as a technical and an ethical requirement in Conservation', ICOM-CC 11th Triennial Meeting, Edinburgh 1996, Edinburgh: ICOM-CC.

Harding, E. and Oddy, W. A. (1992) 'Leonardo da Vinci's cartoon The Virgin and Child with St Anne and St John the Baptist', in W. A. Oddy (ed.) *The Art of the Conservator*, London: British Museum Press.

Hartin, D. D. (1990) 'An historical introduction to conservation', in B. Ramsay-Jolicoeur and I. N. M. Wainwright (eds) *Shared Responsibility*, Ottawa: National Gallery of Canada.

Haynes, M. L. (1993) 'Buried treasures: Wartime and recent uses of underground space for artefact storage', unpublished MA dissertation, Department of Archaeology, University of Durham.

Health and Safety Executive (1993) *A Step by Step Guide to COSHH Assessment*, London: HMSO.

Hedley, G. (1986) 'Cleaning and meaning: The ravished image reviewed', *The Conservator* 10: 2–6.

—— (1990) 'Long lost relations and new found relativities: Issues in the cleaning of paintings', in V. Todd (ed.) *Appearance, Opinion, Change: Evaluating the Look of Paintings*, London: UKIC.

Heuman, J. (ed.) 1995 *From Marble to Chocolate: the Conservation of Modern Sculpture*, London: Archetype.

Hoare, N. (1990) *Security for Museums*, London: Committee of Area Museum Councils and the Museums Association.

Hodder, I. (1994) 'The contextual analysis of symbolic meanings', in S. M. Pearce (ed.) *Interpreting Objects and Collections*, London: Routledge.

Hodges, H. W. M. (1964) *Artefacts*, London: John Barker.

—— (1975a) 'Problems and ethics of the restoration of pottery', in D. Leigh, A. Moncrieff, W. A. Oddy and P. Pratt (eds) *Conservation in Archaeology and the Applied Arts; 1975 IIC Stockholm Congress*, London: IIC.

—— (1975b) 'Problems and ethics in the conservation of metal objects', in D. Leigh, A. Moncrieff, W. A. Oddy and P. Pratt (eds) *Conservation in Archaeology and the Applied Arts: 1975 IIC Stockholm Congress*, London: IIC.

Hollinger, W. K. Jr (1994) 'MicroChamber papers used as a preventive conservation material', in A. Roy and P. Smith (eds) *Preventive Conservation Practice, Theory and Research: 1994 IIC Ottawa Congress*, London: IIC.

Horie, C. V. (1983) 'Reversibility of polymer treatments', *Resins in Conservation*: paper given at Proceedings of the Symposium, Edinburgh 1982, Edinburgh: SSCR: 3.1–3.6.

—— (1987) *Materials for Conservation*, London: Butterworth.

Horie, V. and Francis, D. M. (1984) 'A pilot study of moisture vapour transmission rate through Stewart's plastic boxes', *Conservation News* 23: 13–14.

Howie, F. (1978) 'Storage and conservation of geological material', *The Conservator* 2: 13–19.

—— (1987) *Safety in Museums and Art Galleries*, London: Butterworth.

ICOM-CC (International Council of Museums Conservation Committee) (1984) *The Conservator-Restorer: A Definition of the Profession*, Copenhagen: ICOM-CC.

—— (1993) *The ICOM-CC 10th Triennial Meeting, Washington, 22–27 August 1993*, Washington: ICOM.

—— (1996) *The ICOM-CC 11th Triennial Meeting, Edinburgh, 1–6 September 1996*, Edinburgh: ICOM.

Janaway, R. (1984) 'Textile fibre characteristics preserved by metal corrosion: The potential of SEM studies', *The Conservator* 7: 48–52.

Janaway, R. and Scott, B. (1989) *Evidence Preserved in Corrosion Products*, UKIC Occasional Paper No. 8, London: UKIC.

Jaeschke, R. L. (1996) 'When does history end', in A. Roy and P. Smith (eds) *Archaeological Conservation and Its Consequences: 1996 IIC Copenhagen Congress*, London: IIC.

Jedrzejewska, H. (1976) *Ethics in Conservation*, Stockholm: Kungel Konsthögskolan Institutet för Materialkunskap.

Jenner, C. (1994) 'Gilt-wood restoration: When is it acceptable?', in A. Oddy (ed.) *Restoration: Is It Acceptable?*, British Museum Occasional Paper No. 99, London: British Museum Press.

Jesperson, K. (1985) 'Extended storage of waterlogged wood in nature', in R. Ramiere and M. Colardelle (eds) *Waterlogged Wood Study and Conservation. Proceedings of the 2nd ICOM Waterlogged Wood Working Group Conference, Grenoble 1984*, Grenoble: ICOM-CC.

Johnson, J. S. (1993) 'Conservation and archaeology in Great Britain and the United States: A comparison', *Journal of the American Institute of Conservation* 32: 249–69.

Jones, J. (1997) 'Freeze lifting a neolithic wooden hurdle', in P. Hoffmann, T. Grant, J. A. Spriggs and T. Daley (eds) *Proceedings of the 6th Waterlogged Organic Archaeological Materials Conference, York 1996*, Bremerhaven: ICOM-CC Working Group on Wet Organic Materials.

Jones, M. (1990) *Fake? The Art of Deception*, London: British Museum Publications Ltd.

Jowitt, P. W. (1995) 'Letter: Forth Bridge Future', *The Times*, 9 February 1995: 19.

Kavanagh, G. (1990) *History Curatorship*, Washington DC: Smithsonian Institution Press.

Keene, S. (1994) 'Objects as systems: A new challenge for conservators', in A. Oddy (ed.) *Restoration: Is It Acceptable?*, British Museum Occasional Paper No. 99, London: British Museum Press.

—— (1996) *Managing Conservation in Museums*, London: Butterworth-Heinemann.

Keepax, C. (1975) 'Scanning electron microscopy of wood replaced by iron corrosion products', *Journal of Archaeological Science* 2: 145–50.

Keepax, C. and Robson, M. (1978) 'Conservation and associated examination of a Roman chest: Evidence for woodworking techniques', *The Conservator* 2: 35–40.

Kemp, M. (1990) 'Looking at Leonardo's Last Supper', in V. Todd (ed.) *Appearance, Opinion, Change: Evaluating the Look of Paintings*, London: UKIC.

Kinnes, I. A., Longworth, I. H., McIntyre, I. M., Needham, S. P. and Oddy, W. A. (1988) 'Bush Barrow Gold', *Antiquity* 62: 24–39.

Kirby Talley Jr M. (1989) 'Connoisseurship and the methodology of the Rembrandt research project', *The International Journal of Museum Management and Curatorship* 8: 175–214.

—— (1990) 'The humanistic foundation in the training of restorers', in International Council of Museums Committee for Conservation Working Group on Training in Conservation and Restoration (eds) *The Graduate Conservator in Employment: Expectations and Realities*, Amsterdam: ICOM-CC.

—— (1996) 'The eye's caress: Looking, appreciation, and connoisseurship', in N. Stanley Price, M. Kirby Talley Jr and A. M. Vaccaro (eds) *Historical and Philosophical Issues in the Conservation of Cultural Heritage*, Los Angeles: The Getty Conservation Institute.

—— (1998) 'Miscreants and Hotentots: Restorers and restoration attitudes and practices in seventeenth and eighteenth century England', in C. Sitwell and S. Staniforth (eds) *Studies in the History of Painting Restoration*, London: Archetype.

Kitamura, K. (1988) 'Some thoughts about conserving Urushi art objects in Japan, and an example of conservation work', in N. S. Brommelle and P. Smith (eds) *Urushi*, Marina del Rey: The Getty Conservation Institute.

Kosek, J. (1994) 'Restoration of Art on Paper in the West: A consideration of changing attitudes and values', in A. Oddy (ed.) *Restoration: Is It Acceptable?*, British Museum Occasional Paper No. 99, London: British Museum Press.

Kristiansen, K. (1984) 'Denmark', in H. Cleere (ed.) *Approaches to the Archaeological Heritage*, Cambridge: Cambridge University Press.

Labi, K. A. (1993) 'The theory and practice of conservation among the Akans of Ghana', *ICOM-CC 10th Triennial Meeting, Washington, DC, USA 1993*, Washington: ICOM-CC.

Lambert, F. L., Vinard, D. and Preusser, F. D. (1992) 'The rate of absorption of oxygen by "Ageless": The utility of an oxygen scavenger in sealed cases', *Studies in Conservation* 37(4): 267–74.

Lang, J. and Middleton, A. (1997) *Radiography of Cultural Material*, Oxford: Butterworth-Heinemann.

Larsen, B. (1981) *Moulding and Casting*, Copenhagen: School of Conservation, The Royal Art Academy, Denmark.

—— (1984) *Electrotyping*, Copenhagen: School of Conservation, The Royal Art Academy, Denmark.

—— (1987) 'SEM identification and documentation of tool marks and surface textures on the Gunderstrup Cauldron', in J. Black (ed.) *Recent Advances in the Conservation and Analysis of Artefacts*, London: Summer Schools Press.

Lavedrine, B., Trannois, C. and Flieder, F. (1986) 'Etude experimentale de la stabilité dans l'obscurité de dix films cinématographiques couleurs', *Studies in Conservation* 31(4): 171–4.

Laver, M. (1997) 'Titanium dioxide whites', in E. W. Fitzhugh (ed.) *Artists Pigments: A Handbook of Their History and Characteristics*, Vol. 3, Oxford and Washington: OUP and National Gallery of Art.

Leach, E. (1994) 'A view of functionalism', in S. M. Pearce (ed.) *Interpreting Objects and Collections*, London: Routledge.

Lee, L. R. and Thickett, D. (1996) *Selection of Materials for the Storage or Display of Museum Objects*, British Museum Occasional Paper No. 111, London: British Museum Press.

Leechman, D. (1931) 'Technical methods in the preservation of anthropological museum specimens', *Annual Report for 1929 National Museums of Canada*, Ottawa: 127–58.

Leitner, H. and Paine, S. (1994) 'Is wall painting restoration a representation of the original or a reflection of contemporary fashion: An Austrian perspective', in A. Oddy (ed.) *Restoration: Is It Acceptable?*, British Museum Occasional Paper No. 99, London: British Museum Press.

Lewis, G. (1992a) 'Museums and their precursors: A brief world survey', in M. A. Thompson (ed.) *Manual of Curatorship*, Oxford: Butterworth-Heinemann.

—— (1992b) 'Museums in Britain: A historical survey', in M. A. Thompson (ed.) *Manual of Curatorship*, Oxford: Butterworth-Heinemann.

Linklater, M. (1995) 'Are we letting Britain's greatest bridge rot?', *The Times*, 3 February 1995: 14.

Lipe, D. (1987) 'Value and meaning in cultural resources', in H. Cleere (ed.) *Approaches to the Archaeological Heritage*, Cambridge: Cambridge University Press.

Lister, D. (1991) 'Restoration "ruins ceiling"', *The Independent*, 20 March 1991: 12.

Longman, P. (1992) 'The Museums and Galleries Commission', in M. A. Thompson (ed.) *Manual of Curatorship* (2nd edn), Oxford: Butterworth-Heinemann.

Lord, B., Lord, G. D. and Nicks, J. (1989) *The Cost of Collecting*, London: HMSO.

Lowenthal, D. (1994) 'The value of age and decay', in W. E. Krumbein, P. Brimblecombe, D. E. Cosgrove and S. Staniforth (eds) *Durability and Change*, Chichester: Wiley.

—— (1996) *Possessed by the Past*, New York: The Free Press.

McClure, I. (1992) 'Henry Prince of Wales on Horseback by Robert Peake the Elder', in A. Oddy (ed.) *The Art of the Conservator*, London: British Museum Press.

McCrone, W. C. and Delly, J. G. (1973) *The Particle Atlas* (2nd edn), Michigan: Ann Arbor Science Publishers.

McGhee, R. (1994) 'Ivory for the Sea Woman: The symbolic attributes of prehistoric technology', in S. M. Pearce (ed.) *Interpreting Objects and Collections*, London: Routledge.

MacGowan, G. and LaRoche, G. J. (1996) 'The ethical dilemma facing conservation: Care and treatment of human skeletal remains and mortuary objects', *Journal of the American Institute for Conservation* 35(2): 109–21.

Mancinelli, F. (1991) 'The frescoes of Michelangelo on the vault of the Sistine Chapel: Conservation methodology, problems and results', in S. Cather (ed.) *The Conservation of Wall Paintings*, Los Angeles: Getty Conservation Institute.

—— (1992) 'Michelangelo's frescoes in the Sistine Chapel', in A. Oddy (ed.) *The Art of the Conservator*, London: British Museum Press.

Manitta, S. (1994) 'The care of rugs and carpets: The case for textile conservators', in A. Oddy (ed.) *Restoration: Is It Acceptable?*, British Museum Occasional Paper No. 99, London: British Museum Press.

Mann, P. (1994) 'The restoration of vehicles for use in research, exhibition, and demonstration', in A. Oddy (ed.) *Restoration: Is It Acceptable?*, British Museum Occasional Paper No. 99, London: British Museum Press.

Margolis, H. (1987) *Patterns, Thinking and Cognition: A Theory of Judgement*, Chicago: University of Chicago Press.

Maryon, H. (1947) 'The Sutton Hoo Helmet', *Antiquity* 21: 137–44.

Matero, F. (1993) 'The conservation of immovable cultural property: Ethical and practical dilemmas', *Journal of the American Institute for Conservation* 32(1): 15–21.

MDA (Museum Documentation Association) (1997) *The MDA Archaeological Objects Thesaurus*, Cambridge: MDA.

Mellar, S. D. (1992) 'The exhibition and conservation of African objects; Considering the non-tangible', *Journal of the American Institute for Conservation* 31(1): 3–16.

Merk, L. (1978) 'A study of reagents used in the stripping of bronzes, *Studies in Conservation* 23: 15–22.

Meyer, M. and Booker, J. (1991) *Eliciting and Analysing Expert Judgement: A Practical Guide*, London: Academic Press.

MGC (Museums and Galleries Commission) (1992) *Standards in the Museum Care of Archaeological Collections*, London: MGC.

—— (1993a) *Standards in the Museum Care of Biological Collections*, London: MGC.

—— (1993b) *Standards in the Museum Care of Geological Collections*, London: MGC.

—— (1993c) *Conservation–Restoration, The Options*, London: MGC.

—— (1994) *Standards in the Museum Care of Larger and Working Objects*, London: MGC.

—— (1995a) *Standards in the Museum Care of Musical Instruments*, London: MGC.

—— (1995b) *Working with a Conservator. A Guide for Curators*, London: MGC.

—— (1996) *Standards in the Museum Care of Photographic Collections*, London: MGC.

—— (1997) *Ours for Keeps*, London: MGC.

—— (1998a) *Standards in the Museum Care of Costume and Textile Collections*, London: MGC.

—— (1998b) *Levels of Collection Care: A Self Assessment Checklist for UK Museums*, London: MGC.

Michalski, S. (1993) 'Relative humidity: A discussion of correct/incorrect values', *ICOM-CC 10th Triennial Meeting, Washington, DC, USA 1993*, Washington: ICOM-CC.

—— (1994) 'Sharing responsibility for conservation decisions' in W. E. Krumbein, P. Brimblecombe, D. E. Cosgrove and S. Staniforth (eds) *Durability and Change*, Chichester: Wiley.

Miller, G. A. (1956) 'The magical number 7, plus or minus 2', *Psychological Review* 63: 81–97.

Minolta (1988) *Precise Colour Communication*, Osaka: Minolta.

Molina, T. and Pincemin, M. (1994) 'Restoration acceptable to whom?', in A. Oddy (ed.) *Restoration: Is It Acceptable?*, British Museum Occasional Paper No. 99, London: British Museum Press.

Moore, P. D., Webb, J. A. and Collinson, M. E. (1991) *Pollen Analysis*, Oxford: Blackwell.

Moore, P. G. and Thomas, H. (1976) *The Anatomy of Decisions*, Harmondsworth: Penguin Books.

Mora, P., Mora, L. and Philippot, P. (1996) 'Problems of presentation', in N. Stanley Price, M. Kirby Talley Jr and A. M. Vaccaro (eds) *Historical and Philosophical Issues in the Conservation of Cultural Heritage*, Los Angeles: The Getty Conservation Institute.

Morris, W. (1996) 'Manifesto of the Society for the Protection of Ancient Buildings', in N. Stanley Price, M. Kirby Talley Jr and A. M. Vaccaro (eds) *Historical and Philosophical Issues in the Conservation of Cultural Heritage*, Los Angeles: The Getty Conservation Institute (first published in 1877).

Morrison, C. (1995) 'United Kingdom export policies in relation to antiquities', in K. W. Tubb (ed.) *Antiquities: Trade or Betrayed*, London: Archetype.

Museum Ethnographers Group (1991) *Museum Ethnographers Group Professional Guidelines Concerning The Storage, Display, Interpretation and Return of Human Remains in Ethnographic Collections in the United Kingdom Museums*, London: Museum Ethnographers Group.

National Trust (1999) *The National Trust Handbook 1999*, London: National Trust.

NZPCG (New Zealand Professional Conservators Group) (1988) 'Code of Ethics: New Zealand Professional Conservators Group', *New Zealand Museums Journal* 19(3): 14–15.

Norman, M. (1988) 'Early conservation techniques and the Ashmolean Museum', in S. C. Watkins and C. E. Brown (eds) *Conservation of Ancient Egyptian Materials*, London: Institute of Archaeology Publications.

Oddy, W. A. (1973) 'An unsuspected danger in display', *Museums Journal* 73(1): 27–8.

—— (1975) 'The corrosion of metals on display', in D. Leigh, A. Moncrieff, W. A. Oddy and P. Pratt (eds) *Conservation in Archaeology and the Applied Arts: 1975 IIC Stockholm Congress*, London: IIC.

—— (1980) *Aspects of Early Metallurgy*, British Museum Occasional Paper No. 17, London: British Museum Press.

—— (1994) 'Restoration – Is it acceptable?', in A. Oddy (ed.) in *Restoration: Is It Acceptable?*, British Museum Occasional Paper No. 99, London: British Museum Press.

—— (1996) 'The Forbes Prize Lecture 1996', *IIC Bulletin* No. 5, October 1996: 1–5.

—— (1997) 'Obituary for Harold James Plenderleith', *IIC Bulletin* No. 6, December 1997: 1–2.

Oddy, W. A. and Barker, H. (1971) 'A feature card information retrieval system for the General Museum Laboratory', *Studies in Conservation* 16: 89–94.

Odegaard, N. (1995) 'Artists intent: Material culture studies and conservation', *Journal of the American Institute for Conservation* 34(3): 187–97.

O'Keefe, P. (1995) 'Conservators and actions for recovery of stolen or unlawfully exported cultural property', in K. W. Tubb (ed.) *Antiquities: Trade or Betrayed*, London: Archetype.

Olmert, M. (1985) *Official Guide to Colonial Williamsburg*, Williamsburg, VA: The Colonial Williamsburg Foundation.

Olsen, S. (1988) *Scanning Electron Microscopy in Archaeology*, British Archaeological Reports (International Series) 452, Oxford: B.A.R.

Omar, S., McCord, M. and Daniels, V. (1989) 'The conservation of bog bodies by freeze-drying', *Studies in Conservation* 34(3): 101–9.

Orlofsky, P. and Trupin, D. L. (1993) 'The role of connoisseurship in determining the textile conservator's treatment options', *Journal of the American Institute for Conservation* 32: 109–18.

Orwell, G. (1949) *Nineteen Eighty Four*, London: Penguin.

Painter, T. J. (1995) 'Chemical and microbiological aspects of the preservation process in sphagnum peat', in R. Turner and R. Scaife (eds) *Bog Bodies: New Discoveries and New Perspectives*. London: British Museum Press.

Palmer, M. (1999) 'Romancing the Stone', *Heritage* 48, 12–17.

Palmer, N. (1995) 'Recovering stolen art', in K. W. Tubb (ed.) *Antiquities: Trade or Betrayed*, London: Archetype.

Paxton, R. (ed.) (1990) *100 Years of the Forth Bridge*, London: Thomas Telford.

Pearce, D. (1989) *Conservation Today*, London: Routledge.

Pearce, S. M. (1990) *Archaeological Curatorship*, London: Leicester University Press.

—— (ed.) (1994a) *Interpreting Objects and Collections*, London: Routledge.

—— (1994b) 'Thinking about things', in S. M. Pearce (ed.) *Interpreting Objects and Collections*, London: Routledge.

Perry, R. (1983) 'Tate Gallery Conservation Department records', *The Conservator* 7: 13–16.

Peters, K. M. (1981) 'The conservation of a living artefact. A Maori meeting house at Makahae. A preliminary report', in *ICOM-CC 6th Triennial Meeting, Ottawa 1981*, Ottawa: ICOM-CC.

Philippot, P. (1996a) 'Restoration from the perspective of the humanities', in N. Stanley Price, M. Kirby Talley Jr and A. M. Vaccaro (eds) *Historical and Philosophical Issues in the Conservation of Cultural Heritage*, Los Angeles: The Getty Conservation Institute.

—— (1996b) 'Historic preservation: Philosophy, criteria, guidelines, II', in N. Stanley Price, M. Kirby Talley Jr and A. M. Vaccaro (eds) *Historical and Philosophical Issues in the Conservation of Cultural Heritage*, Los Angeles: The Getty Conservation Institute.

Plenderleith, H. J. (1998) 'A history of conservation', *Studies in Conservation* 43(3): 129–43.

Plenderleith, H. and Werner, A. E. A. (1971) *Conservation of Antiquities and Works of Art*, Oxford: Oxford University Press.

Podany, J. (1994) 'Restoring what wasn't there: Reconsideration of the eighteenth-century restorations to the Lansdowne Herakles in the collection of the J. Paul Getty Museum', in A. Oddy (ed.) *Restoration: Is It Acceptable?*, British Museum Occasional Paper No. 99, London: British Museum Press.

Podany, J. and Lansing Maish, S. (1993) 'Can the complex be made simple? Informing the public about conservation through museum exhibitions', *Journal of the American Institute for Conservation* 32(2): 101–8.

Pollard, M. and Heron, C. (1996) *Archaeological Chemistry*, Cambridge: Royal Society of Chemistry.

Pomian, K. (1994) 'The collection: Between the visible and the invisible', in S. M. Pearce (ed.) *Interpreting Objects and Collections*, London: Routledge.

Prescott, P. (1995) 'Letter: Forth Bridge Future', *The Times*, 9 February 1995: 19.

Prott, L. V. (1995) 'National and international laws on the protection of cultural heritage', in K. W. Tubb (ed.) *Antiquities Trade or Betrayed*, London: Archetype.

Prown, J. (1994) 'Mind in matter: An introduction to material culture theory and method', in S. M. Pearce (ed.) *Interpreting Objects and Collections*, London: Routledge.

Pye, L. and Cronyn, J. (1987) 'The archaeological conservator re-examined: A personal view', in J. Black (ed.) *Recent Advances in the Conservation and Analysis of Artefacts*, London: Summer Schools Press.

Quirke, S. and Spencer, J. (1992) *The British Museum Book of Ancient Egypt*, London: Thames & Hudson.

Railtrack (1997) http//www.railtrack.co.uk/industry/network/97nwms/appenda/proj15.html

Ramsay-Jolicoeur, B. and Wainwright, I. N. M. (eds) (1990) *Shared Responsibility*, Ottawa: National Gallery of Canada.

Rathgen, F. (1898) *Die Konservierung von Altertumsfunden*, Berlin: W. Spemann.

Reedy, C. L. (1992) 'Religious and ethical issues in the study of conservation of Tibetan sculpture', *Journal of the American Institute for Conservation* 31(1): 41–50.

Renfrew, C. (1973) *Before Civilisation*, London: Jonathan Cape.

Renfrew, C. and P. Bahn (1991) *Archaeology: Theories, Methods and Practice*, London: Thames & Hudson.

Riegel, A. (1996) 'The modern cult of monuments: Its essence and its development', in N. Stanley Price, M. Kirby Talley Jr and A. M. Vaccaro (eds.) *Historical and Philosophical Issues in the Conservation of Cultural Heritage*, Los Angeles: The Getty Conservation Institute.

Roberts, M. (1994) *Durham*, London: Batsford and English Heritage.

Roberts, D. A. (1985) *Planning the Documentation of Museum Collections*, Cambridge: Museum Documentation Association.

Roy, A. (1994) *Artists Pigments: A Handbook of Their Histories and Characteristics*, Vol. 2, Washington: National Gallery of Art.

—— (1998) 'Forbes Prize Lecture', *IIC Bulletin* No. 6, December 1998: 1–5.

Roy, A. and Smith, P. (eds) (1994) *Preventive Conservation Practice, Theory and Research: 1994 IIC Ottawa Congress*, London: IIC.

Ruskin, J. (1996) 'The Lamp of Memory, II', in N. Stanley Price, M. Kirby Talley Jr and A. M. Vaccaro (eds) *Historical and Philosophical Issues in the Conservation of Cultural Heritage*, Los Angeles: The Getty Conservation Institute (first published as Chapter 6 in *The Seven Lamps of Architecture* in 1849).

Saunders, D. (1997) 'Who needs Class 1 Museums', *IIC Bulletin* No. 2, April 1997: 3–6.

Scheiner, T. C. (1997) 'Museum ethics and the environment', in G. Edson (ed.) *Museum Ethics*, London: Routledge.

Schulz, E. (1994) 'Notes on the history of collecting and museums', in S. M. Pearce (ed.) *Interpreting Objects and Collections*, London: Routledge.

Schweingruber, F. (1978) *Microscopic Wood Anatomy*, Zurich: F. Fluck-Wurth.

Scott, D. (1991) *Metallography and Microstructure in Ancient and Historic Metals*, Marina del Rey: Getty Conservation Institute and J. Paul Getty Trust.

Sease, C. (1996) 'A short history of archaeological conservation', in A. Roy and P. Smith (eds) *Archaeological Conservation and its Consequences: 1996 IIC Copenhagen Congress*, London: IIC.

Seeley, N. (1987) 'Archaeological conservation: The development of a discipline', *Institute of Archaeology Bulletin* 24: 161–76.

Shashoua, Y. and Thomsen, S. (1993) 'A field trial for the use of "Ageless" in the preservation of rubber in museum collections', in D. W. Grattan (ed.) *Saving the 20th Century: The Conservation of Modern Materials*, Ottawa: Canadian Conservation Institute.

Shell, C. A. and Robinson, P. (1988) 'The recent reconstruction of the Bush Barrow Lozenge Plate', *Antiquity* 62: 248–60.

Skoog, D. and Leary, J. (1992) *Principles of Instrumental Analysis* (4th edn), Fort Worth: Saunders College Press.

Slesinski, W. (1993) 'Conservation of wooden sculpture in southern Poland in the 19th Century', *ICOM-CC 10th Triennial Meeting, Washington 1993*, Washington: ICOM-CC.

Smith, B. (1990) 'Shared responsibility: Welcome and introduction', in B. Ramsay-Jolicoeur and I. N. M. Wainwright (eds) (1990) *Shared Responsibility*, Ottawa: National Gallery of Canada.

Smith, P. (1977) 'Some aspects of commercial restoration and conservation', *The Conservator* 1: 32–4.

Smith, R. D. (1987) 'Mass deacidification at the public archives of Canada', in G. Pethbridge (ed.) *Conservation of Library and Archive Materials and the Graphic Arts*, London: Butterworth.

Smith, S. (1992) 'The Portland Vase', in W. A. Oddy (ed.) *The Art of the Conservator*, London: British Museum Press.

—— (1994) 'Filling and painting of ceramics for exhibition in the British Museum', in A. Oddy (ed.) *Restoration: Is It Acceptable?*, British Museum Occasional Paper No. 99, London: British Museum Press.

Staniforth, S. (1990) 'Benefits versus costs in environmental control', in S. Keene (ed.) *Managing Conservation*, London: UKIC.

Stead, I. M., Bourke, J. B. and Brothwell, D. (eds) (1986) *Lindow Man: The Body in the Bog.* London: British Museum Publications.

The Sunday Times (1995) 'Red Hot, the issue made from girders', *The Sunday Times*, 22 January 1995: SC/8.

Sully, D. and Suenson-Taylor, K. (1996) 'A condition survey of glycerol treated freeze-dried leather in long term storage', in A. Roy and P. Smith (eds) *Archaeological Conservation and its Consequences, 1996 IIC Copenhagen Congress*, London: IIC.

Szrajber, T. (1997) *The British Museum Materials Thesaurus*, Cambridge: MDA and BM.

Thickett, D. (1998) 'Sealing of MDF to prevent corrosive emissions', *The Conservator* 22: 49–56.

Thomas, A. (1998) 'Restoration or renovation: Remuneration and expectation in Renaissance "acconciatura"', in C. Sitwell and S. Staniforth (eds) *Studies in the History of Painting Restoration*, London: Archetype.

Thompson, M. W. (1977) *General Pitt-Rivers*, Bradford on Avon: Moonraker Press.

Thomson, G. (1978) *The Museum Environment*, London: Butterworth.

Tilley, C. (1994) 'Interpreting material culture', in S. M. Pearce (ed.) *Interpreting Objects and Collections*, London: Routledge.

The Times (1996) 'Forth Rail Bridge Neglected', *The Times*, March 1996: 6.

Townsend, J. H. and Tennent, N. H. (1993) 'Colour transparencies: Studies on light fading and storage stability', *ICOM-CC 10th Triennial Meeting, Washington 1993*, Washington: ICOM-CC.

Tubb, K. W. (ed.) (1995) *Antiquities: Trade or Betrayed*, London: Archetype.

Tubb, K. W. and Sease, C. (1996) 'Sacrificing the wood for the trees – Should conservation have a role in the antiquities trade?', in A. Roy and P. Smith (eds) *Archaeological Conservation and its Consequences: 1996 IIC Copenhagen Congress*, London: IIC.

Turner, R. C. and Scaife, R. G. (eds) (1995) *Bog Bodies: New Discoveries and New Perspectives.* London: British Museum Press.

Tweddle, D. (1992) *The Anglian Helmet from Coppergate*, London: York Archaeological Trust and CBA.

UKIC (United Kingdom Institute of Conservation) (1983) *Guidance for Conservation Practice*, London: UKIC.

—— (1996) *UKIC Code of Ethics and Rules of Practice*, London: UKIC.

—— (1998) *Standard Form of Contract* (revised 1998), London: UKIC.

Vaccaro, A. M. (1996a) 'Reintegration of losses', in N. Stanley Price, M. Kirby Talley Jr and A. M. Vaccaro (eds) *Historical and Philosophical Issues in the Conservation of Cultural Heritage*, Los Angeles: The Getty Conservation Institute.

—— (1996b) 'The emergence of modern conservation theory', in N. Stanley Price, M. Kirby Talley Jr and A. M. Vaccaro (eds) *Historical and Philosophical Issues in the Conservation of Cultural Heritage*, Los Angeles: The Getty Conservation Institute.

van Schoute, R. and Verougstraete-Marcq, H. (1986) *Scientific Examination of Easel Paintings*, PACT 13, Strasbourg: Council of Europe.

Viollet-le-Duc, E. E. (1996) 'Restoration', in N. Stanley Price, M. Kirby Talley Jr and A. M. Vaccaro (eds) *Historical and Philosophical Issues in the Conservation of Cultural Heritage*, Los Angeles: The Getty Conservation Institute (first published as 'Restoration' in *Dictionnaire raisonné de l'architecture française du XIe au XVIe siècle*, Vol. 8 in 1854).

Walden, S. (1985) *The Ravished Image*, London: Weidenfeld and Nicholson.

Walker, K. (1990) *Guidelines for the Preparation of Excavation Archives for Long Term Storage*, London: UKIC Archaeology Section.

Waller, R. (1994) 'Conservation risk assessment: A strategy for managing resources for preventive conservation', in A. Roy and P. Smith (eds) *Preventive Conservation Practice, Theory and Research: 1994 IIC Ottawa Congress*, London: IIC.

Walmsley, E., Fletcher, C and Delaney, J (1992) 'Evaluation of system performance of near infrared imaging devices', *Studies in Conservation* 37: 120–31.

Ward, P. (1986) *The Nature of Conservation: A Race Against Time*, Marina del Rey: Getty Conservation Institute.

Watkins, S. C. (1997) 'Science and conservation at the British Museum: A nineteenth century legacy', in S. Bradley (ed.) *The Interface Between Science and Conservation*, British Museum Occasional Paper No. 116, London: British Museum Press.

Watkinson, D. (1982) 'Making a large scale replica of the Pillar of Eliseg', *The Conservator* 6: 6–11.

—— (1996a) 'Chloride extraction from archaeological iron: Comparative treatment efficiencies', in A. Roy and P. Smith (eds) *Archaeological Conservation and its Consequences: 1996 IIC Copenhagen Congress*, London: IIC.

—— (1996b) 'Defining the contribution of non-conservators to conservation: The role of the conservation technician', in J. Cronyn and K. Foley (eds) *A Qualified Community: Towards Internationally Agreed Standards of Qualification for Conservation*, London: ICOM-CC Working Group on Training in Conservation and Restoration..

Weersma, A. (1987) 'Some theoretical considerations on the handling and care of sacred objects in a museum context', in *ICOM-CC 8th Triennial Meeting, Sydney, Australia 1987*, Sydney: ICOM-CC.

Westheimer, F. H. (1994) 'Preservation of books and electronic storage', in W. E. Krumbein, P. Brimblecombe, D. E. Cosgrove and S. Staniforth (eds) *Durability and Change*, Chichester: Wiley.

Williams, N. (1989) *The Breaking and Remaking of the Portland Vase*, London: British Museum Publications.

—— (1992) 'The Sutton Hoo Helmet', in A. Oddy (ed.) *The Art of the Conservator*, London: British Museum.

Wilson, K. (1999) 'Deterioration issues affecting a 20th century photographic archive', unpublished MA dissertation, Department of Archaeology, University of Durham.

Wilson, M. (1977) *The National Gallery London*, London: Orbis.

Wilson, R. J. A. (1975) *Roman Remains in Britain*, London: Constable & Co.

Wollny, K. (1996) 'Investigation and analysis of copper alloy helmets from the De Walden Collection', unpublished MA dissertation, Department of Archaeology, University of Durham.

Woodward C. J. (1888) 'The action of gas on leather bookbindings: A preliminary experimental enquiry', *Library Chronicle* 5.

Wyld, M. (1998) 'The restoration of Holbein's *Ambassadors*', *National Gallery Bulletin* 19: 4–25.

Yagihashi, S. (1988) 'The preservation and handing down of traditional Urushi art techniques in Japan' in N. Brommelle and P. Smith (eds) *Urushi*, Marina del Rey: The Getty Conservation Institute.

Young, C. (1998) 'England's World Heritage', *Conservation Bulletin 33*, January 1988: 3–7.

Yourcenar, M. (1996) 'That mighty sculptor time', in N. Stanley Price, M. Kirby Talley Jr and A. M. Vaccaro (eds) *Historical and Philosophical Issues in the Conservation of Cultural Heritage*, Los Angeles: The Getty Conservation Institute.

Index

Page references in italics are to illustrations